D0010818

Also by Robert Harvey

Portugal: Birth of a Democracy
Blueprint 2000

FIRE DOWN BELOW

*A Journey of Exploration
from Mexico to Chile*

ROBERT HARVEY

Simon and Schuster
New York   London   Toronto   Sydney   Tokyo

Simon and Schuster
Simon & Schuster Building
Rockefeller Center
1230 Avenue of the Americas
New York, New York 10020

Designed by Nina D'Amario / Levavi & Levavi
Manufactured in the United States of America

10 9 8 7 6 5 4 3 2 1

Library of Congress Cataloging-in-Publication Data
Harvey, Robert.
    Fire down below : a journey of exploration from Mexico to Chile
/ Robert Harvey.
        p.   cm.
    Includes index.
    1. Latin America—Description and travel—1981– 2. Latin Amer-
ica—Social conditions—1945– 3. Latin America—Economic condi-
tions—1945– 4. Latin America—Politics and government—1980–
I. Title.
F1409.3.H37 1988
980'.038—dc 19   88-13108
                                                                CIP
ISBN 0-671-61887-3

    Acknowledgment is made to Gordon Brotherston for permission to quote from his translations of poetry
by Pablo Neruda (page 22), Andrés Bello (page 110), Rubén Darío (page 182), and Gonçalves Dias (page
242). These translations originally appeared in *Latin American Poetry*, published by Cambridge University
Press, Cambridge, England.
    Acknowledgment is also made to Jonathan Cape Ltd, London, England, for permission to reprint the
excerpt from *One Hundred Years of Solitude* (pages 121–122) by Gabriel García Márquez.
    We have made every effort to appropriately acknowledge all source material from copyright holders when
required. In the event of any question arising as to the source of any material, we will be pleased to make
the necessary acknowledgment in future printings.

FOR MY MOTHER AND FATHER

My thanks are due to a great many friends in Latin America, some of whom it is better not to name, making it invidious for me to name the others; to my wife, Jane, and Home Types Ltd, who between them typed the book; to the editors, Andrew Knight, Brian Beedham and Gordon Lee, who sent me so often over the past decade to Latin America; and again, finally, to Jane, who put up with me throughout the writing of this book.

CONTENTS

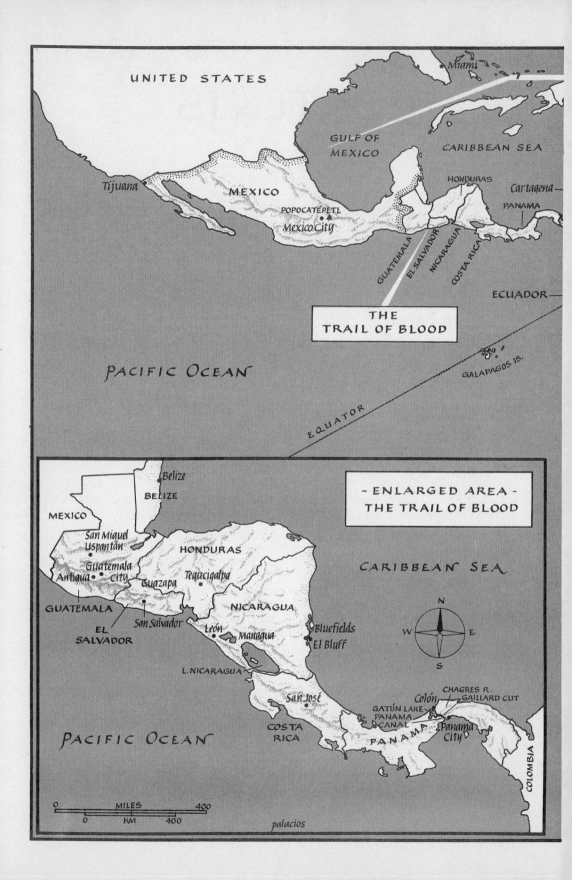

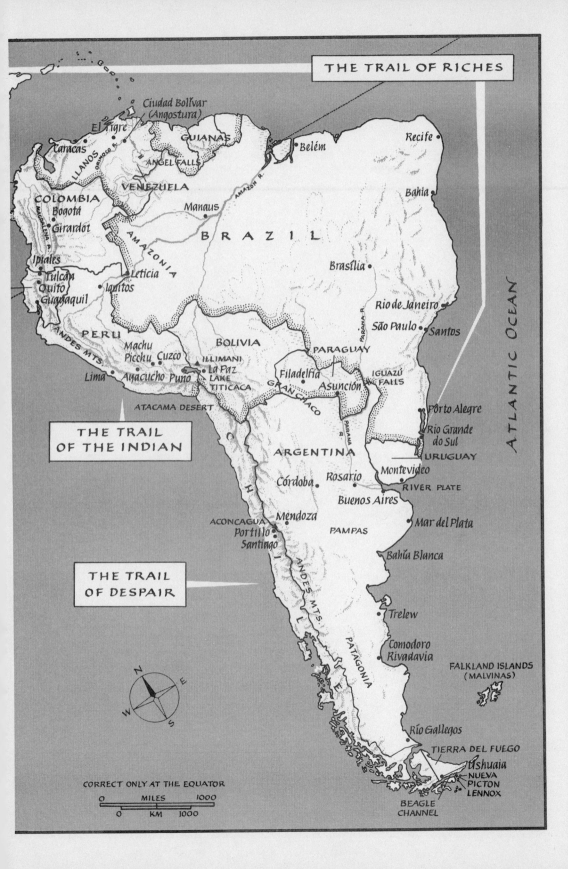

THE TRAIL OF RICHES

Ciudad Bolívar
(Angostura)
El Tigre
Caracas
LLANOS
GUIANAS
ANGEL FALLS
Belém
Recife
COLOMBIA
VENEZUELA
AMAZON R.
Bahía
Bogotá
Manaus
Girardot
B R A Z I L
AMAZONIA
Ipiales
Leticia
Brasília
Tulcán
Quito
Iquitos
Guayaquil
ANDES MTS.
PERU
Machu
Picchu   Cuzco
Lima   Ayacucho Puno
BOLIVIA
ILLIMANI
La Paz
LAKE
TITICACA
PARAGUAY
Filadelfia
Asunción
IGUAZÚ
FALLS
Río de Janeiro
São Paulo   Santos
ATACAMA DESERT
GRAN CHACO
Pôrto Alegre
Río Grande
do Sul

THE TRAIL
OF THE INDIAN
ARGENTINA
URUGUAY
Montevideo
RIVER PLATE
Córdoba   Rosario
Buenos Aires
ACONCAGUA   Mendoza
Portillo
Santiago
PAMPAS
Mar del Plata
ANDES
MTS.
Bahía Blanca

THE TRAIL
OF DESPAIR
PATAGONIA
Trelew
Comodoro
Rivadavia
FALKLAND ISLANDS
(MALVINAS)

N
W   E
S

Río Gallegos
TIERRA DEL FUEGO
Ushuaia
NUEVA
PICTON
LENNOX
BEAGLE
CHANNEL

ATLANTIC OCEAN

CORRECT ONLY AT THE EQUATOR
0   MILES   1000
0   KM   1000

PROLOGUE

NEARLY FIVE HUNDRED YEARS AGO, CHRISTOPHER COLUMBUS STUMBLED across the New World and founded Latin America on behalf of the king and queen of Spain. The friar Bartolomé de Las Casas, who edited the only surviving copy of Columbus's journal in the sixteenth century, tells the story as Columbus's men, openly mutinous and despairing of ever finding land, take new heart.

Thursday, October 11th[, 1492, Columbus's party] navigated to the west-southwest; they had a rougher sea than they had experienced during the whole voyage. They saw petrels and a green reed near ship. Those in the caravel Pinta saw a cane and a stick, and they secured another small stick, carved, as it appeared, with iron, and a piece of cane, and other vegetation that grows on land, and a small board. Those in the caravel Niña also saw other indications of land and a stick loaded with barnacles. At these signs, all breathed again and rejoiced.

After sunset, [Admiral Columbus] steered his former course to the west. . . . And since the caravel Pinta was swifter and went ahead of the admiral, she found land and made the signals which the admiral had commanded.

This land was first sighted by a sailor named Rodrigo de Triana, although the admiral, at ten o'clock in the night being on the stern-castle, saw a light. It was, however, so obscured that he would not affirm that it was land, but called Pedro Gutiérrez, butler of the King's dais, and told him that there seemed to be a light, and that he should watch for it. He did so, and saw it. He said the same also to Rodrigo Sánchez de Segovia, whom the King and Queen had sent in the fleet as veedor, but he saw nothing since he was not in a position from which it could be seen. After the admiral had so spoken, it was seen once or twice, and it was like a small wax candle, which was raised and lowered.

Few thought that this was an indication of land, but the admiral was certain that they were near land. Accordingly, when they had said the

Salve, which all sailors are accustomed to say and chant in their manner, and when they had all been gathered together, the admiral asked and urged them to keep a good lookout from the forecastle and to watch carefully for land, and to him who would say first that he saw land, he would give at once a silk doublet apart from the other rewards the Sovereigns had promised, which were ten thousand maravedis annually to him who first sighted it.

Two hours after midnight, land appeared—at a distance of about two leagues. They took in all sail, remaining with the mainsail, which is the great sail without bonnets, and kept jogging, waiting for day, a Friday, on which they reached the small island of the Lucayos, which is called in the language of the Indians Guanahaní. Immediately they saw naked people, and the admiral went ashore in the armed boat, and Martín Alonso Pinzón and Vicente Yáñez, his brother, who was captain of the nine. The admiral brought out the royal standard, and the captains went with two banners of the Green Cross, which the admiral flew on all the ships as a flag, with an *F* and a *Y*, and over each letter their crown, one being on one side of the cross and the other on the other.

When they had landed, they saw very green trees and much water and fruit of various kinds. The admiral called the two captains and the others who had landed, and Rodrigo de Escobedo, secretary of the whole fleet, and Rodrigo Sánchez de Segovia, and said that they should bear witness and testimony how he, before them all, took possession of the island, as in fact he did, for the King and Queen, his sovereigns, making the declarations that are required, as is contained more at length in the testimonies which were there made in writing. Soon many people of the island gathered there. What follows are the actual words of the admiral, in his book of the first voyage and discovery of these Indies.

"I," he says, "in order that they might feel great amity towards us, because I knew they were a people to be delivered and converted to our holy faith rather by love than by force, gave to some among them red caps and some glass beads, which they hung around their necks, and many other things of little value. At this they were greatly pleased and became so entirely our friends that it was a wonder to see. Afterwards they came swimming to the ships' boats, where we were, and brought us parrots and cotton threads in balls, and spears and many other such things, and we exchanged for them other things, such as small glass beads and hawk's bells, which we gave to them. In fact, they took all and gave all, such as they had, with good will, but it seemed to me they were a people very deficient in everything.

"They all go naked as their mothers bore them, and the women also, although I saw only one very young girl. And all those whom I did see were youths, so that I did not see one who was over thirty years of age; they were very well built, with very handsome bodies and very good faces. Their hair is coarse, almost like the hairs of a horse's tail, and short; they wear their hair down over their eyebrows, except for a few strands behind which they wear long and never cut. Some of them are painted black, and they are the colour of the people of the Canaries, neither black nor white, and some of them are painted white and some red and some in any colour that they find. Some of them paint their faces, some their whole bodies, some only the eyes, and some only the nose.

"They do not bear arms or know them, for I showed to them swords and they took them by the blade and cut themselves through ignorance. They have no iron. Their spears are certain reeds, without iron, and some of these have a fish tooth at the end, while others are pointed in various ways. They are all generally fairly tall, good looking and well proportioned. I saw some who bore marks of wounds on their bodies, and I made signs to them to ask how this came about, and they indicated to me that people from other islands, which are near, and wished to capture them, and they defended themselves. And I believe and still believe that they come here from the mainland to take them for slaves. They should be good servants and of quick intelligence, since I see that they very soon say all that is said to them, and I believe that they would easily be made Christians, for it appeared to me that they had no creed."

Saturday, October 13th. "As soon as day broke, there came to the ship many of these men, all youths, as I have said, and all of good height, very handsome people. Their hair is not curly, but loose and coarse as the hair of a horse; all have very broad foreheads and heads, more so than any people that I have seen up to now. Their eyes are very lovely and not small. They are not at all black, but the colour of Canarians, and nothing else could be expected, since this is in one line from east to west with the island of Hierro in the Canaries. Their legs are very straight, all alike; they have no bellies but very good figures. . . . I believe that in the world there is no better race. . . . They love their neighbours as themselves, and they have the softest and gentlest voices in the world, and they are always smiling."

Sunday, October 21st. "At ten o'clock I arrived . . . and anchored, as did the caravels. After having eaten, I went ashore, and there was no village but only a single house, in which I found no one, so that I believe they had fled in terror, because in the house were all their household goods.

"I allowed nothing to be touched, but only went with these captains and people to examine the island. If the others, which have already been seen, are very lovely and green and fertile, this is much more so, and has large and very green trees. There are here very extensive lagoons and by them and around them there are wonderful woods, and here and in the whole island all is green and the vegetation is as that of Andalusia in April. The singing of little birds is such that it seems that a man could never wish to leave this place; the flocks of parrots darken the sun, and there are large and small birds of so many different kinds, and so unlike ours, that it is a marvel. There are, moreover, trees of a thousand types, all with their various fruits and all scented, so that it is a wonder. I am the saddest man in the world because I do not recognise them, for I am very sure that all are of some value, and I am bringing specimens of them and also of the herbs." ·

He looked at me with cold brown eyes in a leathered, skeptical face. I could not tell, from his slow drawl, whether he was dull-witted or was just allowing his thoughts to be edited by a rich experience of life at its rawest. He said: "One America. Yeah, I guess this is the place you find out that it is One America." The place was Tijuana, Mexico, just across the border from the American customs post south of California's San Ysidro that marks the divide between the United States and Latin America. It was not the dusty, desert town I had expected; it was a thriving, even modern, fair-sized town, a little dirtier but otherwise not unlike its counterparts in Southern California; the flashy cars and smart clothes of many of its people were signs of prosperity. The place was filled with nightclubs, whose names left nothing to the imagination. There were dozens of small bars. We were sitting at a table outside one of them by the main plaza in the afternoon, when it was quiet and there were a few people about. It was pleasant sipping beer in the sun while my off-duty companion from the United States Border Patrol told me about his work, not just stopping illegal aliens, but also, of necessity, protecting refugees of the American third world from bandits as they embarked on the perilous, illegal crossing into the United States.

"The problem is exponential," he said. "Next year there'll be about 1.8 million aliens arrested along this border. That's double the number this year. A third of them come across this sector of the border. That damn fence doesn't stop anyone. How can you ever have enough border guards to police two thousand miles of border? We have our work cut out not just stopping the poor bastards—and, oh boy, some of them are real poor—but protecting them from their fellow Mexicans. This year alone we've had 8 murders, 13 rapes and 165 robberies, and that's just the tip of the problem. Most of them don't get reported. But are the illegals grateful? Like hell they are; the number of attacks on our men has doubled in a year. We're between a rock and hard place down here."

"They all come for economic reasons, for a better life in the States?"

"Yeah, most of them do. Mexico is going through hard times. Some of them are political, though: Nicaraguans, Salvadorans, Guatemalans, people like that, fleeing the fighting further down."

I gazed out over the lazy Latin square in the late afternoon, where a small dog was alternately snapping at, then sniffing another, much larger, dog, which didn't pay much attention.

I considered the figure my companion had mentioned: 1.8 million caught, hundreds of thousands more getting through. It was a human flood, an event of major proportions. The United States was under siege from Latin America. There was already a Hispanic population of some 17 million, plus anywhere between 5 million and 10 million illegal immigrants, forming by far the biggest ethnic minority. They were escaping from a region of nearly 400 million people, which produced goods and services worth $600 billion, to a country of 240 million people, which produced six times as much, nearly $4 trillion worth. Each citizen of the United States produced, on average, about $15,000 worth of goods; each Latin American produced just $1,600 worth of goods. The United States was strong, democratic, peaceful and prosperous; Latin America was weak, precariously democratic, racked by civil wars, and mostly poor. Forty million Latin American kids lived on the streets.

Columbus's paradise on earth had gone terribly wrong. The oldest part of the New World had been far outstripped by the newest. What was the explanation? And could it ever catch up?

To find out, I decided to recross the Latin America that I, like any frequent visitor to the region, had become addicted to.

It was a journey intended to draw upon and weave together my experience of a dozen visits to the continent over more than a decade; to make sense of the patchwork of countries I had visited singly, or in twos and threes during previous trips. To those who know Latin America it is a cliché to insist that the differences between its various nations are more striking than the similarities. For me, that was true only up to a point: the region's history, language and people were also a unity, a series of parallel experiences.

When I first traveled to Latin America in 1975 as a foreign correspondent, to report on Brazil's bleak military regime and the social and economic cauldron bubbling beneath it, I was captivated by the volatility stemming from the country's chaotic politics—a power struggle between extremes of left and right—coupled with the underlying complexity of the society. On subsequent visits I felt increasingly that outsiders' perceptions of Latin America, largely derived from the political struggle, were two-dimensional. The nastiness of the continent's old oligarchy and its newer military rulers was such as to render credible the left's argument that revolution was the only answer to Latin America's problems. I felt, instead, that most Latin Americans, like most people anywhere, would prefer pluralist democracy to either extreme. The chances of that seemed remote; in 1975, there were only three democracies in the region: Venezuela, Colombia and Costa Rica. By 1986, the time of the journey described in this book, there were thirteen.

I resolved, when time permitted, to make a journey that would span the Latin American experience, to see how history, past and present, had shaped the fortunes of some of the fastest-changing, most varied societies in the world. I also wanted to observe the human face of each society as shaped by extreme geography. My principal aim was to answer the question: could Latin America ever rejoin its northern neighbor on the path to peace, democracy and prosperity? I decided to start my journey in the summer of 1986 across a region I knew, but had yet to comprehend, at tacky Tijuana.

Mexico was to be the beginning and end of my journey. I resolved not just to start at this border crossing but to return, full circle, making Mexico my final stop. Mexico is the point where Latin America touches the United States, the closest contact most United States citizens have with their southern fellows. It is, to quote *The New York Times* journalist Alan Riding, the "distant neighbor" of the United States. Successive administrations in Washington have tried to deal with the most tangible threat—the human flood—posed by such unequal nations sharing the same border by making use of the crude armory of immigration controls. I believed that a deeper understanding of—and interest in—the problems of the region might serve the United States better in the long run in coping with a migrant invasion. By the time I returned to Mexico I hoped to have acquired that kind of understanding myself.

The journey, accomplished on a single tour, divided naturally into four sections in my mind: the Trail of Blood, across war-torn Central America—Guatemala, Honduras, El Salvador and Nicaragua, and their two neighbors, Costa Rica and Panama; the Trail of the Indian, across the Andean republics of Colombia, Ecuador, Peru and Bolivia and down into the Indian-populated lowland regions of Amazonia and Paraguay; the Trail of Despair, across Chile, Argentina and Uruguay, developed nations that had fallen on bad times; and the Trail of Riches, across the booming economies of Brazil and Venezuela, returning at last to Mexico.

PART 1

THE TRAIL
OF BLOOD

Come and see the blood in the streets
Come and see
The blood in the streets
Come and see the blood
In the streets

PABLO NERUDA

THE INHABITANTS OF CENTRAL AMERICA—THE LITTLE RIBBONLIKE isthmus, the umbilical cord that connects the United States and South America—have learned to live with the sense of impending disaster. About 150 volcanoes line the unstable chain of the isthmus. From local tongues their names have the sound of ominous gods: Nicaragua's El Viejo (the Old One) soars some 6,000 feet; Momotombo, overlooking Managua, is still active, although its once terrible explosions are fewer and less virulent; Cosigüina, also in Nicaragua, rose to nearly 10,000 feet until an eruption in 1835 blew the top off and reduced it to 3,500 feet. The explosion was heard as far as Bogotá, nearly 1,000 miles away, and the violent storm that ensued for days afterward is celebrated in folk history to this day. Costa Rica's mighty Irazú rises 10,000 feet over San José, casting a giant shadow despite its normally tranquil disposition. But its brother volcano, El Poás, is a troublemaker, erupting forty times during the last century. The San Salvador volcano, overlooking El Salvador, blew in 1910, hurling torrents of lava into the lake in its crater, creating massive explosions of boiling steam. The Santa Ana volcano has four craters and its offshoot, Izalco, in constant eruption, has grown some 1,500 feet in two hundred years. Among its 32 volcanic cones, Guatemala boasts Tajumulco, tallest in Central America at a height of 12,000 feet. Nearby Tacaná is known for its massive crater 1,200 feet in diameter. The others are associated with their most recent eruptions and the numbers of the dead. Acatenango blew in 1924 and 1927; Santa María's 1902 eruption cost 6,000 lives. Atitlán went up in 1932, spewing ash for nearly sixty miles. El Fuego (the Fire) has been in a state of constant eruption, its blasts alternating with those of Pacaya, to which it may be connected underground.

Worse than the volcanic eruptions are the earthquakes to which they are linked. There have been 150 major (in excess of 6.9 on the

Richter scale) earthquakes during the past thirty years. In 1910 the aptly named Costa Rican town of Cartago (Carthage) was flattened. In 1951 San Salvador itself was leveled, with the loss of four thousand lives. Managua was all but destroyed in 1972, with a loss of twelve thousand people. Guatemala's capital, Ciudad Vieja (Old City), was destroyed by an earthquake and floods in 1541. The second capital, Antigua, built close to the volcanoes of Agua, Acatenango and El Fuego, was perpetually troubled by earthquakes until its total destruction, with the loss of 10,000 lives, in 1773. A third capital, Guatemala City, was built fifty miles east of Antigua. The latest capital was shaken badly in 1917 and 1918, but not until 1976 did a major earthquake damage it, taking 23,000 lives, injuring 60,000 and rendering 1 million people homeless.

These calamities understandably induce a certain fatalism in Central Americans. Yet, beginning in 1979, a man-made disaster that dwarfed even the upheavals of nature was to overwhelm the region. Starting in Nicaragua, the isthmus was engulfed in a civil war, in which 150,000 people died in seven years; one in every 150 Central Americans was killed in this eruption of blood, a modern slaughterhouse that stands on a par with the horrors of Lebanon and Kampuchea. How did this occur in one of the world's most underdeveloped regions? Did it mark the end of hope, this unbelievable outbreak of violence just a couple thousand miles away from the southern borders of the United States? Did it prove beyond doubt that Latin America was cruel, savage and backward beyond redemption? It was an easy conclusion to reach. I wanted to move beyond such easy conclusions as I set off along the Trail of Blood, across that Central American killing ground, the first section of my four-part journey across the Second America.

GUATEMALA

THE DAY WAS SULTRY, YET IN THE SHADE IT WAS PLEASANTLY COOL. The scene was picturesque: a small Guatemalan village, a collection of shacks huddled in a fold among the green trees and grasslands of the upland Indian region in El Quiché province just north of Guatemala City.

The village was not the kind of place to attract the tourists; the road that led up to it was just rising dust and there were none of the little shops selling the gaudy pullovers or souvenir knickknacks that amuse the travelers along the main road to the capital, Guatemala City, or to the old Spanish-colonial city of Antigua. In fact there seemed to be no shops or bars at all, though if you stopped at the right shack you could buy a tortilla or a beer for a few pesos.

In the middle of this apostrophe of a place, one shack made of smooth wooden planking stood bigger than all the rest. Its sloping reed roof reached down to touch a corrugated iron one, held up by a pole, which shaded a rudimentary veranda. Around the building was a scrubby wasteland, enclosed by a wooden fence of almost skeletal simplicity, so rickety it seemed hardly capable of standing. On top of the fence perched a boy about five wearing a miniature Stetson. Beside him, a little girl leaned against the fence, her head down, while a much smaller companion gazed out in bewilderment at the long line of people who stood silently in the morning sun, in a queue before the entrance.

The men dressed in rough laborers' clothes, as if they had been in the fields when they heard the news. The women wore fussed-over Indian skirts and shawls. A man carrying a red shoulder bag with a carefully woven motif of a horse entered the building, holding his daughter's hand, under a hand-painted wooden board that announced: Escuela Nacional Rural Mixta Cantón Chamac, Canton Chamac National Rural Mixed School. They might have been going into the school prize-giving session.

It was hot inside, and there was a putrid smell in the air. The visitors filed slowly through, for the most part suppressing open emotion, although some of the women were shaking with heavy sobs. The bodies lay huddled together, without order, over fifty of them, men, women and children. Someone had tried to turn them on their backs so that they could be identified more easily. Beyond that, there appeared to have been no attempt to arrange them at rest. The local mayor ticked off the numbers, in bureaucratic fashion: thirty men, ten women, fourteen children. Some of the frozen faces had their mouths open in grimaces. Some had staring eyes and arms like those of rag dolls—loose and disjointed. Many had had their throats slit. Some of the bodies were swollen by heat and some were hideously disfigured by wounds from jungle machetes.

Outside in the sun again—I could not stay long in the school—men were hammering, making coffins, not tapered at the end, just wooden boxes like those used for the export of local fruits. A large hole had been dug nearby. Later the bodies were put in the boxes. Short services were said. Then the boxes were stacked in the mass grave.

A ten-year-old boy had given the first alarm, the mayor explained to me. The killers—they might have been guerrillas or they might have been soldiers—came in the morning, around nine-thirty. The villagers had only just returned to the little hamlet, after evacuating it when the war came to the region a few months before. They hadn't intended to stay, just to pick up their belongings and stores. But the armed men had come and killed the fifty-four villagers they found there. For some reason, they carried off Miguel Tujin Estayul and his three underage boys. A woman standing by the mayor, her face frozen with incomprehension, said that her husband and five children were gone as well. They also took away clothes, food, grain, pigs and chickens.

This was the hamlet of Macaljab, near San Miguel Uspantán, February 16, 1982. It was only one of the Guatemalan towns to have witnessed such massacres in the last three years.

This was the spot where I had decided to begin my journey: a charnel house in the country, a hamlet of horror in the hills. Back in 1982 it had seemed to me typical of the darkness that lay at the center of the human psyche: the insensate slaughter of innocents. Had the villagers been killed simply because they were in a combat area? Were they murdered as an example to others? Had they perhaps supported the guerrillas, or the army, or delivered supplies to the guerrillas or to the army? Maybe there was a reason, maybe none. It didn't matter, just as it didn't matter who had killed them. They were victims of a cult of violence, an expression of the region's seeming inability to evolve except through destruction, which would condemn it forever to poverty, backwardness, repression and murder.

The banality of evil. How often had I heard the tired phrase; I pondered it as the open jeep jerked and bounced along the potholed, dusty mud track away from that terrible scene. The emptiness of those extinguished lives had been banal to me, certainly, anticlimactic after what must have been a terrible frenzy of human suffering, worse than the scenes of horror in the bloody movies some Americans so admire. And maybe the killers were banal, men of such ignorance and baseness that they derived pleasure, or purpose, from hacking small children to death. Ignorance, primitivism, was the only excuse; if so the killers were not intrinsically evil. They could be cured through education, through the learning of tolerance. Yet if there was such a thing as true evil, as distinct from ignorance, then it was not banal. And I feared that there could be, because atrocity had been part of Guatemala for so long. Where there was ignorance there was hope, where there was evil for its own sake there was none.

The road from El Quiché through the town of Chichicastenango, the highway to the capital, was open. Every few yards along it, I saw Indian self-defense patrols, belonging to the 500,000-strong army set up by the government to police the lonely roads of the highland region. The men looked grimly set in their purpose, walking in twos and threes, bearing machetes or antique carbines across their backs. They were short and stocky, heavily padded against the cold of the upland regions; they had mustaches and the vacant, glazed look of men who had performed routine tasks throughout impoverished lives. Their faces were oval-shaped, rounded, the eyes curved in. When I spoke to them in the Spanish that was their awkward second tongue, they were uncommunicative at first, and did not immediately break into smiles of greeting (only the children did that). But when they did, it was a warm, toothy grin across the lower half of the face.

The women were stocky, too. Their broad hips billowed out into plump legs. They stood at the side of the road, selling knickknacks and melons near the villages. Between the villages along the winding roads through gaunt, rocky mountains, interrupted by knots of thick, wooded country rather like France's Massif Central, walked the patrols. They shuffled along, giving me and the driver surly, suspicious glances, but didn't attempt to stop us. From time to time we passed a fortified army position. These were built back from the road, with rudimentary watchtowers. We could see the soldiers in their camouflage, with their steel helmets or green-and-brown bush hats, watching us.

"Why are the patrols necessary?" I asked my driver, a serious, lugubrious, deferential man with a weathered face and a scrubby mustache. He did not return conversation gladly. He had his work cut out for him dodging potholes. The car, of considerable vintage, was one of Central America's ubiquitous Mercedes. Its front windshield was cracked, but it rattled and bumped its way along at surprising speed. The heating system was out of order and I huddled in my jacket. Guatemala was a hot country, but I had forgotten how high the altiplano—the country's central plateau—was.

"The patrols? *Muy necesario.*" Very necessary. "Against the guerrillas. The guerrillas used to stop buses and burn them."

"What—with the people inside?"

"No. They made the people get out. Sometimes they would take people's belongings or ask for revolutionary taxes. Now the road is open, there haven't been attacks along here for some time. The soldiers guard the towns. The peasants guard the roads between them. The roads serve them, after all; they and their women are the ones who use the buses."

A user of the roads himself, he was not on the side of the guerrillas. When I had been here to cover the worst period of the war in 1982, the roads were virtually impassable, disrupted by frequent guerrilla attacks. The army would travel to its sideshows by helicopter. Villages were abandoned; the crops lay untended by the side of the roads.

The fields were well tended now, and the villages we passed showed every appearance of normal life. The women wore woven, multicolored shawls that gave even the plainest among them a radiance; the hats they favored seemed to be sawn-off tricorns, rather like pirates' hats; they wore beads and jangles, great weights of them, on their breasts. Unlike the men, they went about their tasks cheerfully.

Giant letters were painted on the bare rock along the side of the road, where it widened to two lanes in passable imitation of a highway. "This is a public work of the government," the lettering proclaimed. "The government works for the people." I remembered it from my last trip; it had been put up under Guatemala's most murderous recent ruler, General Romeo Lucas García.

"Do you like the government?" I asked my driver, apropos of the announcement.

"Yes. It has built a good road. The best in Guatemala."

I hadn't really expected him to say anything different. It had built a good road and now protected it. The rest didn't concern him.

I was thirsty and cold after four hours in our jumping jalopy when we reached what my driver had said was a sight I must see: Antigua, the old capital of Guatemala. It lay below the Agua volcano, a majestic, perfectly conical peak that gave the city purpose and a heavy responsibility, like a crown upon its head. The place was not beautiful, but it had a certain stateliness: it was geometrical, with straight streets on a grid in classical Spanish colonial style.

The cobbled streets ran between one-story houses, many of them washed white, others green, garish pink, or gray. There were no soldiers here, no self-defense patrols, just a few kids playing in the street, a few old men in doorways. The squat, reinforced appearance of these colonial towns was explained by the earthquakes they periodically suffered from. The last big quake, which knocked down most of Antigua, was in 1773; an earlier one had reduced Antigua's predecessor as capital city, Ciudad Vieja, to rubble.

We visited the churches, huge buttressed affairs, man's protection against the worst that the trembling earth could inflict. The Monastery of San Francisco was the biggest of them; I left the car and wandered down to the ruined cloisters by the intact church. Through an arch, two monks in conversation could be seen walking on the grass, and I felt a sense of peace and civilization for the first time that day. No wonder the church, a beacon of tranquillity in an outback of small, makeshift dirt villages, was admired.

I didn't want to spend the night in Antigua, though, and even at five o'clock, darkness loomed: my guide wanted to show me one more spot before we reached Guatemala City. After we had driven an hour or so through increasingly dramatic country, the road suddenly plummeted to reveal a huge hole, a lake, calm in the evening stillness, lying in a deep crater overshadowed by two volcanoes. Clouds obscured the top of one of the volcanoes, although I was not sure that they came from the mountain itself. The smooth angle that the volcanoes' long slope made to the surface of the water was reflected in the glassy surface, broken only by the gentle V-shaped ripples that trailed out from two boats crossing the lake. The blue of the lake was an absolute, like its flatness. The scene was one of great beauty, yet the volcanoes, for all their scenic appeal, could be even deadlier than the people who lived beneath them.

The car took an age to negotiate hairpin turns down to a lakeside town. It was a tacky resort, a clutch of bungalows (luxury homes to most Guatemalans). The streets between them were filled with vendors selling bric-a-brac to overweight Americans and Swedes in their early twenties displaying the patronizing contempt and familiarity of those who imagine they are seasoned travelers. The Guatemalans, with their exotic sense of costume, appeared unruffled by the ponytails of some of the male travelers, their overstuffed rucksacks, the girls' well-padded thighs protruding from their chopped jeans. Civil war did not seem to deter the well-heeled international hiker. "What war?" asked one visitor I talked to.

In a little bar, a rather plump, middle-aged man with a weary expression eyed me, then came over. He asked me what I did: when I told him I was a journalist, he told me he was a priest. He had had to leave his parish in the Alta Verapaz in the far north of the country; it got too dangerous. The hard right had murdered some of his most supportive parishioners. He was next on the death list. The people there were now without a priest; but he could go back eventually. The certainty of his optimism was impressive.

"Why did the right attack you?" I asked.

"They said I was engaged in politics," he told me with a shrug. "It is impossible not to be, in a country with social injustice on the scale of Guatemala." But he was a moderate, he said, a Christian Democrat. To the right, there was no such thing as a moderate; so he was a communist.

I wanted to get to Guatemala City that night, and the driver was nervous about driving after dark. We set off as the light began to falter over the crater lake. On the way we overtook a convoy of gaudy buses with a pinball-machine battery of brake lights that lit up in the gloom, like a traveling circus. The road took us in to Chichicastenango, where we were held up by a huge procession. It was the Day of the Kings; men and women wearing grotesque masks and sprouting giant feathers from their bodies jumped about, while others boozed and cheered and laughed.

It is impossible to understand Guatemala without understanding something of the full-blooded Indians who make up nearly half its population. The Indians of Central America are a kaleidoscope of ethnic groups. In Guatemala there are seven—the Mam, the Quiché, the Pokomam, the Chol, the Maya, the Caribs and some Pipils. They speak twenty-three languages, Maya and Quiché being the most important. The pure Indian proportion of the people of Guatemala was 60 percent in 1940, dropping to 43 percent by 1970. Most of them live on the country's high plateau; in Totonicapán province the people are 96 percent Indian, in Sololá 93 percent, in Quiché 84 percent and in Chimaltenango 77 percent.

Guatemala accounts for most of Central America's Indians. In El Salvador, there are far fewer full-blooded Indians, around three hundred thousand, or 15 percent of the population, mostly Pipils, living in destitution. In Honduras nearly two-thirds of the population is mestizo (mixed blood), while only 8 percent are pure Indian: they belong to the Jicaque and Tolupan tribes, the Lencas, the Payas, the Sumos and the Miskitos, whose nine thousand people are scattered about the jungle province of Gracias a Dios (Thanks Be to God). Around seventeen thousand Miskitos, along with sundry Sumos, Payas and Ramos, inhabit the torrid border province of Nicaragua near Honduras. In Costa Rica there are even fewer

Indians—about twelve thousand, or 0.5 percent of the population, divided into Guaymís, Teribes, Huatas, Borucas, Bribrís and Ujarras. In Panama, about 5 percent of the population are Indian— sixty-five thousand people, mainly Chocos from the wild Darién region near Colombia, as well as Cunas and Guaymís.

To the Guatemalan Indian, the family is the center of the social organization. To the women falls the task of bringing up the children, of looking after the house, and of craftworking, as well as selling in the markets. The man's role is to provide the food for the family, to build houses, and to go hunting and fishing. Both men and women help in the harvest, but otherwise the division of functions is absolute. Members of the same family or clan help one another, and if common services are required for the village, all members take part.

Maize is the most common form of Indian food, and *chicha*, an alcoholic derivative, is taken from it. Potatoes, beans, maniocs, chili peppers, cucumbers, pineapples, bananas, avocados, cactus fruits, papayas, mangoes and coconuts are eaten, and tobacco, rice and coffee, which were brought in by the conquistadors, have become popular. Most villages have some common land, although each family farms its own patch.

The children help with household tasks from an early age. Teenage boys are given early independence. Daughters are brought out into the world in a major celebration of puberty, a kind of ritual party. Indian marriages are strictly observed, usually occurring in the late teens, although important members of a community can have second wives. Although sexual faithfulness is not strictly observed among the young, adultery by a married person is frowned upon and can lead to his expulsion from a community. Divorce is allowed in certain cases, such as impotence. The old are taken care of by their families, and burial takes place in a fairly plain musical ceremony, to show stoicism in the face of death. Yet the Indians have elaborate beliefs about the dead, and consider that the soul of a person slain or killed in an accident has been condemned to linger on earth for a time and return to haunt the living. All the dead return to earth on the Day of the Dead.

Ritual looms large in Guatemalan Indian life, and although most Indians are supposedly Catholic, the religious beliefs of the church have been adapted to the original beliefs of the Indians. But the main

Indian religions have always borne striking similarities to Catholicism: baptism, confession, sacrifice, even incense, were known to the Indians before the Spaniards came. The Christian tradition of the Twelve Apostles is reminiscent of the Indian legend of the Twelve Stars that oversee agriculture. The Virgin Mary has become synonymous with the Mother of the Earth. Most Indians believe in a single supreme god of the male sex (although the Paya Indians worship a female called Potatishataha) and also believe in a battle between good and evil spirits.

However, there are also vast differences between Indian traditions and those of the Christians. For example, in the Indian rituals a myriad of spirits are worshiped. The Mams are specters that inhabit the wind, the rain, the lakes, the rivers, the mountains and the railroads. The sun is worshiped as the god of life. The moon is a young virgin, linked to rain, childbirth, menstruation and farming; lunar eclipses are dreaded. Venus is the god of agriculture, hunting and fishing. The god of death is a skeleton robed in white who appears to those near death.

The cross was worshiped long before the Christians came. The Mayan cross represents the four directions to everlasting life. The east is the source of life, the west is where the dead go and the source of malevolent winds. Good spirits inhabit the high ground, bad ones the underworld. The left-hand side of a person is bad; the god of death has an evil left hand. Sundays are good days, Thursdays and Fridays bad ones. The number three is lucky for women, the number four lucky for men. White is associated with death; red with strength. The color yellow is associated with courage, green with fertility, black with sacrificial rites. Chickens and turkeys are still sacrificed.

The Indians believe in bad winds, which possess people and make them ill or indolent, and the evil eye works against people of a delicate constitution. Every volcano has its monster or guardian who sometimes devours the inhabitants of a village and has control of *mozos*, his own band of spirits chosen from among the souls of the dead. Tornadoes can take human shape, as horrible beings dressed in black with mops of unruly hair. Betudo is the devil in the shape of a handsome man. The Judge of Night is a tall man who can take life. The Weeper is a young, sparkling girl who seduces wayward travelers, then makes them ill, lamenting their fate. The Sombrerón—

Hatter—is a small, wizened man who seduces women and leaves them to die. The Teaser leads travelers down the wrong path.

There is an evil wind that invades houses, throwing the plates about and making a noise, and another that shakes trees. Sinsinite is a hideous giant or dwarf who throws stones at those repelled by his appearance. The Black frightens those who are out at night. Juan Dieguito is invisible, and seduces women unable to understand why they are aroused. Chapaneco punishes rich people who ill-treat the poor, and Juan Negro robs the rich to give to the poor. The Phantom Cart has no driver, but passes at night, rendering mad those who see it. The Cadejo is a red-eyed hound that inhabits cemeteries.

The leader in a village is the shaman. A *brujo* is a sorcerer or witch who works evil, often to satiate his lusts or for payment. Every person has a *nagual*, a guardian spirit, that is an animal and it is believed that people can change place with their animal spirits, and thus inhabit animal forms.

The Indians divide their year up into eighteen months of twenty days each; each day has a name and a particular significance. Every local landscape feature has its own particular superstition; for example, the people living around Lake Atitlán believe there is a gold bell at the bottom of the lake that some of them visit in their sleep and that renders them happy forever. Religious rites are an interesting mixture of Indian religions and Christianity. At Easter a stuffed dummy representing Judas is ill-treated and then burned. The twelve days before Christmas are celebrated with nonstop processions and music. Fireworks are a great favorite, and mortars loaded with dynamite charges are sent up as rudimentary messages to God to ask for rain, or seek an end to it.

Indians tend to be reserved, their loyalty more to their communities than to themselves. If this gives them a slightly socialist outlook, their fatalistic belief that the world operates according to the will of God makes them anything but revolutionary.

We crept into the outskirts of Guatemala City in darkness, past the ravines where slum houses perched and sometimes slid down rubble-strewn slopes—because the land cost nothing. We passed the shabby attractions on the city's fringes, the Pizza Huts and hamburger stands and drive-in whorehouses. "That one's cheap," leered my driver. "That one's expensive but it's cleaner."

The road led on past the plaza in front of the old cathedral, square-fronted with two towers, its huge buttresses stained black by the exhausts of countless cars; we passed the skyscrapers at the center of the city, signposts of the country's progress. Life for the Indian peons on the altiplano, who make up more than half the country's population, might not have changed for centuries, but here in downtown Guatemala City it had: big American cars raced about the broken highways past undistinguished modern buildings that might have been lifted from Fort Worth, Texas.

The car left me at a Spanish colonial hotel just off the main road. I rang up a friend, a respected former head of a moderate political party, and arranged to meet him at a nearby steak restaurant. Against the advice of the hotel proprietor who warned of thieves, I walked there. On my last visit fear of ordinary thieves was overshadowed by fear of terrorism. In 1982 a palpable tension hung over the place. It was hard to find a restaurant open then. Concrete roadblocks had been set up at the approach roads to public buildings to frustrate the most common form of guerrilla attack—crashing cars stuffed with explosives. Almost everyone on the streets seemed to be armed, from the angular, bony soldiers in their macho camouflage uniforms to the security guards fondling machine guns. On that visit I could actually hear the distant crump of bombs going off at night.

In the country with the worst human rights record on a bloody continent, death was never far away. In 1981, according to the American embassy's optimistic figures, the number of disappearances was about 300 a month; the Catholic Church claimed that 9,000 people were killed that year, among them more than 250 Christian Democratic Party members and nearly 200 preachers and priests. Fifty journalists had died too, along with union leaders, peasant leaders, students, academics, lawyers and doctors. Guatemala's fellow Central Americans, deriding its slow pace of life, joked that the country's national saying was "Why hurry to your death?"

But it wasn't a joke here. The daily newspapers were speckled with impersonal passport photographs of people who had "disappeared" or whose mutilated bodies had been found by the roadside. I remember on a visit in 1983 hearing the country's president, General Oscar Mejía Victores, declare, "There are no death squads in this country." Who then were the men who one day in September burst into the house in Cotzumaguapa of Isidoro Lech and grabbed him, the woman he lived with and a nine-year-old child? Who were the men armed with submachine guns who, the same day, grabbed Vidal Gómez and his two sons in the capital itself?

Now, in 1986, the terror had eased. At the restaurant where I had arranged to meet my friend, the *jeunesse dorée* of Guatemala, no longer afraid to go out in smart clothes, made merry. My companion was in his late thirties, plump, bespectacled, serious but with a touch of joviality. I shall call him Juan. He wore a loud checked jacket and a broad red tie.

"How do you find Guatemala these days?" he asked.

"Calmer."

"There is a long way yet to go. But yes. Are we still the lepers of the outside world?"

"Not so much."

"Foreigners don't understand us. They think we are still a tyranny, a cruel, right-wing regime. Instead we are in a process of change. Of historic change. The army is being eased out at last. It is a revolution, a civil war. All such things are bloody. But it is for the good, although I wish it had been more peaceful."

"Like one of your earthquakes or volcanic eruptions?" I offered.

He didn't smile. "You would be surprised how after each earthquake, Guatemala City was built on more solid foundations."

He told me that I had to go back a long way to understand Guatemala. All through the present century landowners and generals have fought bitterly for power in Guatemala. The people originally counted for nothing: they were mostly illiterate peasants, the overwhelming majority Indians. The landowners needed the army to defend the nation and their small estates against occasional peasant revolts. But the army was of an inferior class, too, officered by petits bourgeois, shopkeepers, Indians even. It was impossible for any officer to get into the smart clubs of the country. It was all very provincial, very petty.

The struggle between the constitutionalists, as the landowners saw themselves, and the army raged unabated until the Second World War. The soldiers were stronger at times of civil unrest, weaker at times of calm. The last big prewar general was the dictator Jorge Ubico—not bad as dictators go—who lasted thirteen years. He even declared war on Hitler, in order to seize German-owned lands, which he sold off for $150 million, a large sum in those days. Ubico was toppled by a revolution in 1944, the first genuinely popular one, led by university students. It was a sign of the growing strength of the new intellectual classes in the towns.

"They put in a university lecturer, Juan José Arévalo," Juan said. "He was hopeless, an intellectual socialist, an idealist. He despised the Americans and foreign interests. He stirred up the workers in the United Fruit Company, so that they demanded higher wages and had to be laid off."

Juan snorted. "A typical case of a socialist doing more harm than good to his own supporters. He snubbed the old landowners, but, curiously enough, he tried to make friends with the army, believing that with their humble origins the officers would rally to him. Arévalo was succeeded in 1950 by a left-wing officer called Jacobo Arbenz, of German-Jewish origin. Arbenz carried his power to wild excess, confiscating foreign properties, waging war on the landowners, living in unbelievable style himself, traveling about in huge motorcades. He was an Al Capone, a gangster. Arbenz started wooing the Eastern bloc in a childish way. He made his congress stand in homage to Stalin—can you imagine!—when that monster died in 1953.

"And then the gringos intervened. They had had enough. John Foster Dulles sent an invasion force of Guatemalan exiles, headed by Carlos Castillo Armas, and the dictator was overthrown because his own army refused to fight for him. All was peace and light again," he said sardonically, "although it took time to attract foreign interests back to a country which had been so badly burned by the Arbenz experience. Our brief communist interlude was over. Our soldiers were sent to fight communists down the Latin American mainland. We went back to our old power struggle—the landowners versus the army. But the communists managed to assassinate Castillo Armas, who was a good president, and we had a sucession of stupid, brutish generals then. The army was in charge, because the landowners had lost prestige during the Arbenz period. A reformist won the 1966 election, but he was undermined by a guerrilla campaign started by our old friend, Fidel. It was back to the army in 1970."

It was reckoned that through this, though, real change would come. After Arbenz, the economy boomed. Guatemala was the richest economy in Central America. It had oil. It had cotton and coffee, which were fetching good prices then. Its industrialization was impressive for a Central American country. It could feed itself.

The buildings that now adorn the city center were going up. The government was corrupt, but not too bad; the landowners wouldn't let the army plunder the country. Taxes were among the lowest in the Western world and Guatemala's currency was stable. The quetzal was linked inextricably to the dollar: one dollar, one quetzal. Inflation was not allowed to rise faster than America's. It was a brilliant policy. It spared the country from the economic chaos farther south.

Yet, as people got richer, society began to change. A new industrial working class came into being and a new middle class made of new money began to emerge. These people wanted a share in the political actions; it was anachronistic to have a country run by the army, in uneasy competition with the landowners. But how could the army be shifted? Power was its by birthright.

Then things started to go wrong. There was a hurricane in the mid-1970's that destroyed crops; three volcanoes erupted, destroying more and rendering thousands homeless; in 1976, twenty-three thousand people died in the earthquake as their heavy adobe mud houses collapsed in on them. It was one tragedy after another. In Indian Guatemala it was taken as a sign from the gods that things were changing.

Juan continued: "Then we had the economic disaster: the collapse in commodity prices and the jump in energy prices hit the country hard. The urban masses were no longer getting richer, but poorer. They began to veer towards the left. So did the new middle classes, frustrated by their inability to dislodge the army. The guerrillas started up again in a big way. Six thousand of them, in four armies, struck every village: in the north; in the oil-producing area of Alta Verapaz; on the coffee growing estates in the east; in Quiché and Huehuetenango—where you have just been.

"It was serious stuff. A lot of us could foresee the day when the guerrillas would march into the capital. I left the country. Many did. I took up a job with an international agency, and took my family to safety. What was to be done? The army was fat, incompetent, useless. The new president was Romeo Lucas García; just another corrupt general, so we thought. We were wrong. He was a monster as well. His idea of how to stop the revolution was to lash out and kill. In the army there are many people of the most animal kind"— I could not help but wince at the violence of Juan's contempt for the lower classes in his country—"who enjoy killing, who get a kick out of it. And then there were the new wealthy, who wanted to defend their wealth by any means. And the old families, people like myself, we didn't really care what methods were used; we had almost given up hope. Lucas García ran the death squads from his own presidential palace, down the road there." He gestured lazily.

"The reign of terror began. Lucas García's ally was Mario Sandoval Alarcón, the head of the National Liberation Movement (MLN), the country's fascist party. Sandoval is very intelligent, very articulate, although a shadow of his former self. He is old, and has had cancer. You should go and see him. He is still very powerful, very dangerous. He helped make the country a slaughterhouse. Anyone on the left, and even in the center, became fair game. Bodies turned up in the parks, in the countryside, in cars. Lucas García was a brutal man.

"He had a brother, Benedicto. He was just as brutal, but a good general; he pushed the guerrillas away from the main urban centers by using scorched earth tactics. The overall effect of Lucas was to swell the ranks of the left, as even moderates fled for the hills. Lucas García attempted to retain power by appointing a protégé as his successor. There was a coup, staged by that crazy evangelist, General Ríos Montt, supported by junior officers. Ríos Montt was a strange man, part of the new obsession with Protestant cults. He belonged to the 'Church of the Word' and believed God had preordained his power. But he was an honest man, in his way, and a good president. He turned the tables in the war by setting up the Indian self-defense patrols and sending army units into the country on eighteen-hour patrols, in small groups, using the guerrillas' own tactics of harassment against them, getting to know the country.

"He was ruthless too: his guns-and-beans campaign—*fusiles y frijoles*—offered Indian villages guns with which to protect themselves in exchange for their support. If they didn't support the government, so much the worse for them. Along the border with Mexico, he herded the peasants into 'model villages'—fortified and defended from the guerrillas. Anyone the soldiers found outside the villages was in trouble. The army started winning the war. From six thousand guerrillas, the number fell to four thousand. He was a good soldier. A good politician as well, he allowed political parties to organize. He booted the death squads from the presidential palace and had some members of the death squads summarily executed, when his men traced them. But the squads remain a big problem; even now they have so many sympathizers within the armed services.

"Finally, he got the idea he was the savior of Guatemala. He prepared to stay on as president by rigging a promised election for a constituent assembly. That was unacceptable to the gringos, and he had made many enemies within the armed forces. There was another coup, and General Mejía Victores took over. He is a dull, unimaginative officer, but he will carry out his duty. The army wants to get out of office and concentrate on wiping out the guerrillas. The soldiers are unpopular; they know that. They do not want to overstay their welcome. So the elected politicians are to get their chance after all. There you are: we are now an emerging democracy. That is a better picture than you saw from the outside, eh? The tourists should come back to Guatemala."

"How can you say it is acceptable? The killing still goes on."

"Hombre, I told you! They are trying to control the death squads. In the countryside there is a war on. The guerrillas are ruthless. They have been pushed out of the villages now by the guns-and-beans campaign. So they terrorize villages to get their food. It is serious stuff. You cannot take half measures. Even I, a liberal, accept that."

A liberal. He could afford to be one. He had come from a good family, led an easy life, left the country when things got difficult, come back when they got easier. Other, nastier men, whom he despised, protected the social order he belonged to. He was a liberal because he was well educated, well traveled. Yet he lived on the backs of killers. For all Juan's veneer of taste and cosmopolitanism, I found myself almost preferring the Ríos Montts of the world, the men doing the dirty work.

"Does it ever bother you, the poverty round about? Eating in a restaurant like this?" I asked, glancing around as our table was cleared. The people there had the jovial good looks, the smooth skin, of men who have been prosperous all their lives, men who have been spared the struggle of others.

"That is Marxist talk," he said incredulously. "This is a rich country. One that can make all of its people rich. We are not El Salvador, or Peru, or Honduras, where millions of people live off poor soil. If we can sort out our political troubles—and I believe it

will be through democracy—the country can prosper. Then everyone will become richer. There will be a smaller lower class. That is
the ideal in the United States, is it not?"

"I'm not an American," I said.

"I can see that."

I left him early, declining his offer of a lift. He was right: the
contrast between this and previous visits supported my conclusion
that Guatemala was changing and there was hope. But his compla-
cency, his readiness to sanction murder, disturbed me. I walked
home through the deserted streets unscathed.

The ruling class had a lot to answer for. If Guatemala was such a rich
country, why had it not gone the way of the United States? Not
always a backwater for political piranhas, Guatemala was once the
heart of the Mayan empire, the greatest pre-Columbian culture.
Around A.D. 300 Mayan civilization, whose architecture and sculp-
ture rivaled that of Europe, whose practice of mathematics and
astronomy outstripped the Europeans', began in Guatemala, in what
is now Belize. It spread out to other parts of Central America and
Mexico. Temples, pyramids, observatories and ampitheaters flour-
ished. Cities like Tikal, Uaxactún, Copán, Quiriguá and Calakmul
rivaled their European counterparts, though the Mayans knew nothing of Europe. They worked out calendar months, gained skill in
their form of pictorial writing, and practiced what now may be
regarded as a tolerant religion. Yet this civilization was suddenly and
mysteriously wiped out in the ninth century, leaving temples covered in vegetation and a people with vague memories of an earlier
golden age.

The memories quickly dissipated under the reign of the conquistadors. The country's first conquistador ruler was the vicious Pedra-
rias. Its second, the roguish Pedro de Alvarado, held power for
twenty years. His capital, Santiago, was washed away when part of
the volcano it was build upon collapsed on it. But otherwise the
captain-generalcy of Guatemala continued in some prosperity and
semiautonomy until the eighteenth century. The country was run
by a colonial bureaucracy lording it over black slaves and a repressed
Indian population. Guatemala was a bastion of somnolent plantation
luxury. In 1821 the captain-generalcy rather belatedly followed
Mexico into independence, and was soon annexed by a Mexican

army. The Mexicans, made thoroughly unwelcome, pulled out twelve years later, leaving a liberal urban clique in charge.

This faction was overthrown by conservative provincials, who looked for leadership to Rafael Carrera, a charismatic twenty-five-year-old Indian pig keeper of no education who also held the support of the Indians. The liberals became, in effect, the party of the urban oligarchy, and the two groups strove for power under a succession of strongmen. The worst was Manual Estrada Cabrera, who ruled for twenty-two years at the turn of the century, cowing the population but allowing foreign capital to open up the country. The ruling class—the landowners—ridiculed the dictators, but accepted them because they defended the interests of property. Change has come only now that the ruling class has been forced on the defensive by the new middle class and the new wealth.

Juan had suggested I see Mario Sandoval Alarcón, a man with a fearsome reputation, one of the angels of death of Latin America. He represented the old, violent Guatemala.

His larynx had been removed during a cancer operation in 1970, and the metallic tones from his voice box had earned him the title of Darth Vader among local journalists. He described his party as "the party of organized violence."

I decided instead to visit the new Guatemala, in the form of Vinicio Cerezo, leader of the Christian Democratic Party. It took me a while to get a taxi, which drove me over poorly paved streets through the city center to a particularly undistinguished house. There were men on the street looking warily at me as I climbed out. The house had thick wooden boards across the windows; a great slab of masonry was missing.

An earnest, priestly type in a roll-neck sweater asked me who I was and let me in. The room was sparsely furnished, with few decorations, and no light at all. The windows were boarded up. A friendly, good-looking youth fetched me coffee. "My father will be with you in a moment," he said.

"Thanks. You're pretty well guarded," I told him.

"We have to be. I only just got back from the States. My father wouldn't have the family here until recently." He was engagingly frank. "Things are better now, but the killers are still around. I was in a car a few days ago, and we got stuck behind a Land Rover. A

Land Rover—they always use them for the same purpose. This one had no license plate. There was a man trussed up in the back and other men with him. They were on their way to the park. That's where the death squads dump their bodies. There was no doubt what was happening." He paused. "Last week a car went past and opened up on the house; a month ago a mortar was fired at the place. Maybe you saw the impact of the shell on the building."

Yet despite the charged atmosphere, this house—the home of the leader of Guatemala's largest political party—seemed miles away from the normal political circus, the politicians who blare and bluster, democratic, overweight, balding men with ready smiles and crumpled suits. Cerezo, most likely Guatemala's next president, entered wearing cowboy boots, slacks, an open-necked shirt. He was a slim man, with not an ounce of spare flesh. His was a craggy, good-looking face with a small mustache that ran the whole length of his upper lip. I was irresistibly reminded of a Western. He didn't quite look like a bandit, nor quite like a hero either. He spoke in easy American English. He was a man of vigor, youthful in manner, with a relaxed smile that crinkled at the corners of his mouth. There was an engaging informality between father and son that I found attractive. He seemed astonishingly at ease for a man in constant danger. I asked him about it.

He shrugged, with a slightly macho insouciance (but, after all, he was the real thing). "You get used to it. There was a time when I was hardly sleeping in the same house from night to night. This is my parents' house. I don't like the trouble I bring to them. Ah—my son told you about the mortar attack. It was more tiresome than worrying. When I walk down the street, I have to be followed by a carful of armed men.

"At least these days I can walk down the street. Two years ago, I couldn't even ride. They opened fire on my car. The bullet-proof glass and the reinforced steel protected me. We had a ten-minute gun battle. It is safer now. That is why my son could come back. Things have improved a lot under the new regime. The killing goes on, but the government is trying to control it. Sometimes you get a sudden spate of deaths, and then it stops. I think that is to do with the army faction-fighting. I do not understand their internal politics."

I asked him if democracy was really possible in a society where violence is so inbred.

"Sure." He was almost dismissive. "We are not such strange people, the Guatemalans. We are always told that we are not ready for democracy by those who rule us. But they are the ones who practice the violence. When ordinary Guatemalans are given the choice, they vote for moderates. Of course there are too many gunmen in Guatemala. But ordinary people like the violence no more than you or I do."

I was not so sure. I thought there was a cult of murder in Guatemala. A visiting Canadian senator, Peter Stollery, wrote of the horrific assassination of two politicians by the extreme right: Alberto Fuentes Mohr, a leading Christian Democrat, and Manuel Colom Argueta, a prominent centrist.

Two motorcyclists wove between the cars and riddled him [Fuentes Mohr had the misfortune to get stuck in a traffic jam just in front of the main polytechnic] with bullets as he sat at the wheel of his car. They shot the woman in the car behind as well, but she survived. She would not comment about the assailants.

Colom Argueta went down after a spectacular car chase through the streets, also in broad daylight. First the gunmen, again on motorcycles, had to kill his three bodyguards. Colom fought back, but was finished when his car ran into a tree. . . . He had twenty bullets in him when the volunteer fire department arrived. Members of the fire department, the police, and the staff at the morgue earn extra money taking photographs of the bodies and then selling them to the daily newspapers. Guatemala City has a lively press. The most graphic ones are sold to a small paper called *Extra*, which comes out only on Sundays. It has a large circulation and basically only carries pictures of dead bodies.

When I talked to Vinicio Cerezo, I mentioned a newspaper story which had appeared in that morning's *El Gráfico*. Even for Guatemala I thought it was pretty wild. The headline read: THEY ARE LOOKING FOR THE HEAD. Apparently the fire department had found a headless body and their problem was that it could not be identified. They appealed to anyone who found the head to turn it in.

I asked Cerezo if he was a moderate. The MLN had said he was a communist.

He was thoughtful. "I believe in social justice. There should be a land reform and a better health care system. But first we must have democracy. Political pluralism is the prerequisite for everything. Otherwise the moderates will go over to the guerrillas, and the civil war will get worse. Then the real communists will win. The only way of ending the excesses is to get to democracy on schedule. And I believe this president will do so. He understands the political realities."

"Of American pressure?"

"Of course that has some importance, the general likes to get on with the Americans. But we are also very nationalistic. We are a sovereign country; we insist that the Americans cannot push us about. And, after all, the Americans stopped giving us military aid in 1977. So they do not have much leverage over the army here."

I smiled. "Maybe that's why the army is doing so well against the guerrillas: because—unlike in El Salvador—there are no American advisers."

He laughed.

Cerezo's main challengers in the election would be the far right's Mario Sandoval and Jorge Carpio, a flashy middle-of-the-road newspaper proprietor seen by the American embassy as the comer in Guatemalan politics. Perhaps Cerezo was too left-wing for the Americans, although they recognized that his victory would be a good thing and that he was a genuine democrat.

I came away from my meeting with Cerezo immensely impressed. He did not resemble most people's idea of a democratic politician, except for the views he expressed. These included his idea of a Central American federation—certainly this collection of microstates needed it. In Guatemala's desperado politics, you had to be something of a desperado yourself. I thought Cerezo could civilize the country.

That evening, I had one further call to make—to the woman heading a foundation that supported American teaching and academic work in Guatemala. Maybe she would know what really went on there. She worked out of a comfortable matter-of-fact office on the main street. She was the kind that didn't frighten easily and instilled terror in officials. She was friendly at first. I asked her a few questions, sought to provoke strong reactions, but the cooperation went out of her eyes. She stonewalled. She found the conditions in the countryside "okay." There was little evidence of fighting there, she told me. No, her people got good cooperation from the authorities. She thought newspaper reports of the killings and the civil war were exaggerated. It was disconcerting to get this kind of double-talk from a plump, bespectacled, honest-looking American matron. But she had a reason. She wanted to go on working in Guatemala, to protect her people. I understood, but it depressed me.

Back at the hotel restaurant, I fell into conversation with an ingratiating American who was also staying there. He joined me at my table, wearing his clean white shirt and black-belted trousers. He seemed well schooled and clean-cut, his hair cut short, though not absurdly so. His conservative mustache was blond. I guessed he was around thirty years old. Gazing at me with a peculiar intensity, he screwed up his eyes, puffed at a cigarette and asked what I was doing in Guatemala. I told him I was researching a book. "Really? Is that so? That must be interesting. Real interesting." I thought so, but the way he said it didn't suggest he did. He was longing to be asked what he did, so I obliged.

"Well, Robert . . . "—almost the first thing he told me was his first name, David. He was one of those people for whom a second name is too personal. A first, while conveying greater warmth, is more anonymous, identifies you as just one of the millions of Davids out there, who can fade back into the masses without difficulty or trace. "Well, Robert, I'm with one of the evangelical churches out here."

He told me quite a lot, amid a steadily growing crowd of beer cans. The evangelical churches—to which the country's strange ex-president Ríos Montt had belonged—had, he claimed, converted fully a third of Guatemala's Indians. It was a phenomenon that baffled me. As the pieces of this jigsaw of a country fitted into place—the Indians, the civilian parties, the new middle class, the old oligarchy—I couldn't understand how obscure evangelical sects from Southern California could entice the tenacious residents of Guatemala, who had already been baptized by fire. I asked him why he thought the evangelical churches were doing so well.

He responded with a triumphant look. "Well, it's a hard thing to explain. And yet it's a simple thing to explain. Remember, these people are steeped in idolatry. They worship heathen gods plus the Catholic religion, which I guess is the same sort of thing. They were just waiting to be told." He explained as though I was a child, someone untouched by experience. "I would guess, Robert, that

you've never been born again." I told him this was a fair assumption.
"Well, let me tell you, I was; and it was the greatest experience I
have ever been through. It was such a great experience that I resolved to bring it to as many people as I could. Even the poor people.
Or you. Yourself especially. You, Robert, can share in this experience." He wasn't a phony tub-thumper, although he sounded like
one. He was absolutely, passionately sincere.

"Oh, I think I'm beyond saving," I said lightly.

His eyes blazed. "Oh no. You're not, don't ever say that. You can
be saved. Just like those Indians out there. And you can save others."

"What does this experience feel like?"

"The most incredible thing that ever happened to you. Really.
You know, I led a corrupt life before. I got involved in drugs, loose
living. I led a worthless life." He spoke with vehemence. "But He
saved me. Now He can save you."

I changed the subject. "You've done a lot of work with the Indians?"

He was disappointed. He wasn't getting anywhere. "Yes," he
said, in a more normal tone. "Boy, are they poor. Just the very edge
of human existence. You have to see it to believe it. All in the same
room with the animals. Freezing at night except for blankets. Absolutely incapable of raising themselves out of it. All of them subject
to the same low-lying, debilitating diseases. Cholera, leprosy, hepatitis, parasites, you name it. It's despairing at times."

Like all missionaries, the evangelicals did good relief work. But I
was no nearer toward understanding that particular religion's appeal.
Was it merely that most people had so little that they were prey even
to simplistic creeds brought in by the gringos? Was it that Roman
Catholicism—which in some ways reinforced the Indian religions—
had become too much of a formula, too lacking in hope? Was it that
Guatemala was the nearest place for wierdos from California to
travel en masse? Or was it just that the Indians followed the lead of
the generals? Probably a mixture of all four. Both of us were weary
of each other's company after the fourth beer, in the plain little patio
bar with the photographs of Guatemalan wildlife on the walls and no
mosquitos. We said good night.

My last meeting in Guatemala City was with a trade unionist whose
telephone number had been given to me by Guatemalan guerrilla
contacts in Mexico City. He came to see me in my hotel. He was

stocky, honest-looking, with the flat, massive face of a Guatemalan working man. He was not at ease. He told me that his name must not be mentioned. He spoke quietly; although there were few people about, he kept lowering his voice to prevent the proprietor, who moved in and out of the reception area to the bar, from hearing. I asked him the standard question, whether things were improving in Guatemala, as Cerezo had told me. "Hombre, this is a land of terrible injustice. A handful of people have most of the land. Until there is redistribution, there is no improvement. Have you been up into the Indian areas?" I nodded. "It is unbelievable, the poverty. Nothing has changed for centuries. Even here in Guatemala City we have terrible deprivation. The Indians are treated as a people apart, although they are a majority of the population. They are joining the guerrillas in the thousands."

"I am told that has stopped. That they are now fighting the army's war against the guerrillas."

He gestured expressively. "Some of the Indians are frightened. They live in terror. The butchery in the mountains is appalling. The army has the advantage for the moment, but not for long. You'll see."

"And do you see no hope in the elections? Most people think they will be fair."

"Yes, but we have had fair elections before. The results were ignored—as happened when Ríos Montt ran in 1972. If the vote is not rigged, there will be a coup."

"And Cerezo? Isn't he an honest man?"

"Cerezo is an able man. He thinks he can deal with the army. But they will toss him aside when they get the chance, like an old rag. You know our army. We are run by an army of gangsters, crooks."

He was oppressively pessimistic, depressingly like a broken record. If he represented the left in Guatemala—and his views were a foretaste of others I was to hear from left-wing politicians through-out Central America—there was no compromise possible. The guer-rillas were the only hope. Nicaragua, which I was shortly to visit, was the ideal. Nicaragua was the only country that had undergone the necessary eruption.

Miguel Angel Asturias, Guatemala's Nobel Prize–winning writer, has a nicely ambiguous passage about an eruption in his novel, *The Mulatta and Mr. Fly:*

. . . he managed to see it . . . the curving . . . the clouds of dust . . . everything falling to pieces and coming up out of the structures, solid just a moment ago, those great clouds, orange, gray, opaque, without joints, hiding the trees torn up, not by the wind, by their roots, by a subterranean wind in their roots . . . hills and valleys in soapy waves were pushed against the grain by serpentine fissures that flowed along the roads torn out like pieces of hairy skin along with the breaking of bubbling water that ran to hide itself from the moon. . . .

When the devastation is over, Asturias's hero sings:

> *Happy am I*
> *I want nothing at all*
> *the blue of the sky*
> *is my home and my hall.*

Is he merely dead, or truly free? It is a question that Nicaraguans have long been asking themselves.

Terrifying cataclysms, even amid rural poverty and stagnation, are not necessarily liberating, and instead induce fatalism, a fear of change—in ordinary Guatemalans, at least. Fatalism is a national vice, and may turn out to be the most effective brake on Guatemala's progress. Yet economic growth, by contrast, is bringing about real change. Economic growth in Guatemala rose by an average of 5 percent in the 1950s and by 7 percent in the 1960s and mid-1970s. The economy had improved again on this, my latest visit. The economic boom had created the new middle and working classes fighting for power with the old ruling classes. Appalling acts of violence, although not a revolutionary eruption, had ensued in that struggle. Now Guatemalans were beginning to settle their differences through the medium of democracy. If democracy takes real root in the shadow of Guatemala's volcanoes, the lot of the poor and the subjugated Indian will improve. If the place erupts into violent revolution, I doubt it.

At the airport I decided to jet-hop to my next destination, Tegucigalpa, because the jet-hops were so quick (twenty-five minutes on average) and the roads were so bad. A soldier in a gaudy camouflage uniform approached me, fingering his gun. Journalists had been fair game for arrest in Guatemala, although the foreign press was rarely a target, and my heart missed a beat. Perhaps I had said something to offend Mario Sandoval. "You want to swap your quetzals back into dollars? It is not allowed. But I will do it for you." Relieved, I declined his offer, and he went away.

HONDURAS

EVEN FROM THE PLANE, THE CONTRAST BETWEEN GUATEMALA AND THE surrounding countryside was easy to see. It was a brilliant, sunny, early morning, and the lands of conflict lay below in temporary peace. We were not very high up, as the hop was very short. The deep trenches that surrounded Guatemala City, the morning mist that enshrouded the capital, lay behind us, and I felt light-hearted. As the gray and brown of Guatemala's arid desert land-scape drifted below, we moved over a region of fertile hills, appar-ently untraversed by roads. This was El Salvador, the stop after next.

I surveyed the ground in vain for signs of war. Was that smoke over to the west? Was that the Guazapa volcano, where the fighting was supposed to be concentrated? A pair of magnificent conical shapes rose off to the left, neither of them smoking, covered nearly to the tops in green vegetation. But the smoke might have been a forest fire. To the east, where we were headed, the land was higher, less hilly, more lushly vegetated. This was Honduras, a great empty upland, one of the poorest countries on earth, bordering on another country's civil war. If I had found hope where I had expected to find none, in the badlands of Guatemala, what would I find in Honduras, "an asshole of a country," as an American traveling salesman, whose company I fled at the airport, had put it?

The aircraft circled the capital, Tegucigalpa, more than two hundred miles due east of Guatemala City, sprawled below in an uneven saucer of mountains. We made our descent, heading straight toward the nearest mountain. I held my breath: we skimmed the mountain and seemed to be crashing into a deep valley. Suddenly a flat shelf of ground rose up a few feet below and the wheels bumped down, jolting us. The runway was short, so the aircraft pulled up sharply before the next edge.

Feeling a little shaken by the rough landing, I made my way through a long customs line out to a taxi. The taxi coasted from the airport, down a slope, into the outskirts of this strange city that appeared to be just a large spread of shacks covering the mountains, with no rhyme or reason. Some valleys had rows of shacks, others didn't; some had roads, others didn't. Tegucigalpa was incredibly poor, so poor that the embassy district, a row of modest suburban villas with neat, well-trimmed little gardens—labor was plentiful in Honduras—looked like poor retirees' bungalows in a modest American town. Past these, the road arched down to a jerry-built skyscraper that dominated the valley because there were no others. This was the Maya, the city's only tolerable hotel.

The Maya lobby was packed with burly, square-shouldered Americans with crew cuts and wide, good-natured yet impersonal smiles. They sat about in groups, exchanging pleasantries, greeting each other with handshakes, appraising each other as big, self-confident men do.

After a walk, to get rid of the aftereffects of my flight, I went to the hotel lounge for my first meeting. The press counselor of a Western embassy was redheaded, of Irish descent, and strode in with a slight swagger; he had a weather-beaten, cheery look, like a young army officer out of uniform. He was frank and open; I had asked him to help me arrange meetings with his ambassador and military people, so I could learn for myself what was going on in the contra guerrilla camps near the border with Nicaragua.

I had met the Irishman before, on a previous visit in 1982, so it was as familiars that we exchanged greetings on the veranda of the hotel, which overlooked rows of shabby huts dotting the mountainside below. "Christ, am I glad I'm getting to the end of my term here!" he told me. "You sure get tired in a place like this after three years."

"They've been a lively three years," I said. "This place is close to becoming the fifty-first state."

He gave me a sardonic look. "You think Uncle Sam wants it? It's a rathole in the middle of nowhere. We had to put democracy on its feet here. We had to tell the generals to get out. Then what happens? The first civilian president they elect, Suazo Córdova, gets to like the job. He's not allowed to tear up the constitution. So he starts trying to find ways of getting around the constitutional ban on him succeeding himself. First he tried to get a constitutional amendment through to change it. Then he tries to get his protégé appointed as his successor, so he can go on running things behind the scenes. There's a major constitutional crisis brewing up, and the generals are getting fidgety. You can't blame them: the civilians and the army deserve each other." He sighed. "You'd have thought the country's first civilian president in years would have taken the trouble to behave himself."

"It's amazing that democracy survives at all in a place as poor as this," I said.

He narrowed his eyes. The face was hard, freckled; a face with little regard for pen-pushers. But he was an engaging guy nonetheless. "You subscribe to the view that a poor country deserves a dictatorship, huh? Maybe you're right. This is the poorest country in Latin America, except for Haiti, and I don't think that counts. This country's whole national product is smaller than Costa Rica's national debt, and Costa Rica's just a postage-stamp country, for Christ's sake! But I don't agree that they're too poor to look after themselves. When they had an election after years of army rule, they voted for the two big moderate parties, the Liberals and the Conservatives. The far left and the far right were way out of sight. Nah, being poor doesn't make you dumb."

I thought he was right about that: poverty often makes you conservative with a small *c;* you learn to value money, your few possessions, that much more. Particularly so in a predominantly rural country like Honduras, which lies scattered across barren mountainside and torrid jungle. The intellectual left hadn't done much for Honduras: the United Fruit Company was at one stage threatened by an organized left-wing union, and land was collectivized. The company ended up buying the fruit from the workers on contract at a lower price than it had had to pay out as an employer.

Honduras has always been a poor country. Consisting of all the poorest, most unattractive and unsettled scraps of Central America, it withdrew from the Central American Federation in the 1830s. As there was only one big town, Tegucigalpa, and the country was so far-flung, local military leaders, ranchers and heads of small armed forces vied with each other, staging coups and seizing the capital from time to time over the next century. The average term of a president was a year. The country then turned with relief to a period of tough one-man rule by a military caudillo, General Tiburcio Carías Andino, who ruled for fifteen years from 1933. After him, for the first time, a more liberal professional class emerged and a program of education was undertaken; the country, which barely had an economy, began to be developed; some seventy airfields were constructed to pull the far-flung country together. By the 1960s a full-scale economic boom was under way.

The army had taken over again, however. The country's military president during the boom, Osvaldo López Arellano, was considered too conservative by his fellow officers, and a moderate, General Policarpo Paz García, took office. He enacted some modest land reform measures and paved the way for a withdrawal of the army from power. The election gave some 90 percent of the vote to middle-of-the-road parties, with the Liberal candidate, Dr. Roberto Suazo Córdova—a shrewd, tough populist who liked to portray himself as a simple country doctor—taking over.

"People say the army really runs things from behind the scenes," I told the man of Irish descent.

"People always say that. If you're talking about a defense policy, or foreign policy, no president is dumb enough to do something that offends the army. But that's true of any country; the defense establishment in the United States, for instance, isn't a slouch either when it comes to formulating defense policy. But when it comes to economic policy or internal policy, the army's happy enough to let the civilians get on with it. The soldiers don't understand economics."

I was skeptical. "How about disappearances? They discovered a mass grave the other day. That was the army's hand, wasn't it?"

He became cautious. "Yeah. Zambrano. That was a nasty little massacre. But it's the only one we've had. Just a handful of people in

twenty years. Have you been to Guatemala or El Salvador, where
every night the same number are killed? What happened at Zambrano would be just a little Saturday-night unpleasantness in Guatemala. It was actually committed a while ago. And it happened
when our old friend, General Alvarez, was in charge of the army. He
got too tough for the Hondurans. They woke him up one morning
with a pistol pointed at his head. They put him on a plane out of the
country. His successor's a more moderate man, a constitutionalist:
the air-force chief, General Walter López Reyes. He couldn't stage
a coup even if he wanted to, because the air force doesn't have the
firepower. No, I think you'll find democracy has taken root in
Honduras. They're a nicer people than in Guatemala or El Salvador.
They don't enjoy killing people."

"It's taken root because America wants it that way?" I asked
quizzically.

He pursed his lips in irritation. "Sure, America wants democracy
here. I know that argument. It helps Congress to approve supplies of
arms and training for American servicemen down here. This fleapit
has had half a billion in American aid over the past six years. That's
a hell of a lot for a country like Honduras; about the biggest business
in the country. We want democracy down here, because we believe
in it. But you can't install democracy where it doesn't take root.
Hondurans want democracy and they vote for moderate leaders.
They don't like killing. I told you, those are national characteristics."

We left the terrace of that bizarre hotel, which by now was filling
up with energetic American soldiers off duty: there was a primitive
casino in one corner, but it didn't look as if it was ever used. In the
Hotel Maya, many of the floors were built below ground level, down
the slope of the mountainside. I went down to my room.

The barracks was in the center of town. The soldier on guard was a
thin young man, in a forage cap that contrasted with the tin helmets
of soldiers in other Latin American countries. He responded to my
request with an uncertain glance, then pointed at a door, where an
equally young army captain was sitting. He didn't call up to check
whether I had an appointment: he just put on his cap and joined me.
We strode into the main yard of the headquarters of one of the
smallest armies in the world. Men were drilling to one side; evi-
dently there were few parade grounds in Honduras. There were

trucks parked across the way. People wandered over the yard, from one part of the covered walkway, which was a monastic cloister, to another; there were many elderly peasants about, come to see their enlisted sons. It was a busy, informal scene.

The captain pointed: "*Es su oficina.*" He saluted and left me by the doorway. I could have been anyone; the army wasn't overly concerned about security. There was a dark-skinned woman wearing Honduran army fatigues behind the desk. After I explained who I was, she waved me to a chair.

At length a pot-bellied man with spectacles and slow, sloppy way of talking sauntered through. "Come in," he said casually, and I followed him. "How can I be of service to you?" he asked smoothly. He was the colonel who had been assigned to tell the outside world about the dangers facing Honduras and proved quite splendidly unhelpful, parrying every question flat. I asked him about the thousands of contra guerrillas on the border with Nicaragua. "There are no contras in the country," he told me. "They are all across the border."

"But there are full-blown camps down there," I said.

"You have been there?" he asked sarcastically.

"I would like to go."

"That is impossible," he replied triumphantly.

I asked him about the reequipment of the Honduran army by the United States. He was hardly more communicative. I asked him about the attitude of the armed forces toward democracy. "That is a political question. You will have to ask the commander-in-chief."

"Can I see the commander-in-chief?"

"Certainly. When do you leave?" I told him. "Ah, he will not be in town before then."

I stayed only twenty minutes, leaving the tiny headquarters with its busy courtyard for the foreign ministry, where I had an appointment to interview the minister. His office was in a building that must have been distinguished at the turn of the century; it was built around a miniature covered cloister with wide steps ascending behind sturdy pillars to the second floor. There I was shown into a long and—for Honduras—well-apportioned room with uncomfortable gilt chairs, where I took a seat. At length, one side of a double door opened at the end of the room, and a shy little man with a mustache peered out.

He wore a double-breasted suit, which was several sizes too large for him; the cuffs tripped him up repeatedly as he walked toward me with a mixture of self-consciousness and self-importance. I took him to be the foreign minister's flunky, but his smile and handshake were friendly. He looked ill at ease, as though I had come to request a favor. "How can I be of service to you?" he asked in the ubiquitous greeting of the country. He was the foreign minister.

I asked him about the Honduran relations with Nicaragua. "We have correct relations with Nicaragua, as with all our neighbors." What about border violations by the Nicaraguans? His eyes flickered this way and that, and his lips became pursed in a slightly irritable expression. "Any such violations are properly investigated. But I repeat, our relations are correct." What about relations with the United States? "We enjoy warm relations with the United States." Didn't he think relations were closer than that, that maybe they encroached on the sovereignty of Honduras? After all, American soldiers were training on Honduran territory. Couldn't Honduras defend itself?

"We have no American bases here. The troops train here by our consent. We are a country with a strong army and we are grateful to our American allies for their support. Yet, I repeat, we are a sovereign nation, and the Americans are here only as long as we permit them to stay."

After the interview, he came to the door to say goodbye with a shy smile and an automatic handshake. He wasn't a bad foreign minister; he had been interviewed without making any major indiscretion, in fact without saying anything, yet leaving a pleasant impression. But it was frustrating all the same.

That evening I dined alone in the hotel restaurant, which was the only one that looked safe in a country with endemic hepatitis. The food was the bland international cuisine that was featured in any large hotel, even in Tegucigalpa. Two American servicemen were enjoying themselves chatting with whores.

I had two calls to make the next day. The first was to the ambassador of a Western country. The embassy turned out to be only a stone's throw from the hotel, in the diplomatic quarter. It was a relatively high building for the district, and the country's national flag fluttered outside. I was told to go to the second floor by a security guard who didn't look up from his newspaper. I took the

elevator up. There I went into a lobby with a bullet-proof glass
reception area at the end. A matronly local woman glanced at me. I
said I had an appointment with the ambassador. She called through.
At length she let me through a heavy steel door and upstairs to the
next floor.

There a tall, distinguished-looking man greeted me. I took him to
be the political officer or the press officer. It was unusual to be taken
straight to the ambassador. But the post was too small to have a
political officer. He led me into a room with a map on one wall and
a desk at the other end. "Well, and how long are you here for?" he
said brightly.

"Two days," I said. He grimaced. "That's the trouble. No one
stays here long enough. It's a fascinating country, you know. You
ought to get on down to the jungle region by the Coco River.
Absolutely uninhabited. Fascinating area. Little villages in clearings.
The Nicaraguans were rash enough to try a mini-invasion across the
area. They infiltrated a couple dozen men, but the local Miskito
Indians informed on the Sandinistas; they don't like the Nicaraguan
government because ten thousand of their Indian cousins in Nicaragua were made to go on a forced march across mountains and
forests in appalling conditions. Doesn't bear thinking about. Anyway, the Honduran army was quietly tipped off where the invaders
were and staged a successful ambush. They killed six of them,
captured half a dozen others, and left the rest floundering around in
swamp country, trying to survive as best they could while the
Miskitos finished them off."

"Do you think the Nicaraguans pose any kind of real threat to
Honduras?" I asked him. "It doesn't seem a place they would bother
about."

"That's a good question," he said, choosing his words carefully
and playing with his hands as he continued. "El Salvador's the
traditional enemy of this country. You remember in 1969 there was
the football war, so called because a match triggered it off? The war
was really fought over disputed pockets of territory in western Honduras. Honduras has been losing territory ever since it became a
nation. The Salvadorans are tough little men: their country's over-
populated because it has the best land in Central America. So they
want some living space. They attacked, and came off with a bloody
nose. The Honduran army may not be much to look at, but their air

force, which is equipped like a flying museum, can fight astonishingly well. They've now been given twenty-one UH-IH Vietnam-vintage helicopters by the Americans, so they've improved a bit. That's why the air force has such a high prestige in the country.

"But to get back to your question. I don't think for a moment that the Nicaraguans could stage a successful invasion of Honduras, even if they wanted to." He pointed to the map on his wall. "It would be impossible for them to reach Tegucigalpa across this mountainous terrain. Further north, that's impenetrable jungle. The only way they could come in would be down the narrow corridor between the mountains and the Pacific to the west. In theory, they could then gain access to good routes to the capital that way. But it would be military suicide. They could be picked off any time down that corridor. No, I don't think a Nicaraguan invasion of Honduras is on. But they could mount attacks across the border into Honduras to eliminate the contra camps; and at the moment there's not much the Hondurans could do to stop them."

"And the Americans? How strong do you think their commitment is to defend the Honduran government?"

"From an outright invasion, total. I think the Americans would step in. That's another reason I don't think the Sandinistas will try one. Whether the Americans would step in to prevent a crossfire between the Sandinistas and the contras along the border is much more doubtful."

I went back down to the forecourt of the hotel, where the taxis lined up for customers. One took me down to the American embassy complex, which as always was one of the most prominent buildings in town. I mused, as we passed the bustling poverty of the steep streets of the center, that it must be lonely working in a place like this, a rancher's town in the mountains. And yet there must be some excitement to be derived from being the man on the spot in a remote, crisis-ridden capital. Tegucigalpa was, after all, the eye of a storm, although safe in itself. Flying in and out of trouble spots like Nicaragua and El Salvador, while being based in a place like Teguci, must spark the adrenaline, for a while at least.

The American embassy complex was protected by armed Honduran guards and a large steel gate. I was deposited outside the gate by the taxi. A receptionist in a bullet-proof both admitted me as soon as I had told her who I wanted to see and produced a passport.

Standing behind her, an unsmiling marine in a white hat watched as I went through a metal detector. I walked up toward the building, which was laid out more like the center of a university campus than an embassy. There were easy chairs and what seemed to be a library of American publications and literature. People with square faces and spectacles, wearing shirtsleeves and no ties, leafed through magazines.

I was taken upstairs to an office occupied by an oversized military man with a crew cut and a mustache. He was burly in face and body and seemed to regard me with distaste. "I'm not usually supposed to talk to journalists," he told me. "You know the golden rules. It'll have to be off the record. Not even unsourced—just deep background. What is it you want to know?"

He told me his opinion of the Hondurans, which I am honor bound not to repeat. Suffice it to say he made the point that the Americans here got on all right with the Hondurans, and I had to say that in my conversations with Hondurans there didn't seem to be much to suggest that there was a latent anti-Americanism here. The Hondurans, while poor, seemed above envy. They recognized the contribution the Americans were making to the economy. They did not suffer from hang-ups about their native culture. They seemed to genuinely admire the American way of life, and were grateful for the American shield of protection. They expressed no love of their neighbors, Nicaragua and El Salvador. Because of the incredible poverty in Honduras the people had few hopes about what a changed social structure might achieve. The landowning class was microscopic, the middle class was minuscule. Ordinary Hondurans were too poor even to be revolutionaries; they seemed to like foreigners.

The American gave me information about the extensive U.S. operation in Honduras. They had eight to nine hundred Americans moving in and out of an air base at Palmerola, a handful of trainers at a base just outside the capital, and fifteen to twenty trainers at a place called Trujillo. The Americans also used to train Salvadorans, on Honduran soil, to be less murderous and more effective militarily. But the Hondurans began to fear that the Salvadoran army was learning too well and—once it had mopped up the guerrillas—might invade Honduras again. So they booted the Salvadorans out.

The American presence was most noticeable during the infrequent military exercises. There had been four major military exercises to date, involving between one thousand and five thousand men. I was impressed by their seriousness. One exercise involved an amphibious military landing; another included the rescue of a unit cut off and stranded in the jungle. A third was to help the Hondurans defend their territory. The operations had local names, like Ahuas Tara (Big Star) One and Two and Operation Granadero. The continual transfers of American personnel ensured that American boys didn't create too much friction with the locals, and kept their presence discreet. It also meant that the Americans didn't get bored in this remote country with little to do in the evenings. There was no doubt in my mind that the preparations and the training weren't merely to deter the Nicaraguans but to prepare American soldiers for an invasion of Nicaragua, were a decision ever made in Washington to go in. Invasion was a military option, although for the moment not the one favored by the president of the United States.

I flew out the same evening. The drive to the airport was long and slow, the wait for departure interminable. As I gazed out across the ramshackle capital in the mountains while the plane taxied to takeoff, I found myself thoroughly liking Honduras, a realistic, unpretentious country. Then the aircraft was moving and I braced myself against the seemingly impossible takeoff over the lid of the plateau into a mountainside in front of us. It seemed to me that the plane only just made it over the top.

EL SALVADOR

WHERE WAS THE WAR? IT WAS SCANT CONSOLATION NOT TO SEE ANY visible signs. El Salvador's brash, new, empty airport at Ilopango, some 130 miles southwest of Tegucigalpa, looked as calm as any in Central America. At the immigration counter the precautions, as elsewhere in Central America, were surprisingly relaxed—more so than in most Western capitals. My passport was briefly inspected; my intended address was noted, my bags were chalked cursorily with crosses. The agents did not bother to look inside. I shared a taxi paid for at a small booth before I left the airport—a precaution against rip-off operators.

The airport was ten miles beyond the city, built for a tourist influx that had been scared away by the war. (Brochures there still extolled the beauty of Guazapa volcano, long controlled by guerrillas. The taxi driver who later took me to El Playón, the lava bed where the death squads dispose of their victims, was blithely to show off the bed as one of El Salvador's beauty spots.) The splendidly engineered four-lane highway from airport to city curved majestically through the dense foliage and the hills surrounding the inactive, bleary volcano behind the city itself. This highway provided the first stark evidence of war; ours was the only car on the road for twenty minutes until we overtook an old truck. In El Salvador people didn't travel after nightfall—unless they had no choice.

We approached the city on a broad avenue lined with greenery and single-story villas set behind white walls. These were the suburbs, where the prosperous new middle class lived in houses with patios, ample sitting rooms, verandas, large gardens with lawns freshened by sprinklers. A middle-income Californian would have felt at home. We passed a jeep halted on the side of the road. Its occupants, four green-uniformed Salvadoran soldiers with the ubiquitous German-style tin helmets, with submachine guns cradled in their arms, watched us but did not stop the traffic.

Here in the suburbs there were a few more cars, including some large, occasionally battered American convertibles. But nowhere in El Salvador are there many cars; mobility is a luxury in short supply. We quickly reached the Hotel Camino Real. An anonymous yet comfortable building, it provided the security that journalists crave in El Salvador war work: if anyone disappeared, his or her competitors would notice. Telex communications with the outside world were passable. Companionship was to be found there, too.

Rather quickly I was immersed in a situation familiar to all Central American visitors—the foreign-currency-exchange argument. Everyone used the black-market rate because it was two and a half times the official rate. But I was too tired to search for a black-market dealer outside the hotel. A porter came to the rescue with a compromise rate but the transaction was prolonged. After the issue was settled, I noticed a little fiesta and barbecue taking place by the swimming pool beside the hotel, as it did every Tuesday. But only a scattering of people attended. Tourists were the first casualty of war. The nightlife, of course, was also subdued. A restaurant I visited was quite well stocked with food (although wine cost a prince's ransom) and well patronized. But the streets were quiet and dark, as the army units that patrolled the city were edgy and suspicious. And night was when the death squads patrolled. Surprisingly, no formal curfew was in place.

Before I went in search of the war the next day, I was required to get an official pass from army headquarters in San Salvador, just beyond town. At the entrance, my car was waved quickly inside; stopping outside was forbidden. I parked and walked back to the gate where two guards, fifteen years old at most, in gray-green uniforms, scrutinized my passport. These were the people responsible for much of the butchery. Maybe they even belonged to an off-duty death squad. Their faces were broad, puppy fat, their eyes slanted. Their lank, black hair betrayed Indian blood (90 percent of Salvadorans are mestizos, half-castes). There was nothing sinister—or indeed striking—about them at all.

They were eager to give me directions. With wide grins, they pointed me to the center of the camp, and let me proceed unaccompanied, unsearched. I found the press section: a low, utilitarian, military shack, where I eventually got my pass, with its elaborate official seal. The captain who issued the pass was in his late twenties, good-looking and very conscious of it. His feet were on the table, American-style; a crucifix dangled on his hirsute, exposed chest. He wore no tie and his top three shirt buttons were undone. "You want to see some action?" he asked languidly, as a taxi driver might suggest going to a whorehouse. "I suggest Guazapa."

I hired a taxi with ludicrously inadequate protection, a hand-painted sign saying *prensa*—"press"—under the windshield, and we set off out of town. The main road to Guazapa was humming with activity and soon we were stuck behind a truck transporting troops—again those nervous-looking, clean-cut kids with glistening coal-scuttle helmets. Their insignias this time were those of the treasury police, the force most responsible for death-squad killings. Once we got past the truck, there was no sign of war. We approached a bridge. "It has been down many times," the driver explained. "You cannot see them, but there are armored cars camouflaged on either side. They have been attacked too often to be in the open." I couldn't see a thing. The war remained hidden. That, for the most part, was the kind of war it was.

Guazapa looked less like a volcano than a series of low hills studded with stunted trees and shrubs, although there were patches with denser vegetation. The sky was blue, the scene utterly quiet. As we approached the volcano, the traffic diminished; then the town of Guazapa materialized from nowhere. It was a small, poor town, built in the colonial style of the cobbled streets and low one-story buildings with tiled roofs and whitewashed walls. We pushed through the narrow streets until we reached an army roadblock, which consisted of a protected sentry post and empty oil drums drawn across the road. We stopped. Two soldiers were watching, guns under their armpits, lounging against the wall. I asked where their local commander was. One pointed up the road: the roadblock was to prevent a surprise attack on the garrison.

I continued on foot. Further along the road, a soldier lay on his back, surrounded by flies, his foot propped up against a doorway, his gun in his arm, his mouth wide open. He might have been dead but was fast asleep. Inside, the scene was straight out of a B-movie: three men, in a darkened interior, were playing cards. They all rose, wide-eyed, when I came in.

I showed them my press card and asked who the commander was. Away. Who was in charge? A grizzled man in his twenties with a big unshaven jaw and an uncertain smile stepped forward. I asked him about the fighting. What fighting? There hadn't been any in days. What about the guerrillas in the hills? They'd gone. Could I go to the hills? No. He might have been ordered to say that there was no trouble, but the sleepiness of the place somehow lent conviction. I thanked him and returned to the car. We set off back down the cobbles.

This was a war of insignificant, sleepy outposts, grandly called garrisons, which would be suddenly outnumbered by a force of guerrillas. The army would rush in reinforcements, but the guerrillas would have already pulled out. A guerrilla victory, an army repossession.

On our way out, men immaculately dressed in treasury-police uniforms and helmets (the soldiers were typically unkempt) standing by the side of the road waved the taxi down. They trained their Hechler-Koch submachine guns on us. I stepped out warily and showed my credentials. Their commander, a quizzical, fiftyish man with a Clark Gable mustache, inspected these with the suspicion and distance of a man who finds reading difficult. All the while the soldiers kept me covered. I noticed a well-camouflaged camp behind them. The commander told me I should have checked in with him on entering town. He was probably insulted that I only did so with the regular army.

I apologized. I told him it was my first visit to Guazapa, and I hadn't seen his camp. Courtesy, respect, flattery count for a great deal in Latin America. He nodded and let us through. The driver resumed a running commentary, pointing to a nearly deserted prefabricated village of houses that looked like beehives; a few children played in the gutters. "The guerrillas took refuge there: they forced the local people to take them in. Then the army attacked: now most people have gone."

"And the guerrillas, have they really gone?" I asked.

"No, of course they are still in the hills," he said with certainty.

I asked him to drive to El Playón, the dumping ground of the death squads, not out of ghoulishness, but because the killing was so much a part of the place that it seemed an obligation to see it. The sky was clear behind the gentle slopes of the San Salvador volcano; we skirted the mountain, leaving the city on the far side. "El Playón—very beautiful spot," the driver kept repeating, although he knew perfectly well why I wanted to visit it. Like everything else in El Salvador, the clear air and verdant landscape of the foothills of the volcano were disturbingly calm. Only as the road began to wind through a bizarre rockscape across which were strewn large, pockmarked, black boulders, did horror set in. This was the lava bed.

The Black Rock, a great striped boulder, the lower slope of the volcano, extended before me; it was about a third of a mile across, on both sides of the road, where it flattened out. Nothing grew there. Bodies were usually dumped anywhere in this wasteland between the road and the volcano.

We stopped some way from a cart parked by the road, whose occupants gazed at us with blank hostility: relatives of the disappeared maybe, come to check whether one of their family had turned up on the lava bed. We picked our way through the boulders and the litter. I could see bones scattered all over the place and four or five skulls, picked clean by the vultures. You could make out the bullet holes in the backs of the skulls where the victims had been shot. The jawbones were smashed to prevent identification. The vultures did the rest. Nearby, the large, fat, scraggy-necked birds watched. They were so full from feeding on the bodies that they merely waddled when I went near. Sickened by the place, we came away quickly. I thought of the spirits that would inhabit that place for generations to come. Gloom settled over us as we drove back to the deceptive suburban calm of the capital.

El Salvador: the caricature, to outsiders, of what Latin America was all about. Every detail of the caricature was in place. First, most striking and most ghastly, was the cruelty, symbolized by El Playón, where maybe fifteen thousand bodies had been left by the death squads in the past seven years. The cruelty of the far right was soul-destroying, and wholly unwarranted by the occasional excesses of the guerrillas—usually inflicted on villages that refused to give them shelter or informed on their whereabouts.

Second, there were the competing gangs of armed men: the army and the various police forces—the treasury police and the Republican National Guard. The army was no more than an alliance of autonomous local warlords loosely grouped together under the authority of the defense minister who could not fire the most powerful of the warlords, however, for fear of provoking a coup.

Third, there was the old ruling class, the so-called Fourteen Families (actually a few more) who for years ran the country for their personal benefit, using the army as a praetorian guard—until the army got too big for its boots and started to provide its share of the country's presidents and take its share of the money.

Fourth, there was the center—a band of moderate reformists, ridiculed by the gunmen of left and right as corrupt, shop-talking political hacks in a country too polarized for democracy to flourish.

Fifth, there was the Catholic Church, unwillingly dragged into the conflict, bitterly divided, its primate, Archbishop Oscar Arnulfo Romero, cut down in a hail of bullets while saying Mass.

Sixth, there was the American embassy, a concrete fortress in the middle of town, pulling most of the strings.

Seventh, there were the guerrillas, young men in fatigues with earnest faces and black beards on keen chins; young, fresh-faced, prematurely serious young women clutching guns; all belonging to a mad scrabble of Marxist-Leninist acronyms.

If the centers of power and the actors belonged to a caricature Latin America, so too did the history. It could be retold briefly. El Salvador's troubles stem from a century of poverty and backwardness, beginning with its emergence as a nation in the early nineteenth century. The power struggle was brutally simple: a tiny local oligarchy ruled over what was virtually a rural slum until the 1930s. The land, being relatively prosperous, attracted a large rural population, some of whom worked for absentee landlords as laborers. Most of the rest worked small plots in the poorer highland areas. Coffee, planted in the nineteenth century on medium-sized estates, was soon a mainstay of El Salvador's economy, which became relatively prosperous by the standards of its neighbors.

The peasants, their hopes raised by the economic upswing, took part in an uprising led by Agustín Farabundo Martí, a middle-class intellectual inspired by the Russian Revolution. The uprising was crushed by the army in 1932, with the loss of thirty thousand lives. The army's power grew, at the expense of the Fourteen Families, which nevertheless continued to depend on the army to keep the peace.

Like Guatemala and Honduras during the 1960s and early 1970s, El Salvador underwent a minor industrial revolution, with industrial production rising by 6 percent a year. Peasants migrated to the main cities—chiefly San Salvador, which sprouted, in addition to California-style suburbs, a center dominated by skyscrapers of concrete and glass. The city was a gnomic Dallas. An industrial working class also emerged and began to organize. The even smaller new middle class demanded a say in power and vied with the Fourteen Families, which controlled external trade and the banking system.

Then, in 1979, the Nicaraguan revolution took place, suggesting that there was hope for El Salvador's guerrillas, who had all but lost heart after three decades of fruitless struggle. The guerrillas began to recruit among the peasantry and the new working class. Some of the children of the middle class came to join their ranks. A succession of spectacular kidnappings of foreign nationals, including Bank of London and South America executives—for whose release British newspapers were obliged to publish full-page advertisements consisting of impenetrable Marxist-Leninist small print about a country scarcely anyone had ever heard of—supplied the guerrillas with propaganda victories and money.

The beginnings of instability thoroughly alarmed the United States, which feared the spread of Nicaragua's revolution to its neighbors. It was clear that El Salvador's incompetent, repressive ruling general, Carlos Humberto Romero, was incapable of the kind of leadership required. The American embassy made contact with the heads of the Christian Democratic Party and other centrist-groups, with the Church, and with young officers in the army.

With the support of these groups, a coup was initiated at the end of 1979, and sweeping social reforms were promised by the most vocal of the officers, Colonel Adolfo Majano. Local Christian Democratic activists implemented these reforms, including the nationalization of the banks and of foreign trade, and a three-stage land reform. Stage one involved the seizure of estates over 500 acres and their transfer to state-run cooperatives. Stage two provided for the takeover of estates up to 150 acres in size. Stage three consisted of a "land-to-the-tiller" program—all tenants would be given the land they farmed.

For El Salvador, it was full-scale social revolution: that, anyway, was how the extreme right saw it. The right believed that the guerrillas could be stamped out easily enough; more pressing was a campaign to exterminate the American-backed reformists who had used the threat of a guerrilla uprising as an excuse to get their hands on the power and the wealth of the country.

The death-squad horror was unleashed. Men belonging to the security services were recruited and paid by the old interests. (Much of the money came from Miami, Florida, where the oligarchy had fled.) The right found a political champion in Major Roberto D'Aubuisson, a young intelligence officer who was accused by many of leading the death squads. He was accused of having ordered the assassination of San Salvador's archbishop, Oscar Arnulfo Romero, by the then American ambassador in San Salvador, Robert White, who labeled him "a pathological killer."

The violence in El Salvador continued to escalate. By 1981, some twelve thousand people had been killed by the death squads. The savagery created new recruits for the guerrillas, whose numbers swelled to six thousand—a force capable of traveling freely in the remote southeast of the country and of occupying medium-sized provincial capitals by day. The guerrillas were also able to extend their influence into San Salvador, engaging in "economic warfare"—including the destruction of San Salvador's electricity supply lines and of the Puente de Oro, the main bridge spanning the Lempa River, which bisects the country. By 1982 they were able to stroll into El Salvador's unguarded airport and destroy a third of the air force's helicopters, which were vital to the army's ability to shift troops quickly around the country. The guerrillas then occupied the Guazapa volcano, just fifteen miles from San Salvador, building an impressive network of tunnels and earthworks, which withstood many attempts to drive them out.

The army, meanwhile, was an eighteen-thousand-strong rabble

headed by commanders whose main hobby was political infighting, not fighting the guerrillas. Sizable army forces would embark on clumsy military sweeps to purge the guerrillas from the towns. The guerrillas would simply move into other towns, compelling the army to change course. The guerrillas would then return to the areas just vacated by the soldiers. The guerrillas were well-exercised mice, the army a fat and clumsy cat.

By late 1980, with Majano's junta under fire from both left and right, the situation was disintegrating so rapidly that the Americans agreed to postpone further land reform. Majano was ousted and replaced as head of the junta by José Napoleón Duarte.

The most formidable of El Salvador's political leaders, Duarte is a short, stocky man with a bull neck and face sculpted by the endurance and suffering of his political career. He is an impressive stump orator and a sophisticated and persuasive politician who can hold his own in skeptical political circles throughout the world. In 1972 he ran in El Salvador's only recent nonrigged presidential election and demonstrably won, but was imprisoned by the army, tortured and finally expelled from the country. When he returned, he had the best credentials of anyone to become the head of the junta in 1980. Representing the conservative wing of his party, he stopped, as one of his first acts in office, phase two of land reform—the dispossession of estates of between 150 and 500 acres, which would have affected the coffee planters and driven them into the arms of the extreme right—and slowed down the land-to-the-tiller program, which had infuriated many small landowners who had lost their rented fields to tenants. Much of the moderate left promptly deserted Duarte; in particular, Guillermo Ungo, a social democratic leader, left the country to become head of the Popular Liberation Front, the guerrillas' political wing. The war grew worse; the killings escalated. The defense minister, General José Guillermo García, a wily military bureaucrat, provided political support for Duarte but didn't know how to run a war.

The main thing that kept Duarte in power was American aid. President Carter, and later President Reagan, both of whose hands were increasingly tied by Congress, threatened to cut aid off to El Salvador altogether if the right staged a coup. The aid increased steadily to nearly $1 billion over five years. The threats worked;

there was no coup. Slowly, very slowly, Duarte began to overpower the death squads and by 1982 the number of killings had fallen to some seven thousand by the count of the archbishopric's human rights commission (which was hostile to the government). Duarte and the Americans also instigated an election for a constituent assembly.

The election was troubled from the start: the left decided to boycott it. In large parts of the country controlled by the left, campaigning proved to be impossible. As the campaign proceeded, it appeared that the Christian Democrats would be overhauled by ARENA, the far-right party headed by "Major Bob" D'Aubuisson. During this remarkable campaign in the midst of civil war, Duarte visited provincial centers under stiff military guard, surrounded by party bodyguards, to address respectful audiences. D'Aubuisson kept to his strongholds, but, even so, he didn't escape being wounded in the shoulder by a would-be assass in. The incident merely enhanced his macho image.

An astonishing 1½ million Salvadorans voted; most people expected barely half that number to turn out. Forty percent voted Christian Democratic, but D'Aubuisson picked up 29 percent. With the support of the old National Conciliation army party, which hated the Christian Democrats, this gave the far right a majority in the assembly. Intense pressure by the Americans induced enough deputies to defect from D'Aubuisson's group to support a provisional government under a compromise candidate, the banker Alvaro Magaña.

From the low point of 1981, things improved very slowly in El Salvador. The guerrilla capacity to strike inside the capital diminished. The guerrillas remained confined to their strongholds, although still capable of venturing out in strength. The two showpieces of the Salvadoran army—the crack Atlacatl and Ramon Belloso brigades—were trained in the United States while three more were trained at the new American facilities in Honduras. The training had two purposes: to improve Salvadoran army practices and to instruct them in the "rules of engagement"—that is, to desist from shooting blindly at anything that moved in the countryside, from massacring villagers and from raping women. The number of death-squad killings dropped from seven thousand in 1982 to about three thousand in 1983, and fell further in 1984. "Human rights should not be quantitative," an opposition leader commented bitterly to me. Those whose lives were spared might not agree.

A constitution was drawn up. The presidential election was held in 1984, using a ludicrously elaborate system of computerized registration drawn up by the American embassy to prevent electoral fraud: endless lines formed while local officials haggled over the details. Duarte won a runoff election, defeating D'Aubuisson 45 percent to 29 percent to replace the transitional President Magaña. A new defense minister, Eugenio Vides Casanova, started to sort the warlords out into a properly structured hierarchy by firing those who wouldn't take orders and promoting new, younger men.

From desperation, through chaos, the faint beginnings of an ordered state? Or just a sham show arranged by the United States to salvage what it could from a country drifting inexorably toward revolution, as critics in Congress and in Western Europe alleged? Judging by my visit to El Salvador's parliament, an incongruous concrete-and-glass structure by a giant ditch, sham was what it appeared to be. The edifice was poorly guarded, like everything else in this besieged country. The semicircular chamber was presided over by solemn men and women, the floor arranged in lecture-room style and each of the deputies equipped with a desk and microphone. No one was allowed to interrupt as they spoke at interminable length. A plaque on the luxuriant mahogany walls reminded them that they must not be influenced by "outside pressures"—as if the war and the killing outside mattered not at all. The parliamentary ushers were as pompous as such people usually are.

I called on President Duarte's right-hand man, Julio Rey Prendes. His face appeared to be made of thickest leather, toughened by the years of political struggle. He chain-smoked and his eyes were bloodshot, quick, shrewd. Brief and to the point, he avoided all formalities. Was there still any possibility of a right-wing coup? "Some officers in the army still work against democracy, unfortunately." Could the death squads ever be entirely stamped out? He drew attention to the government commission being set up to investigate them, and to the fact that the new constitution for the first time prescribed judicial independence: judges would be appointed for fixed terms and could no longer be fired by the government at will. "But it is a long and difficult problem," he acknowledged.

What about a dialogue with the guerrillas? "We are seeking one; but it must provide for the guerrillas to participate in the political process, by running for election. We will never accept a carve-up of power, as they demand. Just because they have guns, why should they have power? That is not democratic." And the war? "It will be long. But we are slowly doing better." The tone was realistic, his democratic sincerity hard to fault. He hated the extreme right as much as the left. Those glazed eyes, that face pummeled into genial imperturbability had lived, as Duarte had, with the threat of death every day for seven years, and appeared to be above fear. He was summoned to yet another caucus meeting of his group.

A taxi took me to the headquarters of Rey Prendes's bitter enemy, Major Roberto D'Aubuisson. There was no missing the place; it was heavily sandbagged. Three guards lounged on top of the wall with their weapons, covering the small courtyard in front. Each clutched a sawed-off shotgun. Two more guards accompanied the man who inspected my credentials. One wore a bandolier filled with giant cartridges to fit the ugly barrel of the sawed-off shotgun he was carrying—a death machine stunted and disfiguring in its scatter power. A Magnum handgun was strapped to his side. He was large-boned, very dark-complexioned, with a flashing white smile. The others around him had long, rough faces, cool expressions, and the camaraderie of seasoned killers.

I was escorted to the offices of Mario Redaelli, D'Aubuisson's number two. A broad-shouldered man with a heavy mustache and the drawl of a Texas rancher, he ushered me to a chair. I asked him about his party's solution to the guerrilla problem. "We would offer them an amnesty; after that, we would bring about a final solution to the problem." I raised my eyebrows: surely the United States would cut off El Salvador without a bean if D'Aubuisson came to power? How would his side win the war? He reached for a drawer, pulled out a Magnum handgun, slammed it on the table. "We don't need gringo arms! This is all we need!"

Afterward, we pushed through the idle, carbined men in the hall to a giant grille, like a prison gate, which was opened by a guard from the inside. D'Aubuisson seemed to be as much a prisoner as anyone in El Salvador. I remember when I last saw him in 1982 during his tenure as president of the constituent assembly, his eyes

and body nervously twitching from side to side in his seat, bored
rigid by the protocol and procedure.

He was more at ease in his element, his headquarters. The man
most feared in El Salvador—a country where there was a great deal
to fear—was also the middle class's most fiercely masculine figure.
Women were known to faint at his rallies as he slashed melons with
a machete, in demonstrations that were pure sacrificial offerings to
violence. Their purpose was to show that the Christian Democrats
were green outside, red inside.

D'Aubuisson was a short, very trim figure, without an ounce of
fat. His good looks were very Latin: neatly trimmed dark hair curled
up on an oversized head; a thin, fastidious, elegant face; a hard, set
expression and chin. His eyes were quicksilver flashes of nervous
energy, never still for a moment, nor was his body. He jumped up
and down constantly, issuing orders, arguing, looking at papers
brought before him. His office was a jumbled chaos, his dress like
that of most Salvadorans—casual, open-necked shirt, canvas trousers.

He repeated the need for a quick, "final" solution to the guerrilla
problem. "The Christian Democrats are communists," he insisted
bluntly. So when he says he wants to be rid of all communists, that
includes. . . . He didn't answer, fixing me with a stare. What about
the Americans? "We are an independent country. If they stop supplying us with arms, we will win anyway. We can buy arms elsewhere. We are not in America's pockets." He was shrewd,
intelligent, a modern politician using primal methods: he knew what
he was doing. That made his responsibility for what was happening
in El Salvador all the greater. The banality of evil? Nothing about
him was banal: he knew the whirlwind he reaped, the tiger he had set
loose.

My inner tension lifted as I left D'Aubuisson's headquarters. How
very different the extremes were. The far right was fighting to the
death to protect its power and its financial interests—the established
order—although it was sincere enough in its loathing of communism. The far left was fighting for a better, more just society. The
fact that the left's vision was unattainable, and could only be achieved
at unacceptable cost, did not completely detract from the sincere
motivation of the revolutionaries. The far left reached better people
than the far right, however ghastly both their methods were.

On a stopover in Mexico in 1982, I had spoken to Salvadoran guerrilla leaders exiled there. The best-known of these was Comandante Ana Mariá Guadalupe, number two to Joaquín Villalobos, the top military commander of the guerrillas, who headed its most extreme, most strongly Marxist-Leninist faction. She was accompanied by Hector Ocqueli, the roving ambassador for the guerrillas' civilian front.

Comandante Ana Mariá was chubby, with the friendly, shy, intelligent smile of a nun of some years' standing. Underneath her long, dark hair she was serious, careful with her words, but eloquent. Ocqueli was much quieter, an intellectual with a reserved, distant look behind thick spectacles. Ocqueli told me, in effect, that attempts at a dialogue between the government and the guerrillas were doomed. He and Comandante Ana Mariá were both passionate, sincere and reasoned in their loathing for the political and social system in El Salvador.

My question about their concept of democracy was greeted with impenetrable dogma (although Ocqueli plainly took a much more moderate view than Guadalupe). Of course they were in favor of democracy. Would the left take part in elections, as the government had suggested? "The elections are a farce. If we came out of fighting to participate, we would be shot down. They want us to hand in our guns to put ourselves at their mercy." Did they favor elections in their ideal revolutionary state? Elections, in their view, were "a formality. We believe there is nothing wrong with them. But we must impose true democracy—like education for all, giving the peasants enough to eat, giving them hospitals."

It was easy to dismiss the extreme left as the mirror image of the extreme right. Yet its ideals were forged from the genuine perception that power had been in the hands of the right from time immemorial, and that one of the rightist instruments was bogus elections. Against these butchers, violence was necessary to take power; a social revolution must occur. Elections were of secondary importance and always susceptible to manipulation by the forces of the counterrevolution. It did not seem to occur to this enlightened, revolutionary, intellectually superior minority that the people they sought to liberate might want to be consulted. The revolutionary knew exactly what "the people" needed: hospitals, sanitation, houses, education.

The revolutionaries died, too, in obscure, nit-picking fights for their ideals. In 1983, Ana María Montes, number two to Salvador

Cayetano Carpio, the legendary leader of El Salvador's oldest, largest and most orthodox Marxist-Leninist movement, the Popular Liberation Front, was bludgeoned to death in Managua, Nicaragua. At first, the CIA was blamed. Carpio flew back from Libya, where he was seeking financial backing, and, after attending her funeral, committed suicide. The murder had apparently been the work of some of Carpio's men who had misinterpreted his frustration with her mildly softer ideological stance as a command to kill her; his suicide was an act of remorse.

The dull reality confronting the guerrillas was that two thirds of Salvadorans, in two elections that most observers concluded were—give or take a little fiddling—fair, had voted for parties that rejected the guerrillas. The extreme right, judging by the results, had a far bigger popular following than the guerrillas, who had urged electoral boycotts and had been ignored by the voters. Democracy, with a lot of help from the United States, had greater appeal than revolution.

Duarte and the United States had no hope of convincing the extremists of the left to abandon their ideology. But they could work to bring the disaffected socialists and left-wing Christian Democrats back into the arena. That was difficult. As the death squads' principal targets, they were embittered people. I went to talk to a young socialist in the shed that housed Socorro Jurídico—Judicial Aid, the main human rights body—at the back of the archbishopric of San Salvador, where his people enjoyed, in theory, some sort of sanctuary. A young man in spectacles, barely into his twenties, he talked matter-of-factly about how three other members of the governing body of Socorro Jurídico had disappeared recently. He shrugged off the possibility that he too might disappear.

He produced the statistics of those killed, like an accountant presenting his balance sheets: they were broken down by sex and employment—the great majority were peasants and students, but a new campaign against labor-union organizers was under way. He explained that the figures only related to cases in which families had asked Socorro Jurídico to investigate and help; many more went unreported. The total of nearly fifty thousand in four years he tossed in as an afterthought. To reconcile a country, when so many had lost a close relative, and in such a way! "The task is impossible," he said calmly.

I paid a call the same afternoon on the government's agrarian reform institute, where a team of young bureaucrats was seeking to do just that. The large stone building surrounding a spacious courtyard was buzzing with activity. The director of the institute was a tough, alert man in his forties. He pointed at the gaping wall beside the staircase: "A bomb did that." As we sat down, fusillades of gunfire could be heard. "Just the army practicing. Its headquarters is down the road."

Then he described the various stages of the reform, which he passionately believed was successful. Production had fallen on the large cooperatives, he conceded, but that was because of the initial disruption. The intimidation of the peasants by the hired gunmen of the old owners had all but stopped. The problems of the land-to-the-tiller program were being sorted out. One of his predecessors had been gunned down in the coffee shop of the Camino Real hotel, almost certainly by the extreme right, yet he was surprisingly self-confident.

I concluded my trip to the Land of the Savior with a call on the real center of power, and the biggest paradox in San Salvador: the American embassy. American interference in a neighboring country in postwar years had rarely (except in the case of the Dominican Republic in 1965 or Grenada in 1983, where U.S. marine landings took place) been more overt. The Americans had connived to overthrow General Romero; they had prevented Major D'Aubuisson from taking power after the 1982 election; they had insisted on a crackdown on death-squad activity. Fifty-five advisers attempted to enforce reforms in the armed forces, as well as to provide advice on military tactics. American money fueled the economy—and the war.

The greater part of this investment was beneficial, to prevent further violence between the numerous and well-armed extreme-right groups and the guerrillas. No one wanted a Cambodia of the Western Hemisphere. To prevent this a miracle was required: the rescuing of the political middle ground, which was in danger of disappearing.

Prior to American intervention, El Salvador labored drearily under military rule. At that time the Americans' biggest mistake in El Salvador was neglect, despite the presence of some U.S. interests. Nothing much seemed to be happening down there, the U.S. seemed to believe, so why intervene? Actually, American pressure on the earlier military dictators might have prepared the way for reform and avoided the current troubles. Despite the leftist rhetoric, America had taken too little interest in El Salvador for far too long.

The embassy was a remarkable building, approached through a narrow gateway and a revolving steel grille made of giant spikes. Only one person at a time could gain admittance. There were armed guards on the street outside, and there seemed to be guards posted along the tops of the walls, which were several feet thick; gun emplacements straddled the four corners, which presumably also housed guards.

The first body search took place at the gate. Then I was escorted by a guard to the main entrance, where I went through a metal detector and a second body search. As I was ushered into the building, a bullet- and shockproof glass door at least two inches thick clicked slowly open, into a lobby surrounded by thick doors of similar material. There I was greeted by a man encased in a booth, a young granite-faced marine, and the familiar stars and stripes on the wall. My credentials were inspected as I waited under the smiling photograph of President Reagan.

Upstairs, I discussed El Salvador's struggling economy with the American economic attaché, a bright woman in her late twenties with a fine analytical mind, a rather leaden-voiced man from the military mission and finally the ambassador, Thomas Pickering. A career diplomat with a donnish round and bespectacled face, Pickering was professional and admirably unemotional about the place. Somehow he had kept himself insulated from the horrors outside; a sign of Yankee arrogance and insouciance to those unversed in those horrors perhaps, but surely essential for a man responsible for making properly thought-out, often pragmatic decisions. Leaving the embassy, the press attaché weighed me down with "information kits"—telling me a lot more than I needed to know about every aspect of life in El Salvador.

On the drive home, my mind turned back to an earlier trip, when the press attaché's predecessor had invited a group of journalists to his home to talk to the political attaché. The evening had been warm, and despite the reassuring, heavily armored embassy jeep, the vicious-looking armed guards at the gate of the ample villa had been oddly worrying. They appeared much more dangerous than the possible guerrillas.

The house had been recently constructed in the Spanish colonial style by a since-fled scion of one of the Fourteen Families. We sat on the patio in semicolonial splendor, enjoying a gentle breeze across the lawn, ever supplied with stiff drinks by a white-coated waiter. The new political attaché, a tall, earnest young man from a good university, had recently arrived and was genuinely sickened by the place. (He had visited a guerrilla hideout murderously raided by the army only that morning.) The American journalists administered a grilling no lawyer would have inflicted on a murder suspect. The purpose was not to elicit information; it was merely a demonstration of the interrogators' political opposition to the war. "Bullshit! You know the United States is fucking up this place"—and so on, in the same vein. I had been thinking of the American responsibility for El Salvador's situation, the belated attempt to compensate, and the ghastly responsibility of this emissary. It seemed to me that on this occasion the greater arrogance was being displayed by the press, which had no ostensible responsibility, except to report the truth. In conversation later that night, some argued that the problem was "— and I don't want to sound racist—that the guys out there enjoy killing." They all agreed there was no hope for the place, so why not let the left take over, because the right was so appalling?

I thought of the land of El Salvador, its gentle green and yellow slopes, broken only by the occasional low, verdant volcano. I thought of the people: quick, able, hardworking, a trifle sad perhaps. Could one read cruelty into a land, into a people this way?

True, the killers probably enjoyed killing. An interview with a death-squad member by one intrepid *New York Times* reporter suggested, however, that the initial excitement of inflicting death degenerated into the routine monotony of any job. But the great majority desired nothing more than peace, as the votes in successive elections showed. The death squads and the civil war were evidence that killing was part of the culture, a well-engrained method of settling personal and political differences. But that would change as the culture evolved. For frontier societies, including—once upon a time—that of the United States, killing was accepted practice.

A change in this attitude was the slowest and hardest of all to achieve. But it seemed to me that El Salvador had made palpable progress—in the sowing, on such stony soil, of democratic institutions, in restraining the death squads, in the war of attrition against the guerrillas and, above all, in the yearning for an end to the war and democracy expressed by the people themselves. El Salvador's war was ignited by economic progress and its disruption of a stagnant slave-plantation society. Now, after a bitter siege, the political system was adjusting—without reverting to violent revolution. If democracy could find roots in El Salvador, it could find them anywhere in Latin America. There was a hope in hell.

NICARAGUA

MANAGUA WAS JUST A FORTY-MINUTE JET-HOP FROM SAN SALVADOR, around three hundred miles to the southeast, but the contrast between El Salvador's gentle green landscape and Managua's starkness was astonishing. The Augusto César Sandino Airport terminal was as tinny and jerry-built as San Salvador's was sleek.

Lining up for immigration gave me a chilly sense of déjà vu. On a visit three years before, a piece of baggage that had been carried in my aircraft exploded just as it was about to be placed on the luggage conveyor. Four handlers died. It began with a dull flash and thump that wrecked the building in front of me; this was followed by clouds of billowing smoke and a pandemonium of running men warning us to get down. After the bomb had gone off, I felt safe enough; the Sandinistas waving their guns seemed more of a menace than any bomb. But the ceiling of the luggage bay in front of us was reduced to tatters, although no one was hurt inside the building. We then had to wait seven hours to be cursorily interviewed. I knew the airport well.

The screening of entrants was not quite as slack as it used to be, but anyone could get in without a visa, unlike in Cuba. I was soon hurtling toward town in one of the ubiquitous rattletrap taxis with a scarred windshield; the driver did not trouble to dodge potholes, which made every screw of the old machine shake. The road coasted past a mixture of run-down suburban shopping centers, then past the demolished shells of factories—great tangles of girders, relics of the civil war. We skirted the slum quarter, a mass of densely crowded shacks made of planks, with open doorways occasionally protected by sackcloth. The myriad pockmarks on the boards were evidence of where the main fighting had raged. We eased out into the broad avenue of central Managua. But there was no center.

There were broad streets, but no buildings overlooking them: just curbs, overgrown by unkempt, patchy grass. When one came upon buildings, these were huge shipwrecked hulks, gaping skulls. The center of Managua was no more, destroyed by the 1972 earthquake that ravaged the city's crowded heart, leaving a graveyard into which the bodies of twelve thousand killed were plowed.

The emptiness stretched back from Lake Managua, an expanse of water upon which the volcano Momotombo, on its own island, puffed happily away. The earthquake-prone ground—over which the dictator Somoza sensibly did not rebuild the city, and on which Nicaragua's new Sandinista rulers had half-constructed a play area— swept back to the range of low hills beneath which squatted the Hotel Intercontinental, a giant modern pyramid. Its chopped flat top dominated the desolate scene. Beside the hotel, barely concealed, were the squat buildings of El Chipote, the dictator's bunker on the hill, now the Sandinista military headquarters. After the earth- quake, Somoza had the smart suburbs rebuilt around the back of the hill—on land that he conveniently owned. The poor were housed down the road, toward the airport. The car shuddered along the broken road past Sandinista checkpoints to the hotel, which had been badly rocked but stood up to the earthquake. The American multimillionaire recluse, Howard Hughes, was inside at the time of the disaster, occupying the top floor in solitude; his pinched form had to be carried out to yet a few more years of unwanted life.

Modern and ugly as the hotel was, it had an atmosphere. Revo- lutionary tracts were for sale in the lobby. Bodyguards for those senior Sandinistas who resided permanently in the hotel waited around, their guns propped up against the wall. A bevy of plump prostitutes glanced maternally up from sofas by the elevators. The "colonial bar" was a darkened, mercifully air-conditioned room, laden with potted plants; a television in the corner relayed revolutionary propaganda. The bar counter backed onto the little-used swimming pool; below that was a dubious nightclub where middle-aged out-of-towners drank at tables, eyeing overdressed women dancing together. Taking the elevator to my room, I remembered that when on a previous visit, I got out at the sixth floor, which was reserved for Russians, two Sandinista bodyguards pushed me back into the elevator, and not courteously.

It was the landscape and the passivity of the people that characterized Nicaragua, rather than the politics. The country had a curiously timeless air: hot and, in the rainy season, stiflingly humid. It suffered from a problem common to most countries near the equator, the evenness of the cycle between night and day. Perhaps this contributed to the Nicaraguans' defeatist view, that nothing ever changed much. The middle-class suburbs were discreet and few. The overwhelming impression, riding out of Managua, was of villages built on muddy streets trapped in poverty and squalor. Women hung out their washing, children played unselfconsciously, old men sat motionless in slum doorways. There always seemed to be some drunks about.

In the towns the inhabitants were more assertive. I drove out to the old colonial city of León, where there was life and noise in the market and the streets, even though not much had been rebuilt of the devastated rubble in the center. When I had been there in September 1979, two months after the end of the civil war, the place had an eerie, shell-shocked look. The local revolutionary committee was young and enthusiastic: but when I asked an old woman who was standing outside their headquarters selling lottery tickets whether she felt freer under the Sandinistas, she replied, with a cynical grin, "At least they don't kill us. Unlike Somoza." Others relished the climate of freedom, but were apprehensive about the future.

The traces of war lingered. I watched a revolutionary hero's funeral. His coffin was draped in red and black, the colors of the Sandinistas—their slogan was "A free country [red] or death [black]"—and was on a wagon drawn by kids in brown and green uniforms with perfect military precision. Further on, I saw a little knot of men shooting through the doorway of a ruined house, to set off an unexploded bomb. Now, seven years after the revolution, normal life just went on and disillusion had set in among the few who had harbored any illusions.

I had always found the Nicaraguans, despite their passivity, a warm, friendly people. The overwhelming majority were mestizos, but the Indian strain was much more evident than among the Salvadorans. They were taller than their neighbors, with high, sharp cheekbones and dark faces; their eyes were wider and more striking. Many of them were good-looking, but both sexes had a defeatist gaze, an almost pointed air of resignation. Salvadorans seemed sharp and alert, out to make a profit; Nicaraguans appeared to care more about their rights, but could do little to change their fate.

The trembling earth beneath them was probably partly responsible: the 1972 earthquake was only the latest in a series of such engineers of havoc. The volcanoes on every horizon reminded the Nicaraguans just how vulnerable they were to the will of God. Just outside Managua the Santiago volcano could be peered into: it was a giant crater, five hundred feet across, with walls seven hundred feet high, and a gaping, belching mouth through which the smoke rose in a slow, steady column. President Somoza used to toss the bodies of political prisoners into the hole. Earthquakes and eruptions were the backdrop to the populated Pacific side of Nicaragua; nearly half the country was covered with thick jungle, studded only by rackety Caribbean ports like Bluefields and El Bluff, populated by English-speaking Miskito Indians and the descendants of Caribbean buccaneers who had nothing in common with other Nicaraguans.

Yet passivity alone did not explain why Nicaraguans accepted the rule of the Somoza dynasty for so long. Dictators were in Nicaragua's blood: José Zelaya governed the country for sixteen years from 1893 with a ferocity unheard of even in Central America. He was, however, the last truly independent ruler of his country, which became a bone of contention between American and British interests, until 1927, when the marines stepped in. A guerrilla leader, Augusto César Sandino, anti-Yanqui but not Marxist-Leninist, set up a movement in the hills and managed to harass the marines effectively for five years. When the marines withdrew, a liberal president was installed, who said he wanted to make peace with Sandino. After a dinner with the president, the guerrilla leader was murdered in 1934 by the government's new armed force, the National Guard, which had been trained by the marines.

Only two years later the commander of the Guard, Anastasio (Tacho) Somoza, was in power. The first Somoza launched a program for the modernization of the country that also benefited his own extensive business interests. He ruled with an iron hand, elbowing the traditional oligarchy—the Liberal and Conservative parties—from power and suppressing serious opposition. Of this first Somoza, an American secretary of state, Cordell Hull, remarked, "He may be a son of a bitch, but he's our son of a bitch." Tacho's son, Luis, inherited the country on his father's assassination in 1956, and eased the regime's grip. In a tougher mold was his younger brother, Tachito, who took over after Luis's death in 1967.

The Sandinistas were no more than an armed rump by then: their leader, Carlos Fonseca, was killed in 1976, and the other "historical chief," Tomás Borge, was imprisoned. In 1974, however, a group of guerrillas succeeded in taking a number of diplomats hostage at a cocktail party, and secured most of their demands. Tachito Somoza angrily cracked down on the guerrillas. As the country advanced economically, liberal businessmen realized the extent of Somoza's financial interests and began to back his main opponent, Pedro Joaquín Chamorro, who mercilessly criticized the regime in his newspaper, *La Prensa*.

In January 1978, Chamorro was gunned down in broad daylight by unknown assailants, almost certainly Somoza's men. The liberal opposition began to join forces with the Sandinistas; many young scions of the new middle class went to the hills. There they joined Marxist-Leninist hardliners to form the new Tercerista—Third Way—faction. Another organization was set up, the Proletarios, to organize the urban poor. This group was to bear the brunt of the killing during the civil war.

In the years before the war, the dictatorship grew more autocratic and capricious. By 1979 the Somoza family owned about a fifth of the country's wealth, including nearly half of all landholdings in Nicaragua and a quarter of those with the best soil. Somoza's fortune was reckoned at $300 million—enormous by any standards, but especially Nicaragua's. Somoza produced cotton, coffee, beef, sugar, cocoa and tobacco. He owned the country's main shipping line, the airline LANICA, the main cement manufacturer and the main textile firms. He also exported blood purchased from impoverished Nicaraguans. In the last few years of his regime, the nationalized railway was run by one of his cronies, who also owned the main fleet of freight trucks: railway freight prices were hiked up, and the freight pushed onto the roads.

In 1978, after a heart attack, Somoza was flown to an American clinic. On his return he announced a new program of social spending, to use up credits conceded by President Carter on the grounds that the dictator had promised to improve human rights in Nicaragua. The program was to be devoted to heart clinics, for the country's few rich businessmen—in a country where infant mortality and malnutrition rates were among the highest in Latin America.

The Somoza legend was inflated by the Sandinistas. A book published after his death, titled *From Mrs. Hanna to Dinorah*, exposed the dictator's alleged lasciviousness to the prurient gaze of Nicaraguans:

Around the insatiable strong man there grew an extensive network of agents and procurers of sex. People of both sexes, but mainly women, and including soldiers, ran through the countryside and the cities in search, in an odious and despicable clandestine work, of the young virgins (or not) whose physical attributes would awaken the bestial instincts of the dictator. On the level of satisfaction that he demonstrated depended the commission that could be gained. Girls of 10, 12 and 15 years were the most appreciated prizes, and their prices oscillated between 50 and 150 cordobas, this last being paid in a case of proven virginity tied to an extraordinary physical beauty.

These acts were committed in a number of places, according to the book: Las Mercedes, in front of the international airport; a chalet in the province of San Juan, on the Tipitapa River; a chalet on a rice farm in Boaco province; a farmhouse in Azacualpa; another in Nahualapa and one in Rivas. The polemic remarked ironically that Somoza really was in touch with his people, through the women he made love to. His betrayed wife, Hope, evoked sympathy among Nicaraguans; his blowsy mistress, Dinorah Sampson, none.

By early 1979 the guerrillas had unleashed a full-scale insurrection, and Somoza's day of reckoning was close at hand. Their tactic was simple: to move from one ill-defended town to another, occupying them, then withdrawing before the arrival of the National

Guard. Because the National Guard at the time consisted of only eight thousand men, later reinforced by raw recruits to fifteen thousand, it proved impossible to protect all the towns. The Guard was reduced to racing around the country, attempting to enforce its authority. By that time Sandinista ranks had swollen to ten thousand armed men.

Worse was to come: as the increasingly harassed National Guard resorted to greater brutality, the shantytowns erupted. Somoza, whose antique air force had pounded rebel-held León mercilessly (the rebels had no antiaircraft equipment), turned to pounding his own capital of Managua, but to no avail. National Guard demoralization grew more widespread, while the rebel forces consolidated their hold. Reconciled to defeat, Somoza prepared his private aircraft for departure, and set off in style. After landing in Miami, he embarked on a champagne cruise across the Caribbean with his mistress. He eventually settled in Paraguay, where, after ingratiating himself with the mistress of the heir apparent of the local cuadillo, he was assassinated, ostensibly by the Sandinistas.

The region's most colorful, vicious, overbearing single-family regime had gone, leaving fifty-five thousand people dead and a revolution in its place. For the Americans, who had failed to notice the entire nation's growing hatred for the despot who spoke in a perfect Miami drawl and managed to convince American congressmen that he presided over a free system ("We have elections; we have a congress," he would tell visitors), it was a bitter defeat.

Most observers were baffled about what the revolutionaries stood for. The confusion was understandable; the Sandinistas were divided into three main factions. The Proletarios, led by Jaime Wheelock, a tough youngster with an unshaven, tombstone chin and deep-set eyes, were vaguely Maoist. The Prolonged Popular War group, led by Tomás Borge, the revolution's only veteran leader, were clearly Marxist-Leninist—although he denied this when I questioned him shortly after the revolution. He claimed that he didn't believe in the dictatorship of the proletariat as such, but in "the domination of one class over another."

No one knew how to pigeonhole the biggest group, the Terceristas, led by a shrewd, ascetic intellectual, Daniel Ortega, forever peering from behind thick glasses over a thin smile. Ortega was to some extent the key figure. For although Borge was quickly installed as interior minister—in charge of a five-thousand-man police force—Ortega's brother, Humberto, was granted control of the army, now swollen to eighteen thousand. In those heady days I wrote, without much hope, that Nicaragua might be "the revolution Cuba never was," a genuinely nonaligned, left-of-center revolution that could serve as a model for Latin America.

By the time of my next visit, in April 1980, the trend of the revolution was all too evident. Two members of the four-member junta, which had been set up to run the country, had resigned because they had no authority. They said that in reality the nine-man directorate of the Sandinista movement ran Nicaragua. The first was Violeta Chamorro, widow of murdered newspaper proprietor Pedro Joaquín. This frail, dark, intelligent woman loyally refused to denounce the regime during our interview on the splendidly understated patio of her Beverly Hills–style house in Managua. Her younger son defended her refusal to answer what he considered my rather forward questions. Another son, a dedicated Sandinista, edited the revolutionary newspaper *Barricada*.

The second member of the junta, Alfonso Robelo, was more forthright. A well-turned-out man with immaculate graying hair and beard and a deceptively meek smile, Robelo spoke from his more modest Sandinista-guarded suburban house in the capital. He said that during the last few months Cuban technicians had installed the wiring in his office. Cubans had taken over the main telegraph station and occupied two floors of the Intercontinental. According to Robelo, some two thousand Cuban military advisers had already landed in Managua by 1980, along with four thousand teachers. The views of the junta were entirely ignored by the directorate, who were placing the whole nation on a war footing. It appeared that the Marxist-Leninists had taken over the directorate; the Ortega brothers were as pro-Marxist as Borge. Unregulated expropriations were taking place throughout the private sector—even after the nationalization of Somoza's vast land holdings. As for the general election that the Sandinistas had promised on assuming power, that had been postponed indefinitely.

On that visit, in 1980, I attended a mass demonstration in Revolution Square, near the earthquake-ravaged cathedral and the near-ruined national assembly building that fronted on Lake Managua.

Huge posters of Sandino proclaimed: "With their arms and with their lives, the people have already voted." The crowd dutifully responded to the shouts of Sandinista cheerleaders. "Sandino lives," they chanted, along with the old slogan of countless Latin revolutions, "The people, united, will never be defeated." Black and red banners were waved wildly up and down. Squads of brown- and green-shirted young women, eager and disciplined, the new "people's militia," stomped past in the torrid midday sun in front of the platform where I stood. A fat *comandante* with a mustache came up to the podium, sweating heavily. He could have stepped straight out of a National Guard uniform.

Two speakers took the microphone. The first was Comandante Cero, Edén Pastora, the man who led the 1978 assault on the national palace. Craggy, with film-star good looks, wary eyes under dark brows and a flop of graying hair, Cero spoke carefully to the crowd. Although he was the revolution's hero, he had been given a lowly job as deputy interior minister to Borge because he was considered by Sandinista leaders to be politically unsound. After him, his deputy on the raid held forth: she was Comandante Dora María Téllez, a bony twenty-three-year-old with curly, taut, dark hair; bright, sparkling, brittle eyes; and an expression of supreme certainty.

The two linked arms and led the crowd through the wasteland of central Managua. Near the hotel, they stopped to listen to the revolution's real leaders: Humberto Ortega and Bayardo Arce, a Castro look-alike who was Borge's closest crony in the hard-line faction. A guard with a submachine gun sat casually smoking a cigar on the wall above them as they spoke. When they had finished, the crowd chanted, "Cero, Cero." The hero returned to the podium and quietly told them to go home. He was soon to be the Sandinistas' most feared opponent.

By the time of this, my fourth visit, in 1986, things had moved on politically, down economically and barely at all socially. The mobilization of the country was a fact of life. There were fifty-five thousand armed men, counting the army and the men given proper training in the police and the militia: the plan was to train 150,000 men in using a rifle (one in every twenty Nicaraguans). Conscription was being introduced for all. There were four thousand Cuban military advisers and one thousand Russians in the country; a large airport, capable of taking Soviet fighter jets, was being constructed at Punta Huete, just north of Managua. Other airfields had been built on the east coast. The country had been shipped a force of twenty T-55 Russian tanks.

There was a military threat, to be sure: it came in the south from those like Robelo and Pastora, who had fled the country in disillusion. And it came in the north from the ex-members of Somoza's National Guard who set up camps just inside the unpoliceably wild Honduran border. These counterrevolutionaries, or contras, started punching into Nicaragua over the Honduran border in 1982. Two armies were set up there. One of them, the Nicaraguan Democratic Force, was headed by disillusioned pro-Sandinistas, but was officered by former National Guardsmen. It had about eight thousand men and struck deep into Nueva Segovia province, although it failed to capture a single significant town. By 1984 some five thousand casualties had been inflicted on the Sandinistas, and the northern contras had struck as far south as Managua's main port in the west.

On the other side of the country, the Caribbean coast, the Sandinistas were the main cause of their own undoing. In 1982 they began a campaign of resettlement and reeducation of the Miskito Indians, some of whom had left to join the contras. Villages were seized; some thirteen thousand people were forced to undertake a long, terrible march across swamplands to dismal tent villages, in order to relocate them away from the border. This turned the Miskito people against the Sandinistas: a force of one thousand of them began operations from Honduras, inflicting casualities on strategic targets along that pirates' coast.

Down south Robelo and Pastora joined forces to form ARDE, the Democratic Revolutionary Alliance, to force the Sandinistas to revert to their original democratic ideals. Mostly they tramped through the jungle country along the Costa Rican border, but they also struck at the port of El Bluff and captured a few villages. In one of these, Pastora was injured when a bomb went off. The Sandinistas were probably to blame, although by that time Pastora had broken with Robelo, who was urging a merger with the northern contras. For the moment, though, the contras seemed less likely to win than to keep the Sandinistas on edge.

Nor were the contras the Sandinistas' only concern. The United States had sent fleets to cruise off both coasts of Nicaragua in the summer of 1982. The following autumn the Americans had invaded Grenada, a warning shot across the Sandinistas' bow. Between 1983 and 1984 the U.S. had sent six thousand soldiers to perform military maneuvers along Nicaragua's Honduran borders. The Nicaraguans responded with blustering threats to chase the contras across the border; but they knew they were being leaned upon.

One main objective of American policy was to cut off aid from Nicaragua to El Salvador's guerrillas. The volume of this aid has been contested, but the evidence seems overwhelming that substantial quantities were going across from 1980 to 1982. The flow registered a big drop in 1983, and a slight resumption the following year. Some Salvadoran guerrilla leaders openly operated out of Managua.

Nicaragua had cracked down politically too. The tolerant revolution was no more. Borge made much of this tolerance to me when I first went to Managua. "We have abolished the death penalty. In spite of the atrocities they have inflicted on us, we are going to submit the four thousand Guardsmen we have captured to due process of law." Previously the Nicaraguan revolution *had* remained astonishingly tolerant by the standards of its neighbors. But cases of men being shot while escaping custody and of torture grew more frequent. Eastern European–style methods of psychological disorientation were used. A priest was dangled out of an aircraft during interrogation.

The Sandinistas attempted to disband the Catholic Permanent Human Rights Commission—established during Somoza's tyranny—on the grounds that there would be no violations of human rights in postrevolutionary Nicaragua. But the commission stayed in business, reporting scores of disappearances, the arrest of some two thousand political prisoners and the suspension of ordinary courts. The Commission's offices were searched. When I visited it, an earnest young Catholic lawyer told me that Sandinista guards had been stationed outside the Commission that day, although they hadn't been requested. "We don't know if we are to be attacked." Nothing happened. The Commission's president was, however, forced into exile, and the group's work continued with considerable difficulty. A line of some forty relatives of prisoners waited patiently in the courtyard every day.

The crackdown extended to the press. I visited the offices of *La Prensa*, the symbol of the revolution, the murder of whose editor,

Pedro Joaquín Chamorro, sparked the civil war in 1978. "They say we are free to publish," its new editor told me, holding up a sheaf of stories that the censor refused to pass. "So we publish with gaps where these stories would have been. They censor not just stories about politics, but anything that reflects badly on Nicaragua—for example, a ferryboat disaster in which thirty-eight people were killed. They refuse to give us new typewriters when an old one breaks down; they have a monopoly of imported typewriters. Government agencies are prevented from advertising in our pages." An assistant came in to tell him that four pages of the newspaper had been censored. "Then we scrap the issue," he declared, with the despair of a newsman who could not get his message out. The *La Prensa* buildings, a collection of offices and printing works on the road to the airport, were repeatedly attacked by Sandinista mobs, then searched by troops supposedly restoring order. Somehow, the newspaper lived on until 1986 when the Sandinistas closed it down.

La Prensa, like other fragments of freedom, survived so long in Nicaragua because the Sandinistas hesitated to take on too many enemies. The most powerful tribune of the people was the Church, headed by the tough, portly figure of the archbishop of Managua, Monsignor Miguel Obando y Bravo. The Church had been one of Somoza's sternest critics, and mediated when the guerrillas seized his parliament in 1978. But relations with the government deteriorated steadily, as the Sandinistas began to promote a "Popular Church" within it, attacking the regular hierarchy. Representatives of this—Father Miguel D'Escoto, who was foreign minister, and Father Ernesto Cardenal, a poet who was minister of culture—belonged to the government.

The Popular Church certainly had a following in the slums. I went to one well-attended Mass; the jaunty guitar-singing throughout the ceremony was joined in with gusto by the congregation in the simple wooden building, devoid of imagery. The priest criticized the Catholic hierarchy for attacking the government's mistreatment of Miskito Indians. This had provoked a joint statement by the bishops. (Tomás Borge, the interior minister, told me acidly afterward, "I am not afraid of their cassocks.")

Father Bismarck Carballo, the archbishop's right-hand man, an unpriestly figure in an open-necked shirt with a laid-back conversational style, met me in his tiny office, as cramped as a confessional.

He was blunt about the government. "We are against totalitarianism. They are seeking to impose totalitarian solutions. The people of Nicaragua did not die for this. We have every right to express the Church's point of view."

The Pope visited Managua in April 1982, and from touchdown was paraded in front of Sandinista posters. At an open-air Mass, the chanting of Sandinista crowds drowned out his warning against mixing religion and politics. When the Vatican ordered the priests in the government to give up their posts, the Vatican was rebuffed. Yet the Nicaraguan Church held back from calling on Nicaraguans to unite in an uprising against the government. "We do not want to start another civil war," explained Father Bismarck.

The existence of this powerful internal resistence, of the contras at their borders, and the country's appalling economic slump all combined to prevent the Sandinistas from imposing the full-scale, Cuban-style socialism they publicly admired. Economic statistics were horrendous, revealing a fall of about a third in industrial production; a slide of half in industrial investment, which was now almost all coming from the state; and a decline of a fifth in farm production. The country's $600 million in foreign debt had been rolled over only with great difficulty. With a trade gap of $200 million, Nicaragua was largely bankrolled by growing Russian subsidies, which soared to $500 million by 1984. The Mexicans and Venezuelans provided oil on generous credit terms or free, until Venezuela grew disillusioned with the way the revolution was going.

For fear of destroying what little remained of the country's industrial capacity, the Sandinistas allowed about two fifths of the economy to remain in private hands. But machinery grew more and more obsolescent. "Us? Invest? No way," Bill Baez, head of INDE, the country's main private-sector organization, told me. "Besides, there aren't any profits. Where would we get the money? Yet they call our failure to invest 'economic sabotage.' "

The financial and military pressure began to push the country toward accommodation with the United States. The Americans insisted that Nicaragua should hold a direct election; in January 1984, the Sandinistas surprised most people by fixing a date for an election in November. As the year progressed, they relaxed martial law and eased the restraints on opposition. In practice, though, opposition meetings were often disrupted and there was little chance for the

splinter groups—all that was left of independent political thought—
to organize in Nicaragua. A united opposition front formed, calling
itself the Democratic Coordinator, pushing the candidacy of Arturo
Cruz, a former member of the Sandinista junta and ambassador in
Washington with impeccable democratic credentials. The Sandinistas refused to give sufficient guarantees to satisfy Cruz.

The election was contested only by two tiny splinter groups, and
the opposition claimed that it had been denied a real chance to
participate and that the result had been rigged. The Sandinista
promise of democracy was half fulfilled at most.

What of the revolution the Sandinistas started? There was no way
to complete it. The private sector stayed in a kind of huddled,
defensive limbo. The land reform applied only to Somoza's holdings, and was managed incompetently through the country's agrar-
ian-reform institute. The workers had no say. Social services
remained nonexistent. The revolution's sole accomplishment was a
literacy program achieved by importing some two thousand Cuban
teachers and sending the bulk of Nicaragua's literate school-educated
population into the countryside to instruct peasants in the rudiments
of reading with a manual called *El Amanecer del Pueblo* (*The Dawn of
the People*). From beginning to end, this manual consisted of revolutionary slogans such as, Lesson One, "Augusto César Sandino is the
Father of our People." The campaign nominally reduced Nicaragua's illiteracy rate from about 70 percent to about 30 percent.

So what remained? Just *comandantes* in power. A driver who took
me to visit one of them asked which *jefe* I was visiting. *Jefe*—"chief"—
had been the word applied to Somoza's henchmen. I asked him why
he called them that. "They're all *jefes*, just the same," he said con-
temptuously. The *jefes* had moved into the Intercontinental; they
were to be seen eating in the Lobster Inn and Los Ranchos, where
Somoza's men ate before the revolution. They frequented Wilma's,
Managua's classy brothel.

And the revolution? I asked Tomás Borge, its tough man. "It is a
revolution which has learned from the Cuban experience and the
Mexican experience and the Russian experience and even the American experience. But it is more still: it is Nicaragua's own." But he
wouldn't go into specifics of the way in which Nicaragua was,
indeed, different. "We are of course a Catholic revolution." He
pointed to the crucifix on the wall. "And we are an internationalist

revolution. We believe in helping our brothers." So the Nicaraguans were giving help to El Salvador's guerrillas? "We are helping them, yes; but with our solidarity, not with our arms." He would not be drawn into specifics of "solidarity." Outside his office hung a poster: "The revolution has no frontiers."

I asked Sergio Ramírez, the revolution's tame social democrat, a non-Sandinista who had skillfully stayed within the junta by endorsing Sandinista policies. A large, smiling man, "an incredible ball of grease," as a diplomat of Managua unkindly called him, Ramírez pointed to land reform, social progress, the literacy campaign. But he admitted that Nicaragua's straitened circumstances had undermined the achievement of the revolution's goals. To a great extent, I felt that was Nicaragua's own fault: if it wanted money for social reform, it had no shortage of backers—Mexico, Venezuela, even, with strings, the United States—willing to provide funds just to keep it from following the Cuban road. But its stubborn alignment with the Cuba-Soviet bloc slowly choked off the funds.

Borge was the hardliner, Ramírez the opportunist. A common combination. Borge was a short man with an intense, sculptured, humorous, Indian face, penetrating eyes, a long, searching look, polite and gracious in his conversation. A practiced politician wary of conversational traps, he could display great charm, and the curtness of a military leader or a killer. Some of the pain of losing his wife at the hands of Somoza's torturers always showed; his eyes were often remote. Ramírez was an easygoing, Western-educated man, handsome, with all the bogusness of the professional public-relations man. These two, at least, represented no check on Cuban influence.

But the fact was that the Sandinistas wished to remain in power—all, that is, except Tomás Borge, who was perhaps prepared for a martyr's fight to the finish. But Daniel and Humberto Ortega, with their radical, conformist, left-wing, pro-Soviet views, who could see the damage being inflicted on their country by its stiffly anti-American attitude, were said to be wavering. What was the point of a revolution that denied itself the means to achieve social progress? Could pragmatism win over ideology? Nicaragua had been stuck at this crossroads for seven years now, and its easygoing, always optimistic, hard-used people deserved better than to languish much longer in the limbo that had followed the overthrow of the ghastly Somoza.

COSTA RICA

A SENSE OF CALM OVERCAME ME WHEN I ARRIVED AT COSTA RICA'S airport, two hundred miles to the southeast. There were no armed guards there: Costa Rica had a few armed policemen, but the army had been disbanded by President José Figueres, one of the most remarkable men in Latin America. An energetic populist of great character and vision, Figueres was a planter who established a "Caribbean legion" dedicated to opposing tyrants. The legion was viewed with immense suspicion by the United States, particularly as it sought to overthrow the Somoza dictatorship next door; but Figueres was no communist. He took a vigorously anticommunist, anti-Cuban line, and implemented his promise to do away with Costa Rica's army. Without an army, he reasoned, Costa Rica would not succumb to the militarization of the rest of the region. He was right. The country remained a stable, prosperous democracy with a tradition of parties peacefully alternating in power.

How had Costa Rica managed to break the spell of tyranny, poverty and conflict that afflicted its neighbors? To begin with, the country is endowed with a sizable population and a gentle climate: only the coastal belt is hot and humid; the central uplands around the capital of San José are pleasant and fertile. Anything seems to grow on the lava beds in this region. A flock of American time-sharers migrate south to cheap summer houses where they can pass the winter months in comfortable, bungalow-style villas with an acre or two of land. The country has had a ready source of foreign exchange in its exports of coffee, bananas and, later, light industry.

Costa Rica, almost alone on the isthmus, was also free of the unequal land distribution set up under the latifundia—big estate—system further south. The Spanish settlers divided the land into relatively equal parcels and worked it as yeomen, in competition. There was no impoverished peasantry, nor a racial subclass of Indians, unlike that of its northern neighbors. As in much of the United States, the Indians were, where possible, ignored, and, unlike in next-door Panama, the small black population created no racial frictions. The country prospered as a middle-class haven from the start, with a decent source of income and few racial or class divisions. In recent elections there, some 90 percent of the votes went to one of the two almost indistinguishable middle-of-the-road parties.

In a European context, Costa Rica would have been as dull as Switzerland. In Central America, it was a relief. The hotel I stayed in was like a Swiss one, with attentive concierges and comfortable, genteel bars frequented by amiable, elderly people. Over the road from the hotel was a theater, the pride of the capital, where great stars, marooned between flight connections in Central America, would sometimes perform. Built like a miniature La Scala, it symbolized the small-town civility and safety of Costa Rica.

As I walked down the street to attend Mass at the cathedral, another great, yet relatively diminutive, building, a priest expostulated against the prostitutes who flaunted their wares close to the city center. In fact, there were an extraordinarily large number of street-walkers about. But the sermon made a welcome change from the intense political message one would find in, say, a Nicaraguan barrio church. On my way back, I picked up a copy of the *Tico Times*, the local newspaper written for American residents in San José. *Tico* was the fond diminutive used to describe a Costa Rican: it seemed to fit this easygoing, bourgeois people.

My schedule the following day was relaxed, as befitted San José. I paid a call on the American ambassador, a delightful man married to

a young woman of local origins. He knew everything there was to
know about the country. I met a former president who might have
stepped straight from the ranks of Swedish social democracy. His
name was Rodrigo Carazo; he was rotund, well-fed, ginger-haired,
full of empty phrases about the role of the main grouping of world
socialist parties, the Socialist International, in mediating the present
conflict in Central America. Almost single-handedly, this man had
managed to bankrupt Costa Rica, the one solvent economy in Central America, through a generous public spending program paid for
by foreign borrowing.

He refused to take any responsibility for this, however, claiming
that the problem lay in high interest rates. He said that the economy
had needed expansion during his administration. But as the foreign
debt neared $3 billion, Costa Rica's creditors closed in and de-
manded stiff austerity measures. The Carazo administration had
simply refused to meet targets, and the country had been in danger
of default. Repelled by the irresponsibility of President Carazo,
Costa Ricans turned him out in favor of the Social Democrat, Luis
Alberto Monge, a chubby, bookish man whose aura of competence
contrasted sharply with Carazo's extravagance. Carazo had proved
something of a catastrophe. But Costa Rica, it seemed, had the civic
resilience to recover from his rule.

That afternoon, I hired a driver to take me out into the country,
to escape the claustrophobic provincialism of San José and to see the
root of Costa Rica's prosperity. The country was pretty, in a Central
European way, a haven of flowers and trees and market gardens and
shrubs, of well-paved roads and comfortable, prosperous towns that
had nothing in common with the stark, bleached, sad architecture of
Guatemala or Nicaragua. It was like being on another continent.

We ascended the Irazú volcano, which had ruined two successive
harvests by a massive ashfall on the center of the country. Even this
mighty outcrop of nature had been tamed by the Costa Ricans: signs
led up a path that took one to the top where carloads of tourists
peered into a crater that was among the world's largest. There was
a swirling mist about, so I could see nothing but a gaping emptiness
falling away beneath my feet. After twenty minutes I gave up and
returned to a comfortable tea at the bottom of the mountain.

That evening I had dinner with a local newspaper editor. We
talked about Nicaragua, a country the Costa Ricans spoke of as

Muscovites must speak about Outer Mongolia. To them it was primitive, bearing no resemblance to their welfare-state haven. The unspoken object of their contempt was its mestizo culture.

"The Nicaraguans are not a military threat to us. What would be the purpose in their invading us?"

"You have no army. The contras operate across your borders, as well as those of Honduras."

"We have no army, but we have a much more effective barrier. If there was any threat to Costa Rica, the Organization of American States would intervene. The Americans would come to our help. Everyone would; everyone but Costa Rica itself. No, we have a much more effective barrier than the Hondurans have, for example, our moral standing in the world. The contras here are a nuisance to the Sandinistas, but the government tries to keep a lid on their activities. That is good enough for the Sandinistas; they would gain nothing by attacking."

"What about subversion?"

"There has been evidence of people coming across the borders, but mainly to blow up fellow Nicaraguans in exile here. Costa Rica has nothing to fear from the left-wing political primitivism of the Sandinistas. Our left is sophisticated, social democratic. The Marxists, when they run in elections, get only a couple of percentage points. Extremism has no appeal here. There is no depressed peasant class in Costa Roca, nor even much of a working class. What I fear instead is the reaction that Sandinista support for the handful of far leftists in Costa Rica might provoke. We have to be on our guard against militarization."

"But you have no army," I interrupted. "That cannot be a problem."

"Listen." He was a very civilized man, relaxed, in his late thirties, at the pinnacle of his professional success, with an intellectual's way of talking; yet he was too complacent for me. "The problem of Latin America is armies. They have nothing to do, because most of our boundaries are established. Lacking external enemies, they have to invent internal ones. They say there is a Russian threat, there is a communist threat: a threat from a country thousands of miles away! Only it is invented. So it justifies their taking power. This is a country that has gone through a very serious economic crisis; they say that socialism has ruined it. When bombs go off in San José, even ones directed against Nicaraguan exiles, they say there is a terrorist threat. Our police must be armed; our protection is inadequate; that's what they say. And it would be the ruin of Costa Rica if we were to have an army. Figueres is right about that: the army, not the left, is the danger for Costa Rica."

"You really think there is a danger from the right?"

He backed off; he didn't want to admit that things could be going so fundamentally wrong in these elysian fields. Costa Rica had the pride of an insular city-state. "Our democracy is too strong. But it is best that we always guard against such threats."

I believed he was right: there really wasn't much threat to Costa Rica. So what had this country of 2.3 million people to show Latin America? Did Costa Rica prove that the Latin American disease was not inescapable, that Western-style democracy could prosper? My friend thought so. I wondered. If democracy could flourish only under the balmy conditions of Costa Rica, there was not much hope. How could the badlands of Central America, let alone the vast racial and geographical mix of South America, simulate such natural perfection? They were countries with real challenges, unlike Costa Rica.

Costa Rica was a Switzerland keeping to a burgher tradition, not seeking to expand economically or to act as a catalyst for its neighbors. Indeed, until the arrival of the more internationalist President Oscar Arias, Costa Rica was supremely careful in having resisted efforts at Central American integration because it did not want its nirvana disturbed by the problems of others. Latin America as a whole could not be a Switzerland because it was an outback continent, rugged in the mold of the wildest part of the United States.

As we parted in the hotel ballroom, which had been coverted into a bar, with its overweight Venetian-style glass chandeliers, Costa Rica seemed sweet and tired and outdated, like a country in retirement, happy but no longer dynamic or capable of avoiding that disease of elderly countries, welfare statism.

PANAMA

ARRIVING IN PANAMA, THE NARROWEST POINT IN THE UMBILICAL CORD that connects North to South America 350 miles to the southeast, was like leaving Latin America for a moment. Airports are usually poor guides to the countries they introduce, because most are indistinguishable from one another, but this one was misleading in a different way. Thoroughly modern, the place was equipped with the latest in passenger transport belts and satellite terminals, quite unlike the extended prefab appearance of other Central American airports (with the exception of El Salvador's). The airport was named after the man who had built it, General Omar Torrijos, Panama's attractive cowboy dictator for more than a decade, and a man for whom I had always had a slight admiration, not least because he managed to mislead Graham Greene and other romantics into believing that he was a caring leftist. In practice, he was a shrewd, corrupt authoritarian who made cosmetic concessions to the left—resuming relations with Castro, for example—in order to protect himself from a Cuban-supported guerrilla challenge.

He was hard on his own dissidents, and he encouraged Panama to become the banking haven that other Latin American societies craved to be. It was not entirely obvious what made Panama more attractive to tax dodgers than, say, Nicaragua, whose main claim to offshore fame was Howard Hughes. Was Somoza too obvious and crude a despot? What about Costa Rica, which had housed Robert Vesco? Was it perhaps too geriatric? The laid-back, Stetson-and-cigar image of Torrijos was only one ingredient in Panama's success. Another was the torrid climate, with its hint of Caribbean lushness and laziness. A third must have been that airport.

The airport was miles out of town, but the oversized Oldsmobile driven by a black, the first I had met in the region, made short work of the distance. I had booked a downtown hotel to get away from the concrete-and-glass Hiltons and Holiday Inns of the residential quarter. Downtown proved to be a euphemism. The hotel, one of the best there, didn't have anyone behind the counter; I found a hotel employee in a bar where he was serving drinks, and he told me to sign the book and pay in advance, and gave me a key. I took my own luggage up: the elevator barely worked, which was lucky, because my room was seven floors up. My room didn't lock, the air conditioner sounded like a helicopter at takeoff, and the bed was unmade. Apart from that, it was comfortable enough. The crime rate in Panama was supposed to be high. Racist I am not, but the fact that I seemed to be the only white man in the hotel was a little worrying. Still, the hotel was so casual, I don't think anyone even noticed me.

The hotel was centrally located and, dressed in jeans and T-shirt, I walked down toward the heart of the city. Here was a town of old, single-story constructions with built-up verandas made of wooden planks, rather like some relic of the American Deep South. I loved it, and was oblivious to the poverty or where I was wandering until a throaty yell reached me, *"Cuidate gringo!"*—"Take care, gringo." I could not tell whether this was a warning, or a spontaneous burst of Panamanian nationalist resentment. So I made my way back from the backstreets to the main street, and down to the waterfront where the exotic presidential palace and naval base loomed over the still waters. The palace was the kind of pseudocolonial building many of us dream of spending our days in, its landing steps and jetties lapped by the clear-blue Pacific. Ronald Reagan once called Torrijos a "tinhorn dictator." It seemed a pleasant thing to be, judging by his lifestyle.

*   *   *

Panama—the non-Latin part of the Latin American continent, the
noncountry formed because the United States wanted better terms
for its canal than Colombia was prepared to give, the pit stop of
countless sailors on their way between two oceans—was a country
whose burghers, with only partial success, were trying to make it
respectable. Panama's nationalism was the pride of the fallen; not to
be underrated for that.

Panama was created for the Canal, and the Canal was Panama; the
Canal gave it its wealth. Yet Panama resented the Canal. Visiting the
Canal is one of those necessary experiences for the traveler, like
visiting a casino in Nevada, and yet to me it was an anticlimax. The
shabby hotels and bars of the Panamanian town of Colón gave way
to the well-ordered, immaculate, middle-American style of the
Zoners—the inhabitants of that disappearing strip of sovereign
American authority, the Canal Zone; even the tropical vegetation
seemed as ordered as a botanical garden. The five thousand or so
Americans who lived in the Zone with their tennis clubs and golf
clubs, were clean-shaven, short-haired, neatly dressed, a reproof
even to the sloppy American troops, who seemed to prefer the carnal
delights of Colón to the apple-pie sobriety of the Zone. The Canal
itself is a model of order: tranquil, enormously wide for those accustomed to ordinary canals. At a distance it presented the almost
hallucinatory sight of a large ship apparently traveling across land
through dense undergrowth. The vision seemed to symbolize man's
supremacy over nature. The Canal represented, as visibly as anything in Latin America, the clash between the culture of the northern colossus and that of Latin America. But the clash itself was an
exaggeration: there are few places where America has behaved in so
colonial a way; and there are few less typically Latin American
societies than Panama.

The Americans, fond of accusing others of colonialism, always
charge that colonialism is too bald a term. But nothing could have
been more colonialist than the creation of Panama. The 300,000
inhabitants of Colombian-owned Panama at the turn of the century
were neither more nor less Colombian than the inhabitants of any
other part of that disparate country. Yet, America wanted the Canal.
Panama happened to be separated from Colombia by a dense tract of
jungle, still almost impassable, called the Darien Gap. Teddy Roosevelt, that swashbuckling adventurer among American presidents,

thought he had a deal in 1903. Colombia's President Marroquín agreed to sell him a strip of land ten kilometers wide for $10 million plus $250,000 in rent a year. Astonishingly, Colombia's congress refused to ratify the deal.

A spontaneous Panamanian revolution then began, as the fickle mob of Colón, as well as railway workers, took to the streets and set up an independent Panama. The Colombians rushed troops by ship to deal with the uprising, but were stopped by an American cruiser, which was conveniently in their way. The original deal was then offered to and accepted by the new Panamanian republic. Roosevelt boasted of having "taken Panama" from "a bunch of dagos." A later American politician was to say, "We stole it fair and square." America, with its new colonial prize, tried to do its best by the inhabitants: a democracy would be set up overnight. The people of Panama who serviced the needs of those crossing to the American West were told to master civil rights and the separation of powers.

Educating the locals in democracy was, of course, of lesser importance than building the Canal. As an engineering feat it was to be unsurpassed, even by the Suez Canal, whose builder, Ferdinand de Lesseps, had tried to build the first Panama Canal and was defeated by malaria and yellow fever. The Chagres River was damned and became Gatún Lake; the locks that elevate and move ships into and from the lakes are miracles of machinery. The Gaillard Cut, a long section of water literally carved through thick jungle, is the greatest feat of all. From its opening in 1914, the Canal boomed, giving the United States a two-ocean navy and allowing the trade of eastern America to meet that of western America.

What the Panamanians, a bogus people largely imported from the Caribbean to the mainland, thought was of little importance to the Americans. The Canal Zone, supported and protected by American troops, provided the focus of the country's wealth, and that was enough. The United States soon washed its hands of responsibility for the country's chronically unstable political institutions, while the Panamanians lived off the lucre from the Canal. There was plenty of that. There was the rent charge, which they succeeded in raising from a very low base; there was the income of those working on the Canal; there was the money spent by visitors; there was the income from selling the Panamanian flag to ships, allowing them to evade labor laws or safety regulations at home.

And yet . . . nationalism began to grow even in a lawless, third-rate, artificial country like Panama. A pro-Nazi nationalist populist, Arnulfo Arias, raised less on ideologies of left and right than on plain anti-Americanism, was elected president in 1940 and promptly kicked out by the armed police, the National Guard (the Americans had prevented an army from coming into being, saying that the country could be defended by their forces). The country was run peacefully enough for the next sixteen years under pro-American administrations, although the $40 million American income from Panama Canal tolls, compared with a rental of $7 million, got on Panamanian nerves. After the humiliation of Britain and France at Suez, nationalist agitation began in earnest, under a left-wing president, Ernesto de la Guardia. By 1959 a massed popular invasion of the Zone seemed likely to start a major bloodbath. But President Eisenhower took to appeasing the Panamanians through gestures: he allowed a Panamanian flag to fly above the Zone, for example.

But nationalist extremism spread. Panama City is basically divided between the original inhabitants, a few pure Spanish but most of mixed origin, and the blacks imported to build the Canal and then attracted from the Caribbean to take advantage of the immense wealth it generated. Initially the blacks were the conservatives, because they wanted to safeguard their livelihoods. A moderate was elected president in 1960. But he proved unable to stop a Canal riot in 1964, in which four Americans and twenty-three Panamanians were killed. Tension began to calm when the Americans promised a revision of the Canal treaty.

All seemed lost when Arias won the election of May 1968. But after eleven days in power he was kicked out again, and the wily Torrijos took over. Fierily left-wing in rhetoric, right-wing in action, Torrijos let in the foreign bankers. By 1978 he secured the best possible deal he could from President Carter, under fierce attack from Ronald Reagan: the Canal would be handed over to Panama by the year 2000; there would be a gradual transfer of jobs in the Zone from Americans to Panamanians; there would be continuing American military protection. The gangster-dictator, who made huge sums out of the banking boom, had beautifully blended pragmatism with nationalism to extract all he could. If Panama was a whore for America, he was its most successful pimp. He was killed in an air crash in 1981.

Panama's relationship with its colonial power was a typically resentful one. Its anti-Americanism proved impossible for Americans to comprehend. First they had tried to make it democratic. When that didn't work, they had left it to run itself. What more did it want? Yet Panamanians still felt resentful. To them, the Americans were exploiters rather than benefactors. This was obvious nonsense, as the Canal helped both. It remains to be seen whether possession of the Canal will now end that country's extreme anti-Americanism. When the Panamanians came to vote again for a free president, after a brief spell under Torrijos's incompetent successor, it was the aging, erratic nationalist Arias who again topped the poll, and who had to be cheated of the presidency by the National Guard, which was this time run by an incompetent crook, Tony Noriega.

Noriega was later accused by his former second-in-command, Colonel Roberto Díaz, of rigging the election, of murdering an opposition leader and of being involved with the country's drug traffic and arms trade. Senator Jesse Helms, a sardonic observer of Latin American affairs, called him "the biggest drug trafficker in the Western Hemisphere." These revelations created a wave of middle-class demonstrations and brought pressure from the American embassy for his removal, to which Noriega reacted by claiming that, like Torrijos (whose plane he was accused by Díaz of having sabotaged), he was a socialist and nationalist under threat from gringo interference.

But socialism seemed a long way away, as a car took me through the brand-new skyscrapers of middle-class Panama City and back to that glistening airport, with its rows of shops filled with duty-free items. Panama was a newly prosperous country. Its economy had boomed thanks to the presence of some 120 foreign banks, many of them laundering the proceeds of the Caribbean, Colombian, Peruvian and Bolivian drug trades. The country was also, in effect, a duty-free entrepôt, the revenue from this far exceeding its revenues from the Canal. The economic boom was dampened by political unrest but the country's large ex-Caribbean population, which had moved to Panama to earn a living, and its mestizo underclass had become relatively prosperous during the Torrijos years. Noriega was counting on these classes enjoying their new above-the-breadline prosperity—Panama, although poorer than Costa Rica, has none of the real poverty of a Guatemala or a Nicaragua—to keep him in power.

Panama differs from its Central American neighbors in that it has suffered open American interference, not neglect. The trouble in Guatemala, Nicaragua, El Salvador and Honduras has been too little American interference, not too much. Apart from trade—and during the 1930s a policy of propping up local military forces to ensure that trade continued undisturbed—the United States was content that Central America should be in the care of local despots. State Department policy on the region was to a great extent influenced by Americans who did business with Central America.

Of late, the Americans have moved quickly and directly in El Salvador and Honduras, and indirectly in Guatemala, to urge those countries to become democratic. Against Nicaragua, the United States has employed a mixture of military threats and support for the contras in order to contain the revolution. In Panama, the local military strongman clung on. The American fear was that, if the old oligarchs and armies retained power, the eventual winner—after a series of bloody civil wars—would be the far left.

It is much too early to say whether the United States has succeeded in its goals for Central America. The Nicaraguan revolution remains suspended uncertainly between social democracy and full-scale collectivism. Honduras, though, seems safe enough. In El Salvador the civil war continues, although guerrilla ranks seem to be thinning. The struggle there, however, is by no means over. In Guatemala alone has peace returned to much of the countryside, while the economy is improving. The Americans have not saved Nicaragua, but they may be saving its neighbors. The people of those nations, who by their votes overwhelmingly endorse democratic parties, seem to be appreciative that a belated, benevolent interventionism by the United States has at last replaced decades of neglect.

PART II

THE TRAIL
OF THE INDIAN

The memories of early days
Await your lyre; when, in sweet idleness
And happy in native innocence,
Gave easy sustenance to her inhabitants
The first stock of her fertile breast,
Cundinamarca; before the curved plough
Violated the soil or strange ships
Visited these distant shores.
Ambition had not yet edged
Atrocious iron.

ANDRÉS BELLO

I LEFT THE SLEEK, AIR-CONDITIONED PANAMA AIRPORT ON A HUMID, sun-grilled day for a three-hour flight that took me above the Darien Gap, the one impassable stretch in the north-south Pan-American Highway, which links two continents. The second part of my journey was beginning, leading away from the microstates of Central America to a major country, Colombia, along the Trail of the Indian, which would carry me across four Andean countries, Colombia, Ecuador, Peru and Bolivia, and two lowland areas—the regions of Amazonia and Paraguay—dominated by indigenous Indian cultures.

There are three distinct Indian nations in Latin America: the Indians of Central America, described in the last section; the Indians of the Andes; and the Indians of the Amazon and Paraguay. The latter two groups are all that remain of the continent's once-thriving lowland Indian population.

When Columbus landed, he gave the name Indian to the 50 million or so inhabitants of South America, believing he had landed in Asia. Within two hundred years, the total number of Indians had fallen to around 5 million. (Imagine, for comparison, that the British in India had reduced that country's population of around 100 million in the eighteenth century to a tenth of that number, rendering it a territory for large-scale white immigration.) The horrific decimation of those early days was caused mainly by disease, forced labor, slavery and murder. The worst diseases were smallpox, flu and measles, to which the Indian had no natural resistance.

The lowland Indians never recovered; over the next three centuries, however, the highland Andean Indian population grew to around 18 million people. The Andean Indians are similar, in many respects, to their Guatemalan cousins, but there are some differences. The Andeans I visited lived in more solid housing—adobe huts with corrugated iron or straw roofs. Low doors opened into a single, windowless room. Dogs, cats and chickens wandered freely about. There was very little furniture apart from a wooden or stone bench and two or three beds for the whole family—the parents and the children huddled in separate ones, while other relatives slept on llama skins or in their ponchos.

The Andean Indians seem to enjoy greater sexual freedom when young than the Central Americans. Indeed, the art of the pre-Columbian Andean civilizations highlights sexuality. Their explicit statues detail not just straightforward copulation—sparing no detail—but most other practices. All sexual practices are permitted to the young prior to marriage. After marriage, adultery is frowned upon.

The Andean Indians are also more preoccupied with death than the Central Americans, staging elaborate funeral ceremonies. After much preparation, corpses are interred while a beacon is burned on a nearby hill and a dog is killed, so that it can accompany the soul across the lake that separates this world from the next. A week later, the deceased's clothes are meticulously washed and ceremonially burned. A year later, after a small graveside ceremony, the mourning period is over.

The Andean Indian has a religion more comprehensible to the visitor than his Central American counterpart. God, the All-Powerful, has created man. Man's soul, after death, travels to the places he has been during life, drawing up a list of the good and evil he has done. After a week he returns to the cemetery and then travels across a river or lake accompanied by his black dog. The dog, however, will refuse to travel with him if he has been cruel toward animals—although, being fond of humans, dogs usually relent. When he gets to the other side, the All-Powerful is waiting. He adds up the rights and wrongs, then turns the just into white doves that fly to paradise, a flower garden looked after by children where the residents can grow all they want without risk of drought or frost. The unjust are placed at God's left side, and go to purgatory or hell, a mountain covered with thorns, which they have to climb. At the top they roll back down again and have to start all over again until their sins are expiated.

In the Andean religion, God is called Roal, the successor to Viracocha of Inca fame, and dwells on the highest mountain. The religion's symbology includes a Mother Earth figure, Pacha Mama, not to be confused with the malevolent Pacha, god of earthquakes. Apu are benevolent mountain spirits that speak to each other through the winds; the Aukis are spirits that prevent one from accomplishing practical jobs. The Soq'a were the first inhabitants of the earth, who were killed in the Great Flood, when Roal lost patience with them. They wander the earth unable to have normal sexual relations, and are inordinately jealous of those who do. Soq'a Machu dwells in caves, grass and trees, and violates women at night, who then give birth to deformed children. Soq'a Paya, a beautiful woman, seduces men, who afterward go into a torpor and die, vomiting blood. Those who commit adultery are particularly vulnerable.

Inti, the sun, is important, though not all-powerful. His bride is the benevolent moon, Mama Killa. Hail, snow and lightning are malevolent spirits. The Gagones are little dogs that are created whenever an act of incest takes place. Carbucho is a cat that visits the houses of those about to die. Cuzcungu is an eagle that hovers around houses when someone is in agony. Shiro and Chuzalongo live off the blood of their victims. The llama is worshiped for providing transport, wool, food and twine with which to make sandals. The Andean Indians are also respectful of cows, claiming that their milk is not ordinary milk, "but a belt of silk floating in the air."

The Andean Indians' pride are the splendidly embroidered, multicolored clothes they wear. They are also skilled in ceramics and at carving gourds. Otherwise they cultivate poor crops on poor land. In Peru, for example, the area of cultivated land is 4½ million acres, sustaining a population of 17 million. Yields are less than a third those in Europe. Two percent of the people own 90 percent of the cultivated land. On Peru's relatively rich coastland, thirty-seven thousand plots of less than 25 acres make up 20 percent of the territory while 58 percent is held by 2 percent of landowners. In the mountains twenty thousand plots make up 4 percent of the land, while 85 percent is divided among twenty-six hundred estates.

Conditions were still worse in Bolivia until the 1952 revolution: Indians were divided into *pongos*, hired labor in the fields and mines, living on meager earnings, and indentured servants, those in debt to their masters, who lived in conditions of near-slavery. Some sixty thousand small landholders with less than 25 acres held 5 percent of the land, while 95 percent was held by landowners of more than twelve hundred acres. Of the 34 million acres in the hands of large landowners, only 700,000 were cultivated; most were uncultivated mountain areas. The land reform of the 1950s split the large estates into small parcels for the peasants, who are still slowly acquiring the rights to the land. Conditions in Ecuador were a bit better: there the major landowners had no more than 36 percent of the territory, while, on balance, small proprietors had 34 percent.

The existence of a large underprivileged class—a very sizable minority in three Latin American countries, Guatemala, Peru and Bolivia, and a considerable one in Nicaragua, Colombia and Ecuador—largely explains the slow development of these nations. The Indians are hardly to blame, since so little attempt has been made to integrate them. Such revolutionary attempts as have been made to do so—for example, General Juan Velasco's experiment in Peru after 1968—were disastrous, and left them even worse off than before. The most successful revolution—Victor Paz Estenssoro's peaceful civilian takeover in Bolivia—gave Indians a greater sense of pride and emancipation, but left them little better off materially.

Are the Indians, illiterate and tied to the poorest lands, condemned to perpetual misery? Not necessarily. New agricultural methods could considerably improve the yields of all but the poorest lands; but most governments have been reluctant up to now to spend money on agriculture. Indians form a major part of the shanty populations of Lima, La Paz, Bogotá, Guatemala City and Quito: money has been spent improving these slums, but a much greater commitment is necessary to allow these Indians to join the monied economy. Part of the problem is that the Indian has been excluded from the groups that run most Latin American countries. Most armies are staffed at the top by whites or mestizos; banking and business elites are much the same.

Democracy is the greatest hope for the Indians, because they represent a large voting bloc in the countries they inhabit. But historically, their votes have tended to be conservative, antirevolutionary; indeed their ballots, genuine or not, have often stuffed the boxes in rigged elections won by the extreme right. Yet in countries where intelligent, reformist political parties have made the effort to appeal to Indian voters, it has been worth making. In Bolivia, Paz Estenssoro's National Revolutionary Movement won the trust of the Indians; in Peru, APRA has largely done so; and now in El Salvador and Guatemala, José Napoleón Duarte and Vinicio Cerezo have made major efforts to convince the Indians to assert their rights and thus to improve their lot.

By contrast, revolutionary appeals to the Indians have fallen on deaf ears, because the societies they represent are so rural and traditionalist. In Bolivia, Che Guevara was betrayed and killed when he attempted to radicalize the Indians; in Guatemala, where some young Indians for the first time joined the guerrillas in the 1970s, most of their community rallied against them and set up the self-defense forces that threw the guerrillas into retreat. In Peru today a new attempt is underway to radicalize the Indian, through the guerrilla group Sendero Luminoso (Shining Path), which appeals to their most basic complaints against the white man. So far, although a few Indians have joined the group, the reaction of most has been to collaborate reluctantly, at the point of a gun, or to attempt to betray or murder Sendero guerrillas.

But the Indian anger cannot be dismissed as too damp to be ignited by a revolutionary spark. In particular, the urban Indian in the shantytowns has slowly lost his traditional rural roots. As education spreads, so political consciousness will grow. The Indian is becoming more assertive and is voting for the moderate center in greater numbers. But he could become radicalized if the road to improvement is blocked.

Meanwhile, the Andean republics remain two-tier societies, in which a large number of people are marginal to the creation of wealth, producing just what they need to survive, or less. That probably explains why, while the rest of Latin America races to prosperity in uneven fashion, the Andean republics (oil-rich Ecuador excepted) are still lagging behind.

COLOMBIA

COLOMBIA IS THE NONSTORY OF LATIN AMERICA—WHICH MEANS THAT journalists cannot easily package it. But the country is in fact a lively one, a rugged outback with none of the unity that traditionally characterizes a nation. Colombia is a massive challenge of geography and terrain.

Its history has been second to none in its epic quality. Bogotá, the capital, revolted in 1810, one of the earliest cities in Latin America to rebel against the Spanish autocrats who ruled the province of New Granada. Simón Bolívar, the itinerant liberator of Latin America, became president of the new nation although he was absent for the most part, busy freeing other lands. After the liberation, New Granada still included Venezuela and Ecuador, but after Bolívar's death in 1830 it was broken up, with Colombia left as a spacious, largely empty land of just 1½ million people. To rule such a widely flung country, to control it from the center, was a task for a superman.

Colombia resembles a mountain hand reaching out to the sea; the three ranges at the top of the Andes reach to the Pacific on one side and the Caribbean on the other, cutting the territory into two overpoweringly humid sea provinces, three green valleys and a large, sloping mountain plain, Los Llanos, which extends toward the Amazon heartland of Latin America.

The sea strips have remained startlingly different in character. On the Pacific side there is a bandit country of isolated and impoverished settlements, a crime haven from which hundreds of light aircraft take off on dope-smuggling missions into the United States. On the Caribbean coast, there is a well-run society, run by rich whites lording it over a black population in cities like Cartagena, along some of the most attractive coastal scenery on the continent.

The Magdalena valley is a fetid swamp, the river as wide and as long as the Mississippi, but much less inhabited along its banks. To the west, across an almost impenetrable mountain range, lies the Cauca valley, a temperate and fertile region, which is cool even in its higher reaches; the valley boasts farms, ranches and plain towns. The third valley system is actually an immense basin in which sprawls Bogotá, some 8,500 feet up, the proud center of European intellectual tradition, the home of the country's political life.

To this high capital, nearly four hundred miles to the southeast of Panama City, my aircraft bore me on the second leg of my journey, into South America proper, along the Trail of the Indian. The city seemed like a giant saucer high in the Andes, surrounded by a chain of low-lying mountains: its height made its proximity to the equator bearable, but its location made it sodden during the rainy season.

It was raining when I arrived. Clouds covered the mountaintops, and the runway was glistening wet as we landed. When I disembarked, there was a military parade on the tarmac; the president was returning from somewhere. Groups of soldiers wheeled this way and that, and a band played. No one except a few passengers and airport staff were on hand to witness the display of pomp and color.

Bogotá was Danger City. The tension crackled in the air and the traffic moved fast, ceaselessly; no one walked the streets except from necessity. No first-time visitor would suspect this, driving in from the green fields and wide-open cattle country surrounding the airport where men road on horseback and herds of cattle roamed free. Some of this common land was cultivated, much was not, inhabited only by sheep and goats.

The country towns around Bogotá were classic Spanish colonial, with red-tiled roofs and whitewashed houses and geometrical streets and imposing, twin-towered cathedrals. Up across the great green valleys, rugged, unexpected mountains, wooded and wild, trailed back as far as the eye could see, introducing a wilderness that for the most part could only be crossed on horseback. It was wild West country, a country of bandits and guerrillas and great emptiness and great wealth and a few Indian villages. It simply did not prepare me for Bogotá.

Bogotá lay huddled under one of the smaller mountain ranges that encircled the valley. To the south, mile after mile of Indian shanties were divided into streets and neighborhoods in perfect symmetry, in ordered poverty. The city center was a huddle of graceless skyscrapers, department stores and offices, absurdly out of place in this remote upland. Further north lay the rich quarter, acre upon acre of oddly uniform one- or two-story buildings, each with a comfortable back garden, some with swimming pools and garages. These were the homes of the well-fed teenagers who hung around the ice cream parlors and shopping centers and cafés. Furthest to the east, the road curved in under the mountain where the very poor lived in shacks built into the slope. From these wooden-and-tin constructions that looked flimsy enough to be blown over, desultory men in vests and pants gazed unsmilingly over the valley. The women got on with the washing. Small children played and, surprisingly, the school-age ones walked about in smart blue uniforms.

To the east of Bogotá another great urban expanse stretched without inhibition into limitless countryside. Here was the industrial area, a group of similar one- or two-story factories that provided the city with much of its wealth. The workers traveled from the other side of town in packed buses that covered the streets in great sausage strings. The cost of bus fares was one of the most explosive political issues in Bogotá. The government-subsidized buses cost just eight pesos; the private buses, which contained slightly fewer people, eighteen pesos. I had visited Bogotá in 1978 in the middle of a crisis caused by the government's decision to raise bus prices: twenty-six people were killed. A subway system was long overdue.

In a city where, more than in any other in Latin America, the classes were segregated, the contrast between rich and poor was less striking than in Brazil and Venezuela, for instance. But in Bogotá half the city lived rather well on one side, while half lived in poverty on the other, and there was no in-between. The old colonial center, which was burned down in 1948 when the poor went on the terrible rampage called the *bogotazo*, was now the site of dehumanizing modern architecture; it had become a nucleus for those with money but they lived there at their peril, prey to gangs with knives who were known to assault not just individuals but whole groups.

Many Latin American countries are patrolled by the army; but in Bogotá there were up-to-date armored cars in the streets. I was warned to keep the windows of the taxi shut, so as to avoid the men on motorbikes who held up cars at gunpoint. The images from the windows of the closed car were depressing: the urgent, worried crowds of the urban poor; live mannequins, parading in shop windows intermittently, like ghosts come to life; the armed police wearing camouflage uniforms, bristling with radio sets and antennae almost double their size as giant guns in holster straps rode their slim hips. The forces of order were far from idle in this city where the poor were more pervasive than in any but Lima. I witnessed the police moving in on a small, angry crowd, breaking down shop windows. I would long remember the ominous tin hats of the police above their serious, trigger-nervous expressions.

The tension gave a spice to the air. Why Colombia had degenerated into desperado country was a source of passionate debate. The usual explanation was that Ciudad Kennedy, the slum quarter that turned out to welcome popes and American presidents, and then went on lynching sprees against the upper classes, was in a constant rebellion against an oligarchy—the last in Latin America—that had failed to share power. There was only a half-truth here, for the oligarchy had mobilized the hatreds of the working class in its fractious civil wars.

Colombia had a bloodily competitive two-party system. Even upon winning independence under Bolívar, Bogotá, that up-in-the-clouds capital, had the most rarefied political atmosphere on the continent. The ideals of liberalism and republicanism were debated by the high and the literate in coffee shops and bars. Soon after independence, a split emerged between the region of Bogotá, which tended to be dominated by the Liberals, who in the early stages were anticlerical (like their European counterparts), and their Conservative opponents in the widely scattered provinces. In the second half of the nineteenth century, the Liberals took charge of Bogotá and drew up an enlightened and democratic constitution: church and state were separated, divorce was legalized, slavery was abolished, a federal constitution was passed. The country's economy was based at the time on coffee and minerals, a fragile prop.

When, in 1860, the central government tried to usurp the powers of the provinces, civil war broke out. It ended only when a dictator, General Mosquera, took power. At length, the army handed the country back to democratic rule. But a fresh civil war broke out between the Conservatives, now ascendant in Bogotá, and the Liberals: one hundred thousand people died in the fighting. The Colombian writer, Gabriel García Márquez, captures the flavor of Colombian politics, as it has lingered even to this century, in the novel *One Hundred Years of Solitude*:

On one occasion on the eve of the elections, Don Apolinar Moscote returned from one of his frequent trips worried about the political situation in the country. The Liberals were determined to go to war. Since Aureliano at that time had very confused notions about the difference between Conservatives and Liberals, his father-in-law gave him some schematic lessons. The Liberals, he said, were Freemasons, bad people, wanting to hang priests, to institute civil marriage and divorce, to recognize the rights of illegitimate children as equal to those of legitimate ones, and to cut the country up into a federal system that would take power away from the supreme authority. The Conservatives, on the other hand, who had received their power directly from God, proposed the establishment of public order and family morality. They were the defenders of the faith of Christ, of the principle of authority, and were not prepared to permit the country to be broken down into autonomous entities. Because of his humanitarian feelings Aureliano sympathized with the Liberal attitude with respect to the rights of natural children, but in any case, he could not understand how people arrived at the extreme of waging war over things that could not be touched with the hand. It seemed an exaggeration to him that for the elections his father-in-law had them send six soldiers armed with rifles under the command of a sergeant to a town with no political passions. They not only arrived, but they went from house to house confiscating hunting weapons, machetes, and even kitchen knives before they distributed among males over twenty-one the blue ballots with the names of the Conservative candidates and the red ballots with the names of the Liberal candidates. On the eve of the elections Don Apolinar Moscote himself read a decree that prohibited the sale of alcoholic beverages and the gathering together of more than three people who were not of the same family. The elections took place without an incident. At eight o'clock on Sunday morning a wooden ballot box was set up in the square, which was watched over by the six soldiers. The voting was absolutely free, as Aureliano himself was able to attest since he spent almost the entire day with his father-in-law seeing that no one voted more than once. At four in the afternoon a roll of drums in the square announced the closing of the polls and Don Apolinar Moscote sealed the ballot box with a label crossed by his signature. That night, while he played dominoes with Aureliano, he ordered the sergeant to break the seal in order to count the votes. There were almost as many red ballots as blue, but the sergeant left only ten red ones and made up the difference with blue ones. Then they sealed the box again with a new label and the first thing on the following day it was taken to the capital of the province. "The Liberals will go to war," Aureliano said. Don Apolinar concentrated on his domino pieces. "If you're saying that because of the switch in ballots, they won't," he said. "We left a few red ones in so there won't be any complaints." Aureliano understood the disadvantages of being in the opposition. "If I were a Liberal," he said, "I'd go to war because of those ballots." His father-in-law looked at him over his glasses.

"Come now, Aurelito," he said, "if you were a Liberal, even though you're my son-in-law, you wouldn't have seen the switching of the ballots."

In 1930 the Conservatives ceded power to the Liberals, and the country seemed set to continue on a democratic course. But it was not to last. The Liberal Party in power became corrupt and spend-thrift. The benefits of sound Conservative finance, which had ushered in the period of prosperity, were thrown away. Worse, the labor movement started to break away from the Liberal Party, under a fiery radical, Jorge Gaitán. Meanwhile, a far-right party emerged under Laureano Gómez. The divisions afflicting Europe at the time were echoed in Colombia.

The crunch came in 1948, when Gaitán was assassinated. The slum quarter of Bogotá erupted. During the *bogotazo*, an enraged mob surged through the streets of the capital, egged on by people like Cuba's Fidel Castro, then a student. Thousands were killed, and the delegates at the Inter-American Conference were forced to take refuge in suburban houses. The main buildings of the capital were burned and looted, and it took several days to restore order. In reaction, the far-right Gómez was elected president and an appalling administration that pursued a vendetta against Protestantism and "Anglo-Saxonism" came to power. After four years of such rule by Gómez, even the army had had enough, and a military dictator, General Gustavo Rojas Pinilla, took power.

By then a fresh civil war between the Conservatives and the Liberals was underway through most of the countryside. Two hundred thousand were killed with appalling brutality during the period of "La Violencia." This was not just factional fighting, but something deeper: the urban and rural masses joined the Liberal party to fight the ruling class represented by the Conservatives. The fighting continued with unabated savagery under Rojas Pinilla, even though, thanks to his orthodox economic policies, the economy boomed. After the dictator had failed to bring peace, he was unceremoniously dumped in 1965, when the two warring parties, frustrated at being kept out of power, at long last brought the conflict to an end and reached a "National Pact" by which they agreed to alternate in power.

The violence tapered off, but the left argued that the Liberals had sold out, and a large number of leftists continued fighting, taking the revolutionary priest Camilo Torres as their inspiration. The rebels were now avowedly Marxist. But despite their efforts, the National Pact lasted until 1974, when the first genuinely contested election was won overwhelmingly by a right-of-center Liberal, Alfonso López Michelsen. He was succeeded by another Liberal, Julio César Turbay. But this dreary machine politician disillusioned the party's supporters, and an attractive loner—a Conservative, Belisario Betancur—won the ensuing election by advocating populist policies. Turbay, a bow-tied power broker, had been the epitome of everything corrupt and stale. Betancur, aggressive, bright, innovative, seeking a dialogue with the guerrillas, and pursuing imaginative economic policies, did much to rekindle Colombian politics.

The major defect of the Colombian system was, however, the alienation of the working class, which had been loyal to the Liberals and now voted for no one. Democracy survived during the 1960s and 1970s, almost alone on the continent; yet nearly half the electorate failed to vote in presidential elections. In addition, often in order to fight the guerrillas, much of the country remained under martial law. Betancur, to his credit, tried to curb military power, but without much success.

A country of great potential wealth straddling one of the most varied and inhospitable geographies possible, Colombia was ruled from a city in the mountains that was, in effect, divided: a capital with the poor in one area and the rich in another. Colombia was Latin America's longest-surviving democracy, and yet nearly half the population considered itself outside the system.

I met a left-wing Colombian publisher in his cluttered office, filled with books and papers, most of European origin. Like his country, he looked to Europe, not the United States, for his cultural inspiration. He did not hesitate to speak his mind.

"The oligarchy runs this country," he said. "The working masses do not participate. The left is frozen out. One day the revolution will come. Then we will grow and become rich."

My expression betrayed skepticism. "Why doesn't the left take part in politics? This is a democracy. It is no choice not to participate. You have abdicated your influence. You say you could command the votes of half the population."

"On the contrary. It would be wrong for us to take part in the sham of democracy." He waved his finger at me. "It would legitimize them. We tried to play their game, and you know what happened. Gaitán was killed; the killers took power. The oligarchy has been in power ever since. Even the army, which under Rojas Pinilla tried to be fair, is now just a brutal instrument of the oppressor class. Only a complete revolution will change this. Democracy is a sham."

"But the two-party system continues."

"So does the guerrilla war."

"The guerrillas are doing no better than before. Sooner or later they will have to give up. Betancur has offered them generous terms. I haven't seen any decline in support for democracy."

"You will."

I went to meet Betancur. He had a small party office, where he sometimes met journalists; he seemed almost to disdain the splendor of the presidential palace, which was a lovely eighteenth-century construction of cool white and spare black furniture. He was not a man who relished the trappings of public office. He was a plain and simple man with a slightly ugly, chubby face, protruding eyes, and a direct manner, and his conversation lacked the superfluous rhetoric and flowery qualifications of most politicians. Earnest and serious, he smiled only occasionally as he calmly defended his policies. Here was a new brand of Latin American conservative politician—dull, perhaps, by comparison with the old-style caudillos and demagogues, but I found him appealing. His personality, rather than his pedestrian words, made a strong impression.

What about the problem of electoral apathy? I asked him.

"Listen. Half of Americans do not vote in presidential elections. I say that not as an excuse, but just to point out that civic participation is hard to encourage even in a prosperous democracy. Here it is much harder. Of course we are trying to encourage more people to take part. But do not conclude that because people do not vote, they are all against the system."

"And the guerrillas?"

"I am offering them the chance to make peace. They belong to the past, they are an old way of doing things. If they want to win power, then let them compete for votes in elections." It was a refrain I had already heard in countries like El Salvador.

Of Betancur's sincerity I had no doubt: he did not come from the oligarchy himself; he had made his way up from the bottom. He was the real revolutionary—this man dragging his country into the twentieth century—not the guerrillas. But he had a long way to go to limit the power of the oligarchy and the army, whose provincial warlords ran most of the country under the endless state of emergency. The army was in a curious position: it neither dared to seize full power, nor would it give up what power it had. The army had memories of the last time it tried to run the country, when the ebullient Rojas was chased from office, miscalculating how much the people loved him. The people did not love the army, and a coup might trigger the violence always flickering under the surface of Colombian society. All the same, the Colombians wanted the army to hunt down the guerrillas and the narcotics traffic. So it remained powerful, and often ruthless, in extracting money from the peasants whose marijuana plantations it spared. The oligarchy was more of a problem. Betancur did not dare to alienate it by raising taxes or embarking on the land reform that might ignite farm workers' passion, particularly in the coffee-growing areas.

*   *   *

Colombia's biggest export is coffee. But, increasingly in recent years, two other commodities have come to supplement it: marijuana and cocaine. The marijuana is grown in Colombia itself, mainly in the Santa Marta valley and along the sparsely populated Pacific border of the country. The cocaine comes as raw, unprocessed paste from Peru and Bolivia. Processing plants—little huts in the hills of Colombia—turn it into pure cocaine or splice it with lactose and other impurities to make a slightly cheaper product. From Colombia's innumerable airstrips, it is flown in small planes to Florida: the rewards of even one consignment—a markup of around 1,000 percent—make it irresistible to many.

Drug smuggling was by far the biggest preoccupation of the Americans in Colombia. I met with one officer from the U.S. Drug Enforcement Administration branch in Bogotá, an earnest, clean-cut young man with a thin face and spectacles. He spoke quietly, in a jerkily abrupt manner; apart from that, he seemed more like a diplomat than a policeman.

"We have a really big operation here. One of the biggest. But you've got to remember we're just a drop in the ocean compared with the ordinary people who really fight the drugs here—the Colombian army and the police. They're the people who have got to be mobilized on the ground. I spend a lot of my time in this office, unfortunately."

"Do they cooperate?"

"Sure they do. That's the positive side. The debit side is that the army goes in and beats the hell out of the planters. It's big business for the growers and many of them are poor people who couldn't get as much from growing anything else. That's another thing: we need to support alternative crops that provide them with a living, and arrange for financing for new plantations."

I told him that I had heard the army was in with the growers.

He looked awkward. "All I can say is that we have received a much greater degree of cooperation from the authorities since we embarked on this crop substitution program. And you can see their point. For them drugs aren't a problem, but poverty is. The drugs are a problem for the United States. So we've got to pay toward getting to the root of it."

"How's it going?"

"It's a long haul." He showed me a map where the main growing areas were. "The army is achieving considerable success in Santa Marta. But the growers are moving back into Los Llanos—this high, undermapped region here. It's much more difficult to spot the plantations there: there's just so much ground to cover. You should see it yourself from a spotter plane. Some of them have even moved into the Amazon basin, where they operate from remote jungle clearings. Try spotting one of those from the air."

He was a capable, keen young man, doing a tough, professional job against a criminal organization in another country. I respected him, but I wondered how on earth he would succeed. The Colombian government functioned only by recognizing the limits of its authority; that was what successive civil wars had been about. For a foreign power to seek to root out the most lucrative trade of the Colombian badlands was hopeless. The best approach, indeed, was bribery and a helping hand to the country's own forces of order. America was helpless in Colombia, a country too remote and far-flung to take much notice of the outside world, still immersed in its curious imitation of the European politics of the early nineteenth century.

I took a car out of Bogotá, along the rugged main spine of the Andes cordillera to Girardot. The road wound smoothly down the green backbone of the hills into the upper Magdalena valley, and the breathlessness caused by the capital's altitude was replaced by the sensation of sultry heat. Soon, the sky clouded over: great rolling gray shapes smothered the tops of the green-clad hills, providing a heavy, almost claustrophobic, effect. The drive took three hours. The town of Ibagué was undistinguished and we pressed on to Girardot, a larger town, with a fine cathedral square that was airy and well laid out, the kind of middling town where moderately prosperous men led unexciting lives.

The air grew less hot and humid as I traveled. The landscape became drier, harsher, dominated by high, snow-covered peaks— the first I had seen in Latin America. I took a small detour from my route to San Agustín; there I trekked a mile or so uphill before reaching a clearing surrounded by thickly wooded hills. This was the Valley of the Statues, a jumble of stones carved mostly in the shapes of animals and deities—although containing some human figures—created by an unknown culture that extended as far back as 500 B.C. and apparently continued until the Spaniards came. The statues were rough, but their unexpectedness and size in that emptiness made them striking, rather like a reduced version of China's terra-cotta warriors. What did they mean, other than that there had been a civilization in the place long before the Spaniards came?

The statues were a timely reminder that there had been people capable of an art nearly as sophisticated as the European civilizations of Greece and Rome, and certainly more advanced than anything in Northern Europe or, indeed, Spain. Such further evidence of the triumph of brutality under the conquistadors induced melancholy, and I left the company of the statues under the snow peaks.

Rather than stay the night, I chose to press on toward the Ecuadoran border. My car drove on through the deep green landscape, the road becoming a brown ribbon, then paved again as it rose and crossed a gaping, dizzying gorge over the Guaitara River. It had reached a height of more than eight thousand feet by the time I reached Ipiales, a colorful, busy Indian town dominated by volcanoes. I spent the night in the finest hotel in the place, a fleapit.

In the morning I continued on to Tulcán, an uninteresting market center. The road wound on through hilly country, past a lake, to another undistinguished town, Ibarra. From there the country improved slightly: we reached a place called Cayambe, in a desolate, dusty landscape, before plunging into another vertiginous, rocky gorge across the Guaillabamba River. As the car climbed, I considered the extraordinary feats of the original Spaniards who, without roads, had crossed these obstacles. When I had stopped at the border I thought the Ecuadorans seemed more punctilious and courteous than their more surly Colombian counterparts; but perhaps it was just my imagination. From there I took the train down to Quito.

ECUADOR

I WAS NOW FULLY INSIDE A TRULY INDIAN NATION. THEY WERE A PEOPLE who had built great cultures and buildings, had ruled cruelly over their own people, and then were subjugated by European conquerors. Later, the Europeans, while formally easing the shackles of domination, even giving the Indians the vote, continued in effect to dominate them. The subjugation of the Andean Indian was evident in their conflicting attitudes of servility, sullenness and eagerness to please and their characteristic expressions of bland disinterest and indifference. They puzzled me. Why did they endure it? Why, unlike every people oppressed by others in this century, had a consciousness not emerged? Why had race not become an issue in South American politics? Was it that the Indians had created a complete lifestyle for themselves, a kind of remote, folkloric self-sufficiency that had so insulated them from the white man that they felt no desire for political control? It seemed to me the upland Indian had an attitude of independence—a sureness of his greater ability to withstand the rigors of his mountain existence—that made him contemptuous of the white man. Yet resentment was there, as well, and I found it in Quito.

Arriving in a strange place creates a vulnerability that can spark easily into anger. When two small men seized my single case in the bustle of the central railway station at Quito—to carry it for me, no doubt—I was seized by an unreasonable fear that they were stealing it, and yanked it back sharply, giving them a piece of my mind. A respectable, very dark Indian in a brown suit and tie and glasses suddenly turned on me and, in English, shouted angrily, "Why do you speak like that? Arrogant gringo," and so on. I was so startled, and angry, that I yelled back. A small crowd gathered around us. What was it to do with him? Only when someone said they were fetching the police did we both back off.

Later that afternoon, when I was calmer and safely installed in a hotel, I wandered happily through the center of Quito. The city, less than 400 miles southwest of Bogotá, was remarkable. To one side towered the great smooth bulk of a volcano, a bare gray hillside merging with the white ice-cream collar that led to the jagged edge of the summit, a peak ripped away by some giant hand. More pronounced than in Bogotá was the sense of height and altitude: the air was thin, bracing and pure. This was a mountain town, and it sloped down the sides of the mountain to the green bottom of the valley below. On the eastern side were more volcanoes. The open streets provided views of the whole valley and a sense of space, as in Swiss Alpine towns. Walking from the inevitable cluster of minisky-scrapers in the modern quarter to the Indian-inhabited colonial center, I had the feeling that I was an alien intruder, encroaching upon the real civilization of the Andean Indian. For the first time in Latin America, I felt I was on a strange continent. Certainly, the center seemed almost entirely populated by Indians; and yet the impression was slightly misleading, because the fine old cathedral and its square, where the Indians squatted and bargained and thrust things at visitors, was a European creation, set up by an earlier generation of Spanish settlers.

With an Ecuadoran friend I had known in Britain and a Western journalist, I wandered through the elegant, if dirty, cobbled streets, where the smell of urine pervaded the cold mountain air. We turned this way and that, fascinated by the dark doorways that opened onto counters crowded with spices and peppers and animals. Indian women were clustered there, and in the streets, selling vegetables and rag dolls. Many sat but most squatted, their huge dusty bustles billowing out over the pavements, their faces broken in smiles that

revealed bad yellow teeth that chattered and cursed without inter-
mission. Their hair was jet dark, falling in plaits over brightly
colored shawls, woven in patterns of reds and whites and blues and
greens. The shawls were multipurpose, as useful for carrying food as
for carrying babies, serviceable as tablecloths or for displaying their
wares. From their ears hung huge rings of silver and gold, some of
poorer metals, seemingly the key indication to the wealth of their
owners.

On their heads they wore the hats I had first seen in Colombia—
huge squat ten-gallon affairs with wide brims in a variety of colors
below brown hatbands. I never was to find a satisfactory explanation
for the Indian obsession with hats, although it clearly derived from
an imitation of the headgear of the colonial aristocracy and their
ladies. In Peru the fashion was for a white hat with a narrow brim
and a tall peak, rather like a top hat; in Bolivia, most fascinating of
all, the women wore elegant, rakishly tilted bowlers, with a hatband
tied in a bow, similar to the kind popular in Hyde Park at the end of
the eighteenth century.

We visited the cathedral. Behind a finely carved facade, in its
dark, cavernous interior, we were eyed by vivid gory icons and
statues of marginal saints, with staring eyes and gushing red blood.
When we emerged relieved into the sunlight of the square, our
Ecuadoran friend offered to take us to a local bar. Up to now, the
Indians had not paid us much attention, other than trying to sell us
trinkets. In the bar, they eyed us with astonishment as we sat down.
Conversation ceased. The proprietor, after some hesitation, approached the table and we gave him an order casually, continuing to
chat among ourselves. Only slowly did the conversation in the room
pick up. I glanced round the room: it was a basic establishment,
dirty, full of bottle-topped tables, undecorated, unremarkable save
for the men ogling us. They were rough-hewn, wearing simple
working clothes—the pullovers and the woolly ponchos that the cold
required. Whatever their conversation, it was hostile toward us.

One shouted an insult. I could make out nothing except the word
gringo. We continued as if nothing happened. My Ecuadoran friend
was apologetic. "I am sorry. They are drunk. It sometimes happens."
The men at the table with the shouting man seemed to be trying to
calm him. Then the squat, sallow-looking proprietor came forward
and spoke to him; that had no effect. The proprietor sat at our table

and ordered a drink. He didn't apologize, but he was offering us his hospitality and protection. The invective of the drunk turned on him, and the drunk was at last led out by his friends. The tension subsided. "I am honored that you have come," said the proprietor in the tones of a man seeking to make up a disagreement. We were courteous in turn, and left shortly afterward.

The tavern had been a place where no gringo was welcome. I felt the hostility had nothing to do with our being mistaken for Americans—Ecuador is one of the few Latin American countries that has no real quarrel with America—but with our coming from the dominant, monied race, and straying out of bounds into a place where the poor Indian could get away and be on his own.

A pocket-handkerchief country in the Andes, tucked away on Latin America's Pacific coast, Ecuador had no historical reason for its existence as did massive Colombia, the former seat of the captain-generalcy of New Granada, or Peru, the former seat of the viceroyalty of New Spain. It had emerged as New Granada fell apart, and as the feeble grip of the dying Bolívar on his nation was loosened; Bogotá found that it could not enforce its authority over Venezuela in the east or Ecuador in the west. In 1820 a crony of Bolívar, Juan José Flores, a tough, thirty-year-old youngster, had led the state to independence. It consisted of two cities—Quito, a conservative city in the Andes dominated by the colonial class and the Catholic Church, and, unconnected to it, Guayaquil, a torrid, Pacific port detested by sailors as a breeding ground for diseases such as the plague, malaria and yellow fever, which was run by a mixed-blood middle class of traders. The rest of the humid lowlands of the land of the equator were almost unpopulated, while the Andes were sparsely inhabited by Indians. Where the Andes fell toward the Amazon, no one but the most backward Indian tribes lived; much of this area was soon stolen by the Peruvians.

Somehow Flores forged a nation, and even annexed the Galápagos Islands, inhabited by convicts and Darwin's turtles. After Flores's departure, the country lapsed into a ferocious rivalry between the two cities—one conservative and clerical, the other liberal and radical, until a new dictator seized power in 1860. This was the donnish Gabriel García Moreno, a dry, haughty intellectual who for the first time brought some industry and commerce to Ecuador, set up schools, and encouraged the Jesuits to civilize the country. He was madly pro-Catholic and engaged in a quixotic attempt to form an army to rescue the pope, who had been imprisoned by the new Italian state in 1870. Five years later he was hacked to death in his own palace by a band of proliberal guards wielding machetes.

After a short interval, a Guayaquil-based liberal, General Eloy Alfaro, took power and waged war on the clerics. His successor, General Leónidas Plaza, disestablished the church; Alfaro, however, fell out with him, tried to stage a rebellion, and was put in the Quito jail. There he was dismembered by a proclerical mob, which then burned his remains. Ecuadoran presidents did not die pleasantly.

Ecuador underwent a minor industrial revolution in the 1920s, which, over time, created a group of nouveaux riches to challenge the even tinier ruling elite in Quito and the slightly larger one in Guayaquil. The liberal influence of these people produced an instant reaction from the Nazi-influenced army, which took power for several dim years. The country's one sensible president was overthrown in 1944 by a verbose windbag, José María Velasco Ibarra, a shrewd opportunist who espoused every possible ideology in the pursuit of power, but hardly implemented any of them. He was a kind of Ecuadoran Perón, without the military credentials. Velasco Ibarra was to return, election after election, to dominate and paralyze Ecuadoran politics. Altogether, he had five terms of office. In 1960 an attractive, modern, technocratic ex-ambassador to Washington who was passionately committed to constitutional democracy and moderate social reform, Galo Plaza, ran against the demagogue, and was duly defeated. Velasco Ibarra, as before, started stirring up trouble with Peru over the disputed border region, which Ecuador had no chance of regaining, and for good measure engaged in a campaign of vitriolic anti-Americanism. He was overthrown by the army a year later.

However, the Ecuadoran army was fairly responsible: it abdicated power in 1968, allowing a free election to be held. Velasco Ibarra was again elected, at the age of seventy-five. The old man embarked on a wild spending program, seized American tuna ships, and, in 1970, disbanded congress and set himself up as a dictator. Two years later, the army, with every possible justification, moved in. The army, however, had been infected by a curious kind of socialist-nationalist creed, and tried its own rather silly reform program, which went sour. The dictator, General Guillermo Rodríguez Lara, was kicked out by a conservative subordinate—who waited for the president's daughter to have her wedding in the presidential palace before courteously marching in. The new junta handed the country over to constitutional rule.

The election of 1978 looked like a rerun: in place of Velasco Ibarra was a stand-in for the president of the congress, a rough old populist of Lebanese descent, Assad Bucaram; the other candidate was a young technocrat, Jaime Roldós. To general astonishment, Roldós won. His bright, smart style seemed to herald something new in Latin America; other countries soon started imitating Ecuador's example. Tragically, he was killed in a plane crash in 1981 and his vice-president, Osvaldo Hurtado, succeeded.

I went to see the new president in Quito. He entirely lacked Roldós's charm, but he too was a technocrat. Stiff, unsmiling, in a perfectly fitting gray suit with two splendidly braided senior military men in immaculate green uniforms and an Ecuadoran flag resplendent behind him, he greeted me in a lavish skyscraper office that overlooked the remote Andean valley. His answers to my questions were correct and predictable, revealing nothing of himself; the eyes watched cautiously through steel-rimmed glasses, the mouth was closed and pursed. He reminded me of a young priest, or an ambitious provincial bank manager. But he was light years ahead of the old baggy-assed political bosses who had previously made such a mess of Ecuador, provoking military interventions.

It seemed remarkable to me that a country so cut off and insignificant could be so modern in its politics: in particular, that the army could be so levelheaded and that the people could be mature enough to abandon the demagogue tradition.

"The reason," a prominent Ecuadoran commentator told me, "is only in part our oil." Ecuador, a member of OPEC, was the second-largest exporter of oil on the Latin American continent, after Venezuela, and with only seven million inhabitants, the money went far. "We could have behaved irresponsibly with the oil bonanza. I think one reason why Ecuador is so balanced is that the army has always taken its role as defender of the nation's borders seriously—after all, we have so often been at war with Peru. Unlike other Latin American armies, who have nothing to do, the army considers politics beneath it. Our struggle has always been constitutional struggle—though bitter—between the radical populists in the cities and the clerical conservatives in the mountains. I suspect the conservatives have won because the people do not want to see their oil wealth squandered. Also, the wealth is creating a new, solid middle class which is interested in stability. I think our stability is here to stay—even when the oil runs out."

Judging from Quito, conservatism was the order of the day. The elite and the middle class were sober, quiet, reserved, presiding over the grim, long-suffering urban masses, who endured white rule and led their own lives. I traveled to Guayaquil, down the great railway that plunged eleven thousand feet to the coast, to see whether that turbulent city had really become the center of moderation.

The mayor of Guayaquil offered to take me to visit the city's most famous sight, the great stilt slum that had grown up over the years in a torrid swamp between the mountains and the Pacific Ocean. We drove through the port district, clogged with cargo and trucks and the strong, easygoing men who inhabit such areas, to the place where people in the most abject poverty, lacking any means to acquire scarce and expensive land to construct their houses, had built over the swamp by the river that drained into the sea.

There was no land there, so it cost nothing, only the price of the wooden stilts stuck into the swamp to support precarious structures ten feet or so above the water. The slum was like a giant matchwood city, a flimsy construction of spillikins extending out over, and into green slimy waters, linked by an intricate system of catwalks so narrow that you could barely cross them without losing your footing. The whole thing looked so frail, it seemed certain that the slightest puff of wind, much less a storm, would send the spindly structures crashing into the slime. Yet their very frailty was their strength: the water, whipped up below, had very little to push against, and a collapse was rare.

The mayor was a burly man with a bushy black mustache, almost overbearingly self-confident, except that his eyes had a genuine softness. He took us across the catwalks to a place where bulldozers were moving earth into the swamp. "It is a great program. Funded by the Inter-American Development Bank. Thousands of homes will be affected. Then they will be spared the disease that is endemic here. Can you imagine the hygiene problems, with all the waste of these houses going into the stagnant waters beneath? They welcome a storm here because it changes the water."

People recognized the mayor as we walked, and called out friendly greetings. He wore a neat white shirt, which contrasted with their pants-and-vest poverty. Yet he exchanged expansive grins with them. They seemed fond of this hulk of a man as he perspired across the sticks that so improbably bore him above the swamp.

I went into a house, where I was made welcome by a young man; children came out, smiling and playful. The man of the house was thin, undernourished, a body frame without a chest and with thin arms and legs. He had a mustache, a nearly bald head and a cheerful smile. "My parents are out," he apologized.

I stood in the white crisscross shaft of light that shone through the cracks between the planks and bamboo that made up the house. I was dripping with sweat in the heat and humidity, and the flies landed on me with a persistence that had long since defeated any attempts to brush them aside. "You live with your parents?" I asked.

He grinned ruefully. "This is my parents' house."

His wife added: "We want to move; it is not private enough, with his parents in one house." There was only one room, and four children were crawling over its clutter. "It is dangerous, too, for the little ones. Children fall in the swamp all the time. When they are older, it does not matter; they get out. But when they are young . . . about fifty or sixty of them die every year, maybe more, in Guayaquil."

"The government is filling in the swamp," I told her.

"They fill in one bit, but another bit gets added on. I wish they would give us houses on dry land." I thought the criticism understandably overstated: the government was trying to stretch limited resources to meet an insatiable demand.

In the car on the way back, we passed the city cemetery. It was a magnificent affair, full of two-story tombs and temples and stone angels praying for the dead. "They are better off in death than in life," commented the mayor.

AMAZONIA

I LEFT THE REPUBLIC OF ECUADOR, WHOSE OLD- AND OTHERWORLDLI-
ness had cheered me, for Bogotá, whose fetid air of bustle and crime
I had come to dislike. But my return was only to catch another flight
from that great valley in the northern Andes, this time to fly southeast, to where the vast expanse beyond the mountains—the llanos—
descended to the jungle, and the great Amazon basin began.

The first sight of the Amazon from the air lingered long in my
memory. The jungle was endless, a canopy of trees stretching in
every direction, gently undulating. The aircraft hovered, in motion
but apparently motionless, because the scene below never changed.
The Amazon forest is the size of the United States, and it seemed the
size of eternity. Below the canopy, below the green cover, was layer
upon layer of life and vegetation, each layer further from the light,
until the bottom layers mingled with the slime and sludge, a breeding ground of innumerable species that thrive far from the light of
day.

Just occasionally I spotted a little break in the green, a clearing,
where there might be a cluster of brown bamboo houses, or just the
few tree stumps of an uprooted camp. The depth of the hole—the
height of the trees—was startling. A slight chill gripped me: if we

had to land, there would be no place suitable for miles. Certainly these potholes in the greenery were not big enough.

Four hours of buzzing over this green monotony and some five hundred miles later, still within the boundaries of Colombia, the aircraft reached its destination. The jungle below broke abruptly, to yield a sight that resembled the sea, except that one could detect, in the far distance, another green shore to it. This was the Amazon itself, one thousand miles upstream, wider than any river I had ever seen. On the banks of the river, the forest was cleared, and we flew over settlements that eventually opened out into a modern town. The aircraft landed just beyond. I climbed out, and was hit as though by something resembling the hot wet towels they give you on board aircraft. The heat and humidity were overpowering. I felt I could hardly breathe. Within moments I had been bitten several times by mosquitos; I thanked my foresight in taking foul-tasting malaria tablets every day for the previous week.

After clearing customs—a long process because the town, Leticia, was a notorious smuggling point—I took a taxi into town. The taxi banged its way along an uneven road; within half a mile, I had arrived, driving past the main row of shops and the tatty-looking town center. Some way outside the town, there was a low building that opened onto an enclosure of huts that turned out, on closer inspection, to be self-contained hotel apartments. This was to be my stopping place for a couple of nights.

The owner was a wide-shouldered, stocky man with a loud guttural voice and a ready laugh, like a walk-on character in a Hemingway novel. That afternoon he told me about the town. "It's a great place. I fell in love with it years ago, stayed ever since. The greatest wildlife in the world. I'm a naturalist, not a hotel keeper. Started up in the monkey export business. This is just a sideline. We own an island upstream where we breed monkeys. It was a great idea; we brought the monkeys to the island, and they can't get off, so they're easy to catch. We breed thousands of monkeys for export, mostly to hospitals and zoos in the United States. They're good animals for doing experiments on. Now the Colombian government has gone and slapped a ban on the export of live animals. They say the nature here is being depleted. Balls. I breed the monkeys I export. It's just that there are forces here, there's a Mafia here, that doesn't like me; they're too much into that goddamn drugs business."

He was entirely larger than life, like so many who lived in Latin America. He said: "You gotta come alligator hunting. In a canoe tonight."

I decided instead to cross the border into Brazil from Leticia, a curious town that had been built up by the Colombians in an attempt to prevent the Brazilians from quietly moving further into their territory. A Brazilian garrison town was just down the road that led that far and no farther; you could only get out of this clearing in the jungle by plane. The road connected two countries in the middle of the jungle that were cut off from the outside world. Across the Amazon was Peru; from there the cocaine was smuggled across to Colombia in small boats. But that was another story.

A fair-haired, enthusiastic seventeen-year-old German boy who worked for the hotel owner offered to come with me into Brazil. I walked in the dreary heat of the late afternoon sun down the dusty road. "Sometimes there is a frontier check, sometimes not," said my companion. "The two communities depend on each other, so there is little point, even though they were almost at war with each other recently." We passed the hut that demarcated the border, but it was too hot for the frontier guards to be on duty. The sun had come out, although large, woolly clouds threatened. I wished the rain would come. On the Brazilian side the people were darker and had more pronounced features. We found a place that served thirst-quenching beers, and then trudged on into the settlement of Tabatinga.

It was like an early settler town: the roads were unpaved; the houses were made of wood, with saloon bar doors and dark interiors. Men and women on chairs or slouching in doorways called out greetings as we passed. Burly white men walked down the street arguing with loose-limbed blacks. There was a loud argument going on inside one of the drinking places. My guide took me to a tinny, modern building in the shape of a circus tent. "This is where it all happens," he said.

Inside, blinking from the sun of late afternoon, I was greeted by a pandemonium of lights reflected from a golf ball hanging from the ceiling. Garish reds, yellows, greens and blues danced all over the place, to the sound of an overwhelming musical blare. It was a large modern disco, with all the latest hits, in the middle of the jungle.

Men swayed about as sensual young women in print dresses that

exposed voluminous breasts and suggested no clothing underneath
jumped about performing movements that seemed designed to ex-
pose tantalizing glimpses. "Isn't it great?" said the fair-haired boy.
"Beats alligator hunting. Any of the girls will dance with you, if
they're not with someone else. They'll all screw if you pay them
right. I get it free, though. But it's not worth it. They've all got the
clap." He was a confused, likable, worldly kid. He picked up a
young woman and went dancing. Another lingered near the table
where I sat. But I decided to stick with the beer.

The men were mostly off-duty soldiers from the local Brazilian
garrison, the women their whores. Many of the women had splendid
bodies; they were ebony beauties with lithe, vigorous movements
and laughing faces of a kind you saw only in Brazil; they had been
imported from the coast. There must be good money in it, to live in
this hellhole all year round.

It was dark by the time we left, and the shouts and the yells of the
rowdy alleyway between the shops and whisky parlors and by-
the-hour hotels where the soldiers took their women were louder
than ever. It was a relief to follow the boy into the dark peace of the
jungle, along a path he knew, where the chattering of monkeys and
other nameless animals replaced the aggressive babel of human beings. Within moments, we were surrounded by dense undergrowth
in the dark. He said, "I always go this way. You've gotta follow the
path closely, though; it takes only a minute to get lost. People have
disappeared, even this close to town."

At the hotel I thanked him and went to my hut and sat on the
mosquito-netted veranda, dimly making out the great flow of the
river whose far bank I could hardly see.

The next day I took a trip up the Amazon in a power boat with the
boy and a few other hotel guests. The boat, a reliable, rather basic
affair, with no cabins and only a canvas cover to keep the sun off,
departed from a jetty past a row of rickety shops and a unisex "*salón
de belleza.*" Once we were on the river, the sheer expanse of that
moving mass of water became more apparent as we glided along.
The river was like a tidal sea, always on the move. Its swirling,
opaque gray-brown colors eddied and crisscrossed with the currents.
Here was a river entirely uninviting to the swimmer. Apart from the
rush of the currents and the threat of the alligators and the piranhas,

I had heard tales of a fish that entered the sensitive cavities of the body, feeding on the tissue there. One wouldn't last long in that brew.

After we left the town far behind, the riverbank reverted to dense green undergrowth topped by giant trees that seemed to rise from the river. Against this ever-changing curtain of pendulous greenery, peace and torpor reigned as we slowly made our way up that vast waterway, over the mysterious depths below, past the green.

The island the owner had spoken of was a few miles upstream, and was unremarkable apart from the incessant chatter of the monkeys in the forest and a dopey-looking alligator in a pen. The German boy took me in a small motorboat to an inlet in the riverbank where the undergrowth drooped low over muddy brown water and we had to duck to avoid trailing strands. Dugouts paddled out to meet us, carrying thin men with eager smiles in check shirts. I could not make out what they were saying or whether they were only trying to sell us something. We rounded a bend in the river and moored the boat. Four minutes' walk away was an Indian village.

A sturdy, pot-bellied woman in her thirties, her breasts sagging, gazed at us as we arrived, her expression an unchanging scowl. Wearing nothing except a red cloth as a short skirt about her waist, she stared at us disapprovingly as we made our way to a village consisting of bamboo and grass-covered houses built on stakes to escape flooding during the season. Everyone seemed to wear identical red skirts about their waists, men and women, adults and children alike. The men were slender with thick, dark hair cut in bowl style. Their faces were keen and intelligent. The older women, like the one we had just seen, had sagging breasts, perhaps from the feeding of so many children. The younger girls had cheerful faces and slatty limbs. The children were playful, like children anywhere. They did not seem undernourished.

The Indians sold us bark paintings and piranha-teeth necklaces. "The hotel owner pays them so that we can take visitors to see them," my guide explained. That seemed to be the extent of their exploitation. I had expected to see ill-treatment of the Indians; but they were merely a curiosity, protected by the local settlers. "Not on the Brazilian side, though. That's where they get beaten up," the owner later told me.

*   *   *

The plight of the Amazon Indians is very different from that of the upland ones. Unlike the large, self-sustaining upland tribes, the Amazonians face extinction. Where racial subjugation is the charge leveled against the oppressors of the Andean Indian, genocide is the charge leveled against the oppressors of the Amazon Indian. And genocide is not too strong a word, for once. Most local governments are trying feebly to save the Indians from the profiteers, but the attempt to preserve the jungle Indian's way of life has itself opened up a great debate about what is in their best interests. Is it best, they ponder, to keep the Indians apart from the world, untouched by progress and the material improvement that almost everyone else can enjoy? Or is it best to absorb one of the last holdouts from the modern world?

The Indians are too scarce to survive in Amazonia, where they are prey not only to the diseases of the white man that have already decimated thousands of them, but also to the intermarriage and miscegenation that will eventually transform their civilization. The highland Indian has a style of dress and art that guarantees the continual visibility of the culture—even if the economy of that culture is improved. Yet if the Amazon American Indians lose their poverty, they will become the antithesis of their culture, which is based on the rejection of materialism. The absence of consumer materialism is what appeals to Westerners most about the Amazon Indians. But how can the Indians' lot be improved without losing all that? And how can an outsider say their lot should not be improved because he believes them to be happier in a nonmaterial condition? It is more of a dilemma than the defenders of the Amazon will admit.

The onslaught upon the one million or so lowland Indians who survived the exploitation of the rubber planters in the nineteenth century was unleashed by a massive development of the Amazon river basin toward the end of the 1960s; it has continued unabated since. The latest attack has begun with the opening up of the Trans-Amazonic Highway and assorted roads by the Brazilian government, and has continued with the associated resettlement program, the laying waste of jungle for cattle grazing lands and the construction of major projects. The effect of all these changes on the Indians has been traumatic. Some remote tribes have been abruptly exposed to the challenges of Western civilization. Others further into the jungle have been threatened with absorption or extinction.

The Yanoamö and the Jívaro have traditionally been among the most isolated tribes. The Yanoamö live in the jungle regions between Venezuela and Brazil, and until recently roamed the most inaccessible part of the rain forest. But this changed with the beginning of mineral development and other new projects, including a road to be constructed connecting Manaus, at the heart of the Amazon, with Caracaraí to the north. This project, which will eventually link Venezuela to Brazil, has already brought lethal disease, cutting into the Indian population of around thirty-five thousand—the largest group in Latin America.

The Yanoamö wear no clothes, except for a string around the waist, which the women hang small aprons from and the men tie their foreskins to, a supposedly hygienic practice. They wear small twigs through their noses and ears. Their hair is cut in bowl style. In place of clothes, they wear traditional paints, using red dyes from plants and black dyes from soot. The tribe has recently taken to small farming, although it still hunts and fishes. The Yanoamö remain warlike, using bows and arrows, and chanting, "I, the vulture, am hungry for flesh" before going out to hunt their enemies. This usually takes the form of blood feuds against neighboring tribes. The tribes also engage in ritual fights, with giant wooden clubs, and in boxing contests with no holds barred. There was a story told of Padre Cocco, a missionary, who arrived in the area and bribed the natives to abandon a large number of weapons; they simply fashioned new ones.

The Indians also indulge in ritual incantations and drugs. The Jívaro sniff a hallucinogen called *ebena*. During their trances, they imagine that their souls are translated into the soul of an animal, usually a jaguar or a bird, which can roam great distances in the forest, casting an all-seeing eye. Michael Harner, the Indian affairs scholar, describes how boys are initiated into these trances, usually after being cleansed by the waters of the "magical" waterfalls:

If the Arutam-seeker is fortunate, he will awaken at about midnight to find the stars gone from the sky, the earth trembling, and a great wind felling the trees of the forest and thunder and lightning. To keep from being blown down, he grasps a tree trunk and awaits the Arutam [acquired soul]. Shortly after the Arutam appears from the depths of the forest, often in the form of . . . giant jaguars fighting one another as they roll over and over to the vision-seeker. When the apparition arrives, the Indian must run forward and touch it, either with a small stick or with his hand . . . After nightfall the soul of the same Arutam he touched comes to him in his dreams. His dream visitor is in the form of [an old warrior] who says to him: "I am your ancestor. Just as I have lived long, so will you. Just as I have killed many times, so will you." These rituals involve dancing, the playing of drums and musical instruments and the wearing of masks.

The Yanoamö believe in a system of myths, much of it centered around sexuality. In their lore, the moon is cold, spotty and sullied by an act of incest committed by its sister, Mener-yo, who darkened its face. Woman, according to Amazon Indian mythology, used to rule man until a male spirit seized the sacred flames that were the source of her power. The source of the flames was hidden between her legs, which became her vagina. Indian ritual carvings concentrate on the themes of phallus and vagina, many of the carvers invoking the phallus as the physical world and the vagina as the spiritual world. Another group of Indians, the Makuna, dance wearing outsize phalluses as fertility symbols.

The snuff the Yanoamö use for their trances is said to date from Father Sun's attempted incest with his daughter, who rejected his penis, spilling the "seed of the sun." The Indians believe that animals live in a giant reserve, to which their medicine men, the shamans, can go to procure new life, keeping the supply of jungle beasts constant for the Indians to live on. In addition to these functions, the shamans are healers, using the technique of rubbing an afflicted person with an egg or a guinea pig to transfer a disease to it.

It is hardly surprising that when Indians do encounter Western civilization, they tend to be attracted by its clothes, canned foods, radios, cooking stoves and, in particular, medicine. The healing herbs are sometimes useful, but the Indians also need other medicines. (A vaccine against AIDS is being developed from an Amazon bank product long used by the Indians.)

In one area, housing, it is impossible to argue that the Indians' talents were not better adapted to their surroundings than modern inventiveness. Their designs are simplicity itself, yet with an elegance that makes them preferable to modern tin shanties. The simplest house is a windbreak, which is no more than a circular series of bamboo stems and leaves mounted on a small, low wall of adobe, with a hole in the roof, in which a tribe can live communally. The opening allows the smells and hot air to escape while the shade provides a surprising coolness: this is known as a *shabono*. Another common type of building is the *maloca*, a large barn of wood and grass, airy enough to allow cool air to circulate. Often the *malocas* are fortified.

One of the staunchest defenders of the Indian way of life is Fritz Trupp, author of *The Last Indians*, an account of the various tribal cults. He concludes sadly:

The Auca who once lived on the meat of monkeys, on larvae and berries, are now dependent on the white man, working as day laborers and spending their hard-earned money on things they had found for nothing or did not need. But now their system of values is characterized by imported canned food, transistor radios and guns. Their hair, once groomed with pride, is now cropped short with a pair of old scissors. That way it is not "savage" anymore. Their ear plugs are missing, leaving the stretched lobes to flap unaesthetically around their necks. And for clothes they now wear faded shirts and ill-fitting shorts courtesy of the USA and, often enough, woollen socks, baseball caps and sloppy old sneakers. Men who were used to walking around naked only 50 miles away, now bathe in the river fully clothed. They have learned to be ashamed of their unspoilt nature.

But even the Auca living in self-imposed isolation on the Río Cononaco cannot expect to live undisturbed for much longer. In 1979, when we wanted to pay them a visit, we found that the landing strip once laid out by an oil company and since abandoned had been blocked with oil drums. Only when Samuel Padilla, whose mother is Huaorani, dropped a basket woven by that group of Indians as a recognition signal did they remove the barrier. But, also in 1979, white visitors introduced influenza to the area, which led to the death of two children. The children's father could not understand what had happened, presumed it was the result of an evil spell, and slew his neighbor. And there are other problems, too, such as an acute shortage of partners for marriage. The two groups that still live in isolation are now so small that it is almost impossible for them to observe the strict rules of exogamy to which any marriage is subject.

Consequently, a girl who wishes to marry must leave the jungle behind her.

But in any case it is only a matter of time before the bulldozers, drilling rigs and construction gangs arrive in the jungle of the Cononaco, which will then become the former hunting grounds of the last of the Auca. Then Mengha, Tita and Nape will lay aside their blow guns and take up the spade to build another helipad. And the world will have lost out on another of its people and another piece of its history.

Some people have little sympathy for this view, including a young Amazon Indian in Leticia who said: "They talk rubbish, these Indian protectors. They want to keep us apart from the world, they think we are not strong enough to fend for ourselves. But we can do so. . . . There are parts of our lifestyle we wish to protect, of course. But we must be allowed to enjoy the things the white man has— proper medicines. We need better health, not people who come to inspect us. We have a right to a good life."

On my last evening in Leticia, a car suddenly raced down the road, hurtling crazily from side to side. It screeched toward us, and the German boy only escaped in the nick of time. The car came to a halt ten yards away. "For Christ's sake!" I exclaimed. We ran over to argue with the drivers: they were girls of ten or twelve years old, giggling and squealing with the fun of it all.

It was a frontier town where the laws had scant sway. Its main trade was in cocaine, ferried by dugouts across the Amazon; the Indians took risks doing so, because sometimes the dugouts were swept away by the currents in midstream. The drug trade claimed hundreds of victims in the area every year. With the raw violence of a garrison town nearby and the drug trade to fight, the authorities could not be bothered to enforce the law against a couple of kids who had borrowed a car. The veneer of civil authority was marginal, in that slight encroachment against nature that man had made in the jungle town of Leticia. It was something I noticed in many places along my journey.

PERU

I TOOK A BOAT UP TO IQUITOS, IN PERU, AS, BY NOW, MY SPIRITS WERE beginning to be dampened by the jungle. There was a claustrophobia about it that a sudden glimpse of iguanas, perching on trees like miniature prehistoric monsters, and huge flame-colored parrots did little to dispel. There was the monotonous greenery, the hovering cloud, the torrid heat, the gloom of that huge river that never grew smaller, draining millions of square miles of jungle. I felt surrounded, unable to escape.

But when I flew out of Iquitos, my spirits lifted as the green canopy below grew less dense, merging with green hills that eventually climbed to a barren region of long grass, then a vivid red earth, interspersed with sharp, emerald lakes and white-topped peaks, some chopped off in volcanic stateliness. The plane was crossing the Andes again. Yet now the three Colombian fingers had merged into one mighty range that would run down as South America's vertebrae all the way to the far south.

The mountains were majestic and varied, a relief from the green carpet. Millions of years ago the Amazon flowed from east to west, draining into the Pacific. But when, tens of thousands of years ago, great plates crashed at the bottom of the ocean, the Andes were lifted from the water, and the continent tilted the other way. As a result, the water sluggishly changed direction, flooding the vast basin of central South America, turning it into a swamp, a reverse estuary. These were the peaks around its edge.

The elation I felt was diminished by the sight of Lima nearly six hundred miles to the south of Iquitos. Lima was not a lovely city. The taxi ride from the airport took me across a ghastly dust bowl, the Atacama, one of the world's largest, least-known deserts, which runs down to central Chile between the Andes and the Pacific. Not surprisingly, the Lima area has one of the smallest rainfalls in the world. The day I arrived, the city surroundings were crowned by a gray cloud that rarely lifted and rarely poured. There was an overpowering stretch of urine in the city because its streets, on which so many people lived, were rarely washed by rain.

After the dust bowl came a slum of houses in various stages of construction, the homes of the upwardly mobile in Lima. People added to them, a room at a time, if they could obtain the money and the materials. The suburb resembled a city blasted by a nuclear bomb, with its half-finished rooms and its unpaved streets. As I approached the center, the city's elderly, shabby office buildings, constructed in a kind of derelict turn-of-century Gothic style, came into view, as did the people. Huge crowds packed the streets—some going to work, some at work, most with nothing to do. I drove down the main thoroughfare, and still the crowds grew bigger, until I reached the thronged Plaza San Martín. The taxi dropped me at the Gran Hotel Bolívar and I thankfully made my way out of the madding crowd into one of the world's great hotels, rendered all the greater by the contrast with the dirt and poverty outside. The need to escape dirt and squalor makes elitists of all but the saints among us.

To step from the smells and noise of the street into the hotel was to move in an instant from one world to another. The attentive doorman helped me make the passage. A conspicuously bemedaled man in a smart blue uniform, a kind of colonel of footmen, stepped forward to direct me to the conciergerie, while benevolent porters greeted me with a friendliness that was not obsequious, just courteous. Their commander was a white-haired man with glasses and the air of a president of the republic, who checked me in. I turned from his desk into the lobby, which led into a circular hall with a stained glass dome, potted plants and gilt-and-blue chairs. A piano quartet— one man on a piano, three on violins—played classical pieces, with questionable success. Beyond the lobby rose a magnificent staircase with embroidered carpet, but I chose the elevator, which was made of wood and stained mirrors, a mobile antique itself.

My room was as large as a tennis court, with a magnificent Edwardian bed, an elegant desk and other fine furniture of comparable vintage. The bathroom contained a splendid large tub with brass taps and an elaborate Heath-Robinson machine for cranking the plug into place. I washed off the humidity of the Amazon and the dust of Lima and descended, like a turn-of-the-century potentate, to the hotel bar to meet the political officer of a nearby embassy.

Middle-aged, mustached and voluble, he briefed me on the political situation. The new ruling party was led by Alan García, a thirty-six-year-old political prodigy, who had been the protégé of Víctor Raúl Haya de la Torre, the father of APRA—the American Popular Revolutionary Alliance. The party was a Latin American hybrid founded by the charismatic Haya from an amalgam of political and metaphysical ideas dating back to the beginning of the century. A much-traveled intellectual, Haya had elaborated a theory of political relativity, based on Einstein and socialism, with the concept of "historical time-space." He believed in an "Indian America" in which there would be an equal distribution of wealth and land for all races.

Although he was not a communist, Haya's message had been anathema to the country's ruling oligarchy and the army. In 1931 he was first cheated of electoral victory by the army and imprisoned. APRA won the 1936 election, but again was robbed of victory by the army, and began a campaign of political violence and assassination, which in turn drove the army to greater and greater repression. After General Manuel Odría, a hard-nosed dictator, took office in 1948, Haya fled to the Colombian embassy, where he lived for five years under police floodlights, with a permanent guard stationed outside. He was instructed to keep his distance from the windows to avoid being shot by Odría's marksmen. In 1962 another election was held, and Haya came back to win it, only to be prevented from assuming office by the army once again. In 1968, the civilian president, Fernando Belaúnde Terry, was deposed by the army to prevent an election that was certain to result in another victory for Haya. Only after Haya died in 1980 was his successor, as APRA leader, Alan García, permitted to take power.

I remember hearing the old man speak, in 1978, on the eve of a constituent assembly election that his party won. He was in his eighties then, a sturdy figure with a cascade of scruffy white hair over his collar, and deep-set Old Testament eyes. His voice was a distant echo of the booming, sonorous intonation of earlier years but his presence and flaming eyes commanded the overflowing square in front of his party headquarters in Lima. He had been a man with ideas ahead of his time, who stirred the imagination of a terribly poor people. Latin American unity, socialism, the emancipation of the Indian, nonalignment, Víctor Raúl Haya de la Torre had been thinking about these things in the 1920s, and thrusting them into the Latin American consciousness. He was an authentic, original voice on the South American left, for all his failings.

Now, Haya's successor, Alan García, personified Peruvian hope amid the squalor and despair of everyday existence. Young (thirty-six years old), good-looking, articulate, modeled on Spain's Felipe González, García was prepared to defy the world and stand up to the big stick of the International Monetary Fund, which stronger economies in Latin America shrank from doing.

The remainder of the political spectrum, as outlined by the political officer, seemed less captivating. There was an orthodox conservative party, headed by ex-president Belaúnde, a grandiose visionary. "El Arquitecto" had promised to redesign Lima but he and his ally Luis Bedoya, an able, urban machine politician, changed nothing.

The far left was headed by an aging ex-guerrilla sporting a graying Castro beard. Everyone considered Hugo Blanco so harmless that he was allowed to run for president, collecting a remarkable 30 percent of the vote.

What about the army? I asked the embassy official. "The army got its fingers burned between 1968 and 1976. It became bitterly unpopular. People spat when they saw a man in uniform. The army likes to be liked in Peru. They're not a problem, so long as young Alan doesn't go and do anything crazy."

The 1968–1976 military dictatorship had been traumatic for Peru.

Juan Velasco Alvarado, the general who had seized power in Lima, was a strongman, but an idealistic one, whose views had been formed when he saw service in the mountainous regions and witnessed the poverty of the Indians there. He wanted to improve their lot. A revolutionary "Plan Inca" was drawn up, followed by a "Plan Tupac Amaru." The banks, the railways and the electricity grid were nationalized. Foreign assets were seized, including those of Anaconda Copper and the Cerro de Pasco copper mines. Sugar and cotton plantations were confiscated from their owners and handed over to state cooperatives. The education system was to be trilingual, in Quechua and Aymara Indian, as well as Spanish. Using the army—which had so often denied power to the left—Velasco sought to impose socialism through a military dictatorship.

It was a harebrained experiment, and it ended in appalling economic collapse, political disorder and a serious riot in Lima in 1975 in which dozens of people were killed. Ordinary workers were the first to suffer. Industrial production plummeted by an average of 5 percent a year between 1971 and 1974; workers' living standards were slashed by a third. Peru's chronic problems of poverty and unemployment were exacerbated. In 1975 Velasco was deposed by a conservative general, Francisco Morales Bermúdez, and died of gangrene from an amputated leg the following year.

I had witnessed the fall of this curious regime of revolutionary soldiers on a reporting trip in 1978. General Leónidas Rodríguez, the dashing thug who had led the coup in 1968 by driving a tank that broke down the gates of the presidential palace in Lima, made a last stand for the revolution. Although he was wanted by the government, he emerged suddenly from hiding before constituent assembly elections were due. He turned up at the presidential palace demanding to speak to President Morales Bermúdez. The president's startled secretary prevaricated. General Rodríguez then leaped onto a motorbike and made a getaway before he could be arrested.

A couple of days later he showed up to vote. I accompanied him, along with a cavalcade of pressmen whom he hoped would act as his protection from the authorities. A man with a handsome face, a ready laugh, a loud voice and hair slicked to the top of his scalp, he was full of bluster in the press bus that accompanied him. We followed him into a school that had been turned into a polling station, past uneasy policemen, under the glare of television lights and popping flashbulbs. It was all a great carnival. Then we followed him out to the steps of the school.

Four men in plain clothes moved in wordlessly. One was square and world-weary; the others were thin men with dark glasses, open-necked shirts, gray-brown trousers and casual, deadpan faces. The world-weary fellow said distinctively—I was standing just behind the general—"You must come with us, General."

The general, so boisterous up to now, turned red with anger and tension. He said, "You have no right to arrest a general of the army. Only another officer can arrest a general of the army." The man merely repeated what he had said and put an arm on the general's shoulder. Rodríguez shrugged it off, shouting, "I am not coming with you!" In an instant the four men had grabbed him, and more or less marched him down the steps towards a waiting car. The general was a strong man, and they had quite a struggle getting him in; his bewildered, furious face and shouting, open mouth were the last glimpse we had. The press and the crowd looked on in mute astonishment. The car sped off. It had been like a scene from a Costa-Gavras film. The general was put on a plane the following night, and spared the torture he himself had meted out to political prisoners while interior minister. All the same, it was an ugly scene.

Now, in 1986, the army had relinquished power and a young civilian belonging to the party that the army had so bitterly opposed was in charge of Peru. But things hadn't changed much. I remembered Plaza San Martín as the place of riots where I had once been chased, with fleeing mobs of others, by a small armored car equipped with a water cannon. Today there was a demonstration, connected with a price increase, and tear gas wafted in from the open windows of the hotel. "Cover your face with a handkerchief and take your contact lenses out," advised the political officer. The gas smelled sweet and sickly, and my eyes smarted slightly, but it didn't do me any real harm.

I went out the following morning into that Calcutta-cramped mass of humanity. The idle poor meandered through the streets while the crippled and moribund who lived there sold peppers, avocados as big as footballs, and tempting corn on the cob from stalls. Despite its appearance, the produce would have wreaked havoc on my unsuspecting system.

The city was as dirty and shabby and smelly as always—poor Lima! —and yet almost alone of Latin American capitals it had not been ruined by new development, by the dreary Salt Lake City skyscrapers that made the most unusual Latin American site or tradition seem banal. Lima retained its colonial heart, maybe because there had been no money to rebuild it, perhaps also because the Limeños were more conscious of their history than their neighbors were. The streets were narrow. The elegant houses were adorned with moorish-style, dark wood or covered balconies from which, in the past, the women of the houses could take the air unseen while admiring passers-by through grilles. I have never seen such beautifully worked balconies anywhere.

The churches were the finest in Latin America: the cathedral has a brilliantly intricate carved-stone facade, though inside it is a little disappointing. Next to it is the most elaborate covered wooden balcony, that of the archbishops' palace. La Merced also has a good facade; San Pedro is a baroque display; and San Francisco boasts a catacomb, in which great heaps of bones are on display, arranged into neat, circular patterns like flowers, making even death decorative. The most sinister are the shriveled, gaping skeletons in monk's habits standing under the church—as though a statement that eternity is, after all, just the gaze of an eyeless socket.

The cathedral contains a mummy—the shriveled remains of Pizarro, the savage conquistador of Peru. Lima is, after all, the city of the first colonists. The main square reflects this; it is one of the most attractive in Latin America. The center of the square is the low, elegant presidential palace, guarded by squat mestizos in ceremonial plumed hats. The hats recall the days when Peru had been the heart of the Spanish colonial world, the source of the silver that eventually corrupted Spain itself. Peru remains in many ways the repository of the continent's militaristic traditions.

It all began with Pizarro, who, after several failed expeditions, arrived in 1530 with a motley band of 180 men and 27 horses. He learned when he disembarked on that torrid coast that a civil war between Atahuallpa and Huascar, the legitimate Inca king, had just ended with victory for the former. Pizarro did not stay to hold the territory, but marched straight for the Inca capital of Cajamarca, in the mountains, to seize the new king. The expedition party trekked across the Atacama desert, up the soaring Andes, fording streams and scrambling across gorges on precarious rope bridges. They were not attacked by the Incas, for Pizarro said he merely wanted to pay his respects to the king. When they reached the city, they found that the monarch had gone into retreat in the mountains.

On November 16, 1532, Pizarro invited the god-king of the Incas to come and meet him. In the evening a magnificent Inca procession of warriors in feathers came down the mountain; Atahuallpa was carried on a litter behind them. Pizarro's chaplain, Friar Valverde, met them and began to lecture the king in the rudiments of Christianity, ending with the statement that the entire city had been placed in the possession of the Spanish crown.

The furious Inca replied that he was subject only to the authority of the sun, and grabbed a prayer book from the priest. The Spaniards ambushed him with their guns, scattering his men and killing several, capturing Atahuallpa and his nobles. With this swift stroke, the Inca empire fell, because all authority had been concentrated in the god-king. Courteously treated at first, Atahuallpa was eventually garroted. Pizarro's men went on the rampage through the Inca empire, pillaging and plundering and melting down gold and other treasures for bullion. Pizarro founded a coastal capital, Lima, which he dubbed "the City of the Kings."

The Spaniards were barbarians compared to the civilization they had usurped. It had dated back to 3000 B.C., spawning successive cultures like the Chavín, and the societies at Nazca, Paracas, Mochica and Pachácamac. A civilization at Tiahuanaco, near Lake Titicaca, seemed to have gained power about A.D. 400. Eight hundred years later, the Incas, a warlike, minor tribe, came to the fore. The Incas believed that the world was created by the god Viracocha, who had once fled the world in displeasure with man, and then reemerged from Lake Titicaca to redeem him and to create the sun and the moon. The sun, jealous of the moon, threw ashes at it, to make it shine less strongly.

Viracocha then departed to the west, but centuries later a family of eight emerged in the Cuzco region claiming to be his heirs. They established the remarkable social system of the Incas, which, in its collectivist attitudes, resembled some of the Eastern cultures and later provided a seedbed for modern Peruvian socialism. At the top was the emperor, who was the son of the sun. Below him were provincial governors. Below them were chieftains, each of whom ruled ten thousand Incas; those below governed smaller factions, directly responsible to those above. The smallest faction was about fifty. This precision was also found in the extensive network of stone-paved roads across the mountains, and in the terracing that allowed the mountainside to be cultivated scientifically. Above all, it emerged in the architecture. Palaces were constructed of giant stones that fitted carefully into one another, requiring no mortar; during earthquakes, the stones would separate, then fall back into place undisturbed.

Peru was conquered by a tiny group of adventurers with guns and horses, but it was very far from subdued. A people with the Incas' self-esteem was not going to submit easily. A puppet emperor, Manco Inca, was installed by Pizarro. He turned on the conquistadors and laid siege for ten months to the hill city of Cuzco, surrounding it with 180,000 Incas. Even after his forces were repelled, Manco Inca dominated a large part of Peru from the mountains.

The Indian nation in the mountains continued to stage incursions against the Spaniards until, in 1571, they trapped its new young king, Tupac Amaru. They took him in chains to Cuzco, where they beheaded him in front of his people; the groan of the assembled Indians is said to have haunted the Spaniards for decades afterward. The Indians were forced to pay tribute to the Spaniards, and to work for them in the silver mines, tilling their soil and building their cities. Occasional fierce rebellions flared up in the seventeenth and eighteenth centuries.

Meanwhile, a long way from the mountains, Lima developed into one of the great cities of the Americas, funded by the silver wealth.

A rebellion in the late eighteenth century came as a rude shock to the complacent life of central Lima. The head of the revolt was not an Indian, but a wealthy mestizo, José Gabriel Condorcanqui Noguera, who claimed descent from the Inca princes. In the late 1770s he started agitating against the iniquity of central rule and set himself up as Tupac Amaru II, the rightful Inca king. After he had executed a government official, the sullen mountain Indian population rose in a terrifying settling of scores with the white man, butchering thousands and laying waste to towns and villages.

Inevitably, after assembling an army 60,000 strong, the white man won, and Tupac Amaru II was betrayed into the hands of the Spaniards, to be pulled apart by horses in 1781. The insurrection spluttered on in Bolivia (Upper Peru), with two sieges of La Paz. The Spaniards tried to improve the Indians' lot after that, paying the Indians for their labor for the first time. But the jewel in the Spanish crown began its inexorable decline; the crushed Indians in the mountains by now amounted to no more than 600,000, as against 135,000 Europeans, 244,000 mestizos and 80,000 Negroes.

Peru, the center of the empire, remained loyal to Spain to the end. During the wars of liberation, General José de San Martín, after freeing Argentina and Chile, landed near Lima with an expeditionary force commanded by the British commander, Lord Cochrane. There he occupied the port, Lima's main source of food, and the governor-general withdrew from the city. San Martín was able to enter it unopposed. He presided over a period of semianarchy and eventually was overthrown by his subordinates while he was away, attending a meeting with South America's other great liberator, Simón Bolívar.

The capital continued in chaos, and the Spaniards briefly recovered it. Bolívar at that stage marched south, seized Lima, and, in a series of decisive battles with the pro-Spanish army in the mountains near Cuzco, finally defeated the forces of the peninsula. The battle of Ayacucho in December 1824 marked the end of Spanish rule in South America. Bolívar proclaimed himself Peru's dictator and tried to unite all of South America in a giant federation under his rule.

As soon as he was gone, Peru's generals revolted, and embarked on a miserable and oppressive period of vying for power: in its first forty years of independence, the country had no fewer than a dozen constitutions. The main instrument of power became the army, a wretched band of men press-ganged and locked into their barracks; the country degenerated in a series of power struggles between the few rich men dominating a sullen subproletariat. Thus was the greatest, richest country in Latin America brought low; and, although a fount of ideas in the twentieth century, it has never revived.

Peru was transformed by a surge of economic growth in the 1950s; a great urban shantytown grew up around Lima, contributing to the squalor and impoverishment of the city. A middle class also grew up to challenge the oligarchy and the country's clique of ruling generals. President Belaúnde was the representative of the new class; the army, however, had a final crack at power under General Velasco. After his government fell apart Belaúnde returned. He was succeeded by the moderate left-winger, Alan García.

Ghastly echoes from Peru's past remained: Sendero Luminoso, a mysterious, Maoist guerrilla movement based near Ayacucho, staged a series of spectacular and bloody terrorist attacks. As the guerrillas began to massacre Indians who failed to cooperate, the army organized them in "self-defense groups" armed with sticks and machetes. Appalling bloodbaths in the mountains ensued between the two groups, a reminder of the primitivism of the mountain people of the Andes. On one occasion a group of journalists visited the mountains; they were hacked and bludgeoned to death by villagers who mistook them for guerrillas.

It is encouraging, though, that, despite the terrorist attacks and the election of a left-wing president, the army has so far made no move out of the barracks. Peru might seem doomed to remain trapped in poverty. Half of its population of 18 million are mountain Indians. Most of them are illiterate, two fifths are undernourished, and 99 percent have no running water. The country's main racial group is still on the underside. It is hard to see how a country with so many disadvantages of geography and racial mix—a land dominated by the successors of a rich colonial class and underworked by the remnants of a once-proud Inca nation—can ever, sadly, be much of a success.

I took a train out of Lima from the Desemparados station, my destination the great Indian outback. The train chugged off at 7 A.M., through dusty suburbs, past crumbling mud-brick walls, across the misty dryness of the coastal belt. Then it began to climb. With the tenacity of a centipede on a wall, it rose steeply up the side of the barren brown valley, until it passed another line shelving steeply upward. The points were switched, and the train rolled back downhill, onto the second line, where it climbed again.

The process was repeated, down one switchback and up another, and we climbed sideways, almost vertically up the cliff face, leaving the barren valley floor far below. Finally we reached the top, found ourselves at the bottom of yet another valley system topped by still higher mountains. Here there were fertile, lush green fields to break the monotony of the brown-and-purple rock.

We started climbing up the side of the next mountain. On the most elaborate switchback the engine was not strong enough to push the train up from behind, so it was decoupled from the train and rolled down onto a turntable, which was operated by men who, with a lever, hauled the engine around on the beautifully oiled surface, and sent it off to the front to pull us up. Thus we climbed, further and further into the skies, until we reached the top, which was the bottom of another valley system, and repeated the process.

It was on the fourth such system that we reached a little mining village and made our first stop—none too soon for me. As we had climbed, my head had felt constricted and my mouth had a curious metallic taste that, coupled with the smell of cooking oil in the train, was making me quite sick. We were thirteen thousand feet up. I walked out into the cold thin air of the Andes, where the sun beat mercilessly down on the settlements. The houses were plain wooden shacks, built by the mining company, and the men were hardened, prematurely grizzled and bent by their work—only Indians could do backbreaking work like that at such high altitudes. The women had the small, squat shapes of their counterparts in Ecuador and wore wide hats, but there was little finery about them. Children wandered about with colored woollen caps that had flaps over their ears. The town so clearly existed for mining alone that I found it oppressive. We had reached the highest point on our climb, and descended to Huancayo in the late afternoon, where we spent the night. Another train proceeded on the way to Cuzco across another Andean valley the next day.

Cuzco, more than three hundred miles to the east of Lima, was impressive, and a bit of a fraud, because it had been rebuilt in the old style after the last earthquake. Its open main square was situated at the end of a fertile valley. The square was teeming with women selling goods and packed with hippies who had settled there in the late 1960s, sniffing cocaine and smoking pot. The crisscross streets were built in Spanish colonial style but laid out according to the original Inca plan. Just outside the city, a huge stone fortress, built of the irregular slabs that fitted into one another, loomed; it had withstood countless earthquakes.

I wandered about the city's museums, with their displays of the many cultures of the Andes, so superior to the rule of the postcolonial white man. I spent two days there, and on the morning of the third took the train down to Machu Picchu, the legendary lost city of the Incas. My taxi got me to the station just a few minutes too late, but he was not put out; he accelerated through the slum streets that climbed up the hillside overlooking Cuzco, and on the other side came down the valley slope, where I glimpsed the train meandering lazily through fields of maize. The driver raced his cab parallel to it, banging frantically on his horn, bringing the train to a stop, and I was hurried across the fields and helped up onto the train.

The scene around us was one of the most beautiful on my journey yet. We were in a wide, cultivated valley, with a long range of high mountains on either side. The Incas had designed an extensive network of stone terraces on the sides of the mountains, which were still cultivated; the lines of green and yellow cut into the brown of the rock and harmonized with the yellow of the valley floor, which was rich with crops and wildflowers in the bright sun. The impression was of tranquillity and peace. The Inca civilization of the upper Andes had been a place of prosperity and order, not of backwardness and starvation, which had followed its demise.

The train wound its way slowly down that green valley, and the mountains began to close in on us. Soon we were in a narrow gorge, and a torrent of water thundered along beside the track. This was the journey the American explorer Hiram Bingham had made at the beginning of the century, in pursuit of the impossible, a fantasy, the lost city of the Incas. The gentle vegetation grew lush, coating the now steep-sided mountains wherever it could find a hold; elsewhere, forbidding brown cliffs rose far above us. We were descending the eastern side of the Andes, into the Peruvian jungle, toward the Amazon region.

In the inner bowels of that mountain chain, where the jungle was impenetrable, the crags overwhelming and the torrent at its fiercest, the train stopped. It was the middle of nowhere. I and the other passengers climbed out, and we were herded onto a bus, which set off at a cracking pace on a road that zigzagged up the side of the nearest mountain. It roared around the hairpin turns, which became more terrifying the higher the bus climbed. Finally when it seemed we must be touching the clouds, we arrived at Machu Picchu. The two tacky hotels that greeted us were a monstrous disappointment. I fled the gaggle of tourists, along a steep slope and out onto a terrace that would give a view of the lost city.

I stopped, openmouthed, at what lay before me. Cascading down over a mountain shelf was a large city without roofs but with its walls intact, symmetrically arranged. There were squares and streets and public buildings and suburbs, fashioned in those eternal Inca building blocks. The degree of organization required to create a city like this—and at this height from the valley floor!—was astonishing. So was the location: a huge green summit soared up and beyond; on every side cliffs plunged thousands of feet; the clouds rolled in and out of the surrounding peaks. My trance at the beauty and imagination of the place was interrupted by the babel of those behind me. I fled before them to explore the city's doorways and passages and stairways, built at impossible angles in sheer rock. Four hours was not long enough to appreciate such a sight. I could only acknowledge my despair that such a civilization could have been wiped off the face of the earth, and a goverment as poor as that of Peru's over the past six hundred years could have been substituted.

I took the train the next day to the edge of what had once been Upper Peru and is now Bolivia. It was a spectacular journey over barren rock interspersed with high-altitude, fertile valleys. It was a land of cliffs, far-flung settlements, and fair-sized towns peopled with colorfully dressed Indians; these people were Quechuas, taller and rounder than their counterparts in Lima. They absolutely ignored the white man except to sell to him. It was as though this was an unwritten rule of passive resistance, an assertion of independence, not to speak to the occupier.

The train climbed to Puno, some 170 miles to the southeast of Cuzco, a bleak place on the shore of Lake Titicaca, the edge of the central plateau of the Andes. I spent the night at Puno, and was given a ride out to the "floating islands," constructed on reeds, where a rather sad-faced group of Indians eked out an existance, as far as I could see, selling artifacts such as model reed boats to the tourists. I felt slightly relieved to leave the dingy port, as the boat I had hired took me across the lake the following day.

BOLIVIA

THE LAKE IS THE HIGHEST OF ITS SIZE IN THE WORLD. BUT, TRAVELING on it, you wouldn't think so. Surrounded neither by mountains nor by snow, it was a vast blue expanse, almost perfectly reflecting the blue of the sky above in its inlets and subordinate lakes. The land around it was an arid yellow desert of rounded slight hills that barely tickled the junction between the glass-smooth surface of the lake and the sky. The air and the water were cold, yet the sun at that altitude burned; even my very dark-complexioned boatman raised his pullover grotesquely over his head to protect himself. I took the hint and stayed under the rough awning. It was a peculiar sensation, floating across this absolutely still lake past yellow rocks on the roof of the world: there was nothing in sight—not a tree, not a house, not an animal. Just the water, the sky, and the yellow rock.

This surreal effect was enhanced about halfway across the lake, when a long, jagged jawbone of teethlike mountains appeared on the horizon, growing larger as we progressed across. They seemed unbelievably high and distant—snow-covered mountains sticking up out of a desert.

On the other side, I disembarked at an isolated jetty. A little way beyond, there was an Indian village of shabby adobe mud huts. I took a taxi and set out on a road with no traffic. The vivid blue of the lake faded in the yellow distance behind us as the car trundled into the emptiness, until that great sea on top of the world was no more than a blue streak in the landscape. Occasionally we passed a dingy settlement of whitish mud huts clustered closely together or women tending scrawny cattle or building houses. The women seemed more square-shouldered than those in Peru; they seemed to be absolutely circular in girth, a roundness that their bowler hats and round rough skirts emphasized. This was my first glimpse of a matriarchal society, where the women reared families, did the work, and commanded while the men were content with a passive role.

Now and then we passed herds of alpacas, a beast with a kind of idiot curiosity, a mixture of a camel and a furry sheep, unfrightened by the approach of our car. A people had started a wondrous civilization in this barrenness, understandably worshiping the sun. To me it was an emptiness. It seemed impossible that there should be a modern metropolis up here; supposedly twenty minutes away, we wondered where La Paz could have got to.

The answer came very abruptly. The car reached a particularly shabby village, the kind of rundown place with old jalopies and shops with swing doors and dogs picking their way through the dust that you see portrayed in old movies about the American dust bowl during the Depression. A little way beyond, the horizon seemed to stop: a woman sat motionless there, her baby wrapped in a cloth and perched on her back, a dog beside her. She was gazing down where the plateau suddenly crashed into a vast gorge, and the position of the mountains, which seemed always one step ahead of the horizon, became clear.

Below lay a big, surprisingly modern-looking city. It straggled down the center of the gorge floor, as though Los Angeles had been placed at the bottom of the Grand Canyon. The shacks of the poor were terraced up the sides, all around. Across the other side, perhaps seven or eight miles away, a giant range of white mountains loomed as a backdrop. They were the eastern range of the Andes, the rim of that strange upland; behind them the land fell three miles to the jungle. Illimani was the greatest, at 19,500 feet. The others included Chacaltaya, which boasts the highest ski slope in the world. And there before them lay La Paz, a ribbon city in a gorge, its puny skyscrapers so utterly dwarfed by the skyscrapers of nature that they made a bizarre harmony. It was the strangest, most spectacularly placed city I had ever seen.

We made our descent on a winding road through the shantytowns on the slopes, and I found a hotel. I didn't feel well, and the only edible things on the menu were palm hearts and pepper steak. Exertion made me breathless, and a metallic taste was always in my mouth. That evening I walked through the streets with a journalist friend from a previous visit to Bolivia. We passed the white-trousered, red-jacketed presidential guard and the lamppost from which they had hung a president years before, the post in front of the oddly tilted presidential palace which had lost its presidents at an average rate of one every ten months in the country's 150 years of independence. We visited the little tea shop where Bolivian high society met and plotted and gossiped, the men in double-breasted suits that mixed incongruously with the attire of the Indian majority.

The dresses of the Indian women were striking. A typical twenty-year-old wore a bustled blue skirt descending to her calves, dark blue stockings underneath, and ballerina-like shoes. Over the skirt, a plain protecting apron. Above the waist, a short red pullover. Over this, a beautifully embossed pink shawl with long trailing fringes. On her shoulders would hang a magnificent embroidered cloth used for a variety of purposes. In one case, it was used to carry a plump child who peered over the top, a sun hat perched on its head. From the mother's ears hung the finest earrings she possessed. The women competed with one another in dress, to show off their prosperity, and, as they were in charge of the finances, their own efforts were on display. They looked proud, independent; when young they were extremely good-looking, with delicate, china-pretty features of an almost Asiatic cast. The men, by contrast, seemed a sullen, prematurely aged, oppressed lot.

Bolivia is in some respects a travesty of a country. It is remarkable that any freedom survives there at all. Unlike Peru, whose disorder is man-made, the result of appalling crimes committed hundreds of years ago, in Bolivia the problem is of a wholly unhospitable land and the desperate men that it breeds. Yet human decency insists on coming to the surface.

Consider the topography. Bolivia is about twice the size of Spain, yet only 5½ million—a seventh as many people—live there. Much of the population lives in the central region on the altiplano I crossed from Lake Titicaca (thirteen thousand feet high), which provides the sparest of livings for those who farm there. To the east lies the Eastern Cordillera with its magnificent, twenty-thousand-foot-high peaks. The Andes then fall to the one fertile area of Bolivia—the Yungas, where most of Bolivia's cocaine is grown—to the lowland region stretching to Brazil, Argentina and Paraguay, which accounts for two thirds of the land area. This land is inhospitable, consisting largely of jungle swamps and arid scrub adjoining the great, desolate Chaco of Paraguay. The country's chief natural resources are its minerals—the Cerro Rico, a mountain of solid tin, silver and manganese, was discovered by the Spaniards in 1545. It was quickly worked out of its silver, although tin is still mined. In recent years, cocaine has become important. Locally, the coca plant is grown as a mild stimulant and provides protection for the Indians against altitude sickness. Coca has become Bolivia's largest export; to the country's endemic poverty has been added the corruption associated with harvesting an illegal crop and exporting it to Colombia for refining.

Most of the inhabitants of the altiplano are Indian. In La Paz itself about half are; the other half is mixed. They are all dominated by a white ruling minority (La Paz has a strong German influence; it is marvelously clean, by comparison with Lima, and its beer cellars are its best night spots). Most of the inhabitants of the Yungas are mestizos. The Indians, as usual, are largely outside the political life of the country, although they fought the Spaniards harder than any of their compatriots: there were uprisings against the Spanish in 1661, 1730, 1776 and 1780.

Bolivia won its independence in 1825, when one of Bolívar's generals, Antonio José de Sucre, defeated the Spanish forces. The nation was named after the Liberator himself. Then Sucre's second-in-command, General Andrés Santa Cruz, became president and attempted to link Bolivia with Peru to make it a more viable state. He failed.

Since then the country has been gradually dismembered. During the War of the Pacific, Bolivia lost its port of Antofagasta to Chile, as well as a slice of the mineral-rich Atacama desert. The Bolivians still lay claim to one outlet to the sea, and have an admiral and a navy, consisting of patrol boats that steam around Lake Titicaca (Bolivia ran out of money to maintain its sole frigate).

In 1927 war broke out between Bolivia and Paraguay over the country's undefined eastern border, the Chaco, a terrible wilderness of flat, hot country, some of it grassland, some of it densely packed with a gorse so hard that it can cut through leather. The Chaco War was one of the bloodiest in Latin America's bloody history, decimating fifty-two thousand Bolivians and thirty-six thousand Paraguayans. Gangs of men wandered about the bush, fighting each other to get to water holes, bogged down during the rainy season, suffering disease and insects. Bolivia ceded nearly all of its Chaco territory during the war.

Until then, Bolivian domestic politics had been dominated by military groups of the most vicious and venal kind, groups that were occasionally pushed out by the country's oligarchy. After the Second World War, however, Bolivia took a giant step toward mass politics with the development of two important movements. The first was a trade union movement of the left, led by the charismatic Juan Lechín; the second was the National Revolutionary Movement (MNR), which despite its name was a moderate, democratic movement with some left-wing elements. It was headed by Víctor Paz Estenssoro, an economics professor and one of the most enlightened, thoughful men in Latin American politics. I met him in 1978 on my first visit to Bolivia, when he was running for election in opposition to the dictator General Hugo Banzer. He was already an old man, living in a modest home in a suburb of La Paz; he was calm, impressive, thoughtful, with the gentle humor and *gravitas* of an elder statesman. But his energy and courage were not yet exhausted.

In 1951, contrary to the ruling junta's expectations, the MNR had won a general election. The army promptly responded with a coup, but a massive popular revolt flared up. Paz proved to be a skillful politician, establishing good relations with the United States, beginning the construction of roads and major public works to bring the far-flung country together and exploiting the country's mineral and oil resources. He set a land reform in motion that parceled out plots to the Indians, turning them into a smallholding conservative class. He also allowed Lechín's unions to organize.

The democratic golden age continued with the election of 1956, when Paz's vice-president, Hernán Siles, was elected president. Under Siles, however, the economy began to deteriorate, as the tin mines, nationalized from the Patiño and Aramayo families, began to be managed in the interests of Lechín's workers. The land reform resulted in outbreaks of lawlessness. But Paz won the 1960 election and proceeded to restore order and prosperity.

Within a few years, Bolivia's economy was growing faster than any other in Latin America. Paz appeased the unions by installing Lechín as his vice-president. But Paz relied increasingly on the army, which saw its chance to regain influence after ten years without power. In 1964 Paz was foolish enough to take an army general, René Barrientos, as his running mate; Barrientos, an appealing figure for a soldier, ousted Paz, who was by now unpopular for his policies of austerity, in a coup.

The army chief proved surprisingly populist but was killed in a helicopter crash in 1969. An extraordinary workers' revolution soon took place, led by a faction of the army headed by General Alfredo Ovando. A "People's Council" was set up under Juan Lechín, who preached that it was the beginning of a Soviet-style revolution. A year later an extreme left-wing general, General Juan José Torres, staged another coup (Bolivia's 186th). Torres befriended a French revolutionary, Regis Debray, who had worked alongside Che Guevara, the legendary guerrilla who had fought with Castro in Cuba. The country seemed set for sweeping nationalizations and economic collapse.

In 1971, however, General Hugo Banzer, representing the conservative majority within the army, staged a coup. Few Bolivians rushed to defend the workers' revolution. Banzer was a tough, able, unimaginative man who simply crushed the opposition and led the country back to economic growth, financial solvency, and stable government. His rule lasted seven years until the movement for democracy led to his removal.

In 1979 an election was held and won by Hernán Siles, the head of one wing of the MNR, who was supported by Lechín and the left; the runner-up was Victor Paz. The army promptly staged a coup, but the protests grew so strong that a countercoup was staged by officers who promised a return to democracy and a rerun of the election the following year. The election was duly held, and Siles won again; but a gangster clique of army officers connected with the drug trade headed by one General Luis García Meza, took over, supported by the nastiest character in Bolivia's recent history, Colonel Luis Arce. The colonel was a protector of the cocaine dealers, and he had a reputation for utter ruthlessness. He had won his military reputation as a young man by tossing hand grenades into dormitories that housed the wives and children of striking tin miners.

Sitting at a restaurant table in La Paz, I remembered vividly my last visit, in 1980, to this peculiar, politically volatile capital in a canyon on top of the world. *The Economist*'s correspondent, the American journalist Mary Helen Spooner, had filed a story from La Paz detailing Colonel Arce's past. As the colonel had been behind the coup the previous weekend, and as there were only two telex lines out of the city, both of which were being monitored by the colonel's men, she was promptly arrested. As I was the editor who had commissioned the story, I flew in to try to negotiate her release along with J. D. F. Jones, the splendidly combative foreign editor of *The Financial Times* (for which she also wrote). Our arrival in La Paz was inauspicious; we found ourselves surrounded by men with electronic protuberances and equipment that we assumed to be torture devices; it turned out that there was to be a total eclipse of the sun that weekend, and that these were professional eclipse watchers who chased the moon's shadows across the world.

We went straight to the British embassy. We were told by the ambassador and his staff of two ("Can you imagine those men cooped up there for three years?" remarked J. D. F. Jones) that we were unwise to have come. "You won't do any better than I did through official channels. And you may end up getting yourselves arrested."

We went to the American embassy, where they were glad to see us. The chargé told us that what Mary Helen had written was "absolutely right. They're a gang of crooks." He suggested how we should proceed. As America had withdrawn its ambassador in protest of the coup, we were advised to seek a meeting with the interior minister through the British ambassador. The British ambassador agreed.

The interior ministry fixed a meeting the following day. We were met by a tableful of squat, sinister officials. We were told that Miss Spooner had committed a grievous insult to the minister and to the nation, and must stand trial under Bolivian law. She would be formally charged in a couple of days' time. The only person of any consequence at the table was Rosaria Poggi, the secretary-general at the ministry who, it was said, was very close to the infamous Colonel Arce. She wore tight black leather and her severe appearance was enhanced by her long dark hair, swept up into a tight black bun. Her long fingernails were a vivid crimson. "They have been writing the most terrible lies about us. It is unbelievable," she said passionately. "They have said that I personally tortured people. Can you imagine?"

We had been groveling as far as was possible without compromising Mary Helen. We had told them that our newspapers hadn't published her story—which implied that we had disbelieved it. In fact we hadn't published it because they had locked her up and we didn't want to get her into worse trouble. At Mrs. Poggi's remark, I said, with a gracious gesture towads the glamorous lady, "I can't imagine anything more ridiculous than to suggest you could have tortured anyone." She blushed and the hatchet-faced men around the table roared with laughter. J. D. F.'s version of the story was that I said, "My dear, it would be a pleasure to be tortured by you"—but I don't think I had the wit or the temerity.

In any event, the ice had been broken with these monsters. We were depressed, though, as we went back to the hotel. Just down the road, Mary Helen had been kept for four days in a four-by-six-foot cupboard without windows or much air. If she were committed for trial, the proceedings would take months, and if she were moved to a rat-infested Bolivian jail, I imagined she would go mad or die—even if she were eventually acquitted. We considered going to sing morale-boosting songs outside the ministry of the interior, but thought better of it. Our concern was to get her out, and we decided that it was better that our newspapers should end up with red faces than that she should linger there a moment longer than she had to.

The following day, Rosaria, who seemed to have taken personal charge of the case, summoned us to a meeting with the minister of communications. This slippery individual said that the only way Mary Helen could be released would be if our newspapers apologized handsomely for the insult to the Bolivian people and the minister of the interior. We retorted that, as our newpapers had published nothing defamatory, there was nothing to apologize for.

He said that in that case we must apologize on her behalf for the lies she had transmitted across the telex lines, because a telex was just as much a public communication as a newspaper. We insisted that a telex was not public, and that in Britain no one had seen the phrases she used about the interior minister. We adjourned, agreeing to meet later to see if a compromise was possible.

We worked on a statement of our own that afternoon, and returned to a full meeting with the minister and his officials. It took two hours of hard bargaining to agree upon wording that, in our opinion, did not cast any slur on Mary Helen's professionalism. The statement "expressed our regret at the consequences that have arisen as a result of Mary Helen's article"—which we took to mean not that we regretted the article, but that we regretted her subsequent arrest. We thought we had done rather well to get this language; but, in order to save her, we would have gone a lot further.

We had limited concern for our newspapers' reputation, or even Mary Helen's own, because her life was as stake. But we did not want to provide them with any statement that might be used against her in court, and we did not want to provide a document that might encourage other third world countries to lock up journalists in order to extract apologies. A further condition of her release that J. D. F. insisted upon was that she should not be present when the statement was read out, so that she would not in any sense be humiliated before a kangaroo court. A press conference was fixed for the evening.

Exhausted, we returned to the hotel to liaise with the American consul and to make plans to get out on the first available plane— which left the morning after the press conference—a long wait when there was still the possibility that Colonel Arce might change his mind. To clear my thoughts, I took a ride down the canyon to La Paz's fabled Valley of the Moon. The city seemed despondent after the coup, with soldiers everywhere, and people going quietly about their work, keeping off the streets. They had every reason to be cowed: perhaps seven hundred people had been killed, and pockets of resistance were still being mopped up. The miners had gone on strike, and had locked themselves into the tin mines. The army was attempting to starve them into surrender. Thousands of political prisoners had been taken. Lechín, the miners' legendary leader, had disappeared, and many feared he had been murdered.

People were especially elusive that day: the few that were about looked constantly toward the sky. My taxi driver drove me past the luxury suburbs down the canyon, past the river where Indian women were washing their clothes, down to the Valley of the Moon—an extraordinary congregation of stone shapes, a broken-up, cracked bed of rock that had been eroded into thousands of level spikes, tapering off to points a few inches wide, rather like a gigantic, flattened hedgehog's back. In that desolate, terrible scene, the driver told me that the eclipse was underway, and offered me dark glasses to witness it.

I viewed it through them briefly. The sun had turned into a black globe surrounded by brilliant white. I took the glasses off, and saw that the light had changed. The countryside was dull and gray and in shadow, even though there wasn't a speck in the sky and to the naked eye—such was the brightness of the corona around the sun—the sun was as bright as ever. The sky was overcast, although there were no clouds. The sight was like one of those film effects that denote hell or limbo, a kind of twilight at midday. Eclipses were not infrequent at these latitudes, and I understood now why the Indians worshiped and feared the sun: the desolate altiplano could not be a more impressive place to observe an eclipse. I turned and, only for an instant, did what one is not supposed to do: I looked straight into the sun. The brilliance of the surrounding light was such that it engulfed the moon, giving the impression that a teardrop—elongated and transparent—was passing across the face of the sun, a teardrop shed at the barbarity and desolation that had befallen the sad land of Bolivia.

Two hours later, the press conference was held. We met in an atmosphere of tension. We were told Mary Helen was being held in the next room, and would be brought in shortly. J. D. F. was furious. "She is not to be paraded before the press. We have an agreement on that. Otherwise we call the whole thing off." Alarmed, the communications minister agreed to keep her in the next room. The room was crammed with journalists and television equipment.

The notorious colonel made his appearance. The man the Americans had described to us as a "pathological killer" was short and pudgy, with close-cropped, wiry hair, a snub nose and a dreamy-looking smile over protruding teeth. His eyes had a peculiar glazed expression that I will never forget: it was as though he had deliber-

ately insulated himself from the human race in order to behave with
absolute cruelty. It was a look I have seen in some doctors—but their
work requires it. In his eyes, though, was a look of enjoyment. He
relished power and, it seemed to me, the inflicting of pain. I was told
by Mary Helen afterward that he would masturbate quite openly in
front of her, in front of his men, while interrogating her; even his
men were disgusted. It was an exhibition of power over normal
human inhibition. Like Mario Sandoval in Guatemala and Roberto
D'Aubuisson in El Salvador, Colonel Arce was anything but banal;
he had elevated himself into something quite out of the ordinary in
his quest for money and power. His appearance may have been
bland; his expression was not.

He seated himself at the head of the table in his smart green suit
with immaculate red epaulets, and I read aloud our statement in
Spanish while the cameras clicked and whirred. Then, in violation of
our agreement, an interior ministry official opened the door, and
Mary Helen stood there, disheveled, confused. J. D. F. and I rushed
to protect her and the press were pushed out of the room by officials.
The Colonel then came forward, jovially shaking hands with everyone, patting us on the back, seeking our approval. "I am glad it has
ended this way. I treated her well, didn't I?" he said, approaching
her with a smile. We had shaken hands with the monster. Out of
confusion, or hatred, Mary Helen ignored his outstretched hand and
he withdrew, with a look of puzzlement and anger.

We drove her to the hotel; she was as thin as a waif, and very
teary. She had her first bath in a decent room in four days and
J. D. F. plied her with pills to put her to sleep. I went with the
American consul, a practical, sympathetic man who every day had
to fight harder cases on behalf of imprisoned drug offenders, to get
her belongings at the interior ministry. The place where she had
been held was a cupboard at the end of a long, low, impersonal guard
room where angular hard men with broken teeth in shabby suits
gazed at us with contempt. I had no doubt that the men were
torturers; one of them, according to Mary Helen, boasted that he
was the killer of Che Guevara. I was relieved to be out of the place;
J. D. F. and I spent the evening celebrating.

The next morning, we left the hotel in apprehension, waiting at
any moment to be stopped and for Mary Helen to be rearrested. Our
fears did not diminish until the plane was in the air; then we drank

champagne. She was extraordinarily lucid, talking nonstop, which was probably therapeutic. She told us that Colonel Arce had interrogated her repeatedly, had pointed a gun at her, and had threatened to kill her several times. The press was out in force when we landed in Lima, a city that for once I was glad to see.

On the way out, J. D. F., who had traveled through the Miami airport without an American visa, had been placed under guard during our stopover, to his fury. After Peru, he continued to Chile; on my way back, as I went through Miami customs, I was asked what I had been doing in Bolivia, one of the drug capitals of the Western Hemisphere. "Helping to get an American citizen out of jail," I said in pompous, exhausted irritation. "Step right through, sir," said the customs inspector, in the broad accent of a Miami Cuban. When I got back to London, a prim letter from Lord Avebury to the editor awaited, attacking us for kowtowing to a despicable military dictatorship. Avebury got the short end of my editor's tongue.

Now I was back in La Paz. General García Meza and Colonel Arce had lasted less than a year before another coup pushed them out and steered the country toward democratic elections. Siles had won the election, and his government, although presiding over the most severe economic difficulties in the country's history, survived long enough to hand power over to another democratically elected successor—Víctor Paz Estenssoro. Democracy had survived even in this harsh, unpromising soil; force could not prevent it from growing roots and putting out its shoots, however often they were cut down. Colonel Arce had fled to Argentina. I did not doubt that he and his military friends would try to hijack the country again. The democratic government had declared war on the cocaine growers, and Roberto Suárez, the country's drug king, had fought back viciously. The killers would seek to return; but the forces of minimum decency were fighting back, even in Bolivia, and so far prevailing.

PARAGUAY

To descend to Paraguay from the hard mountain country of
Bolivia is to descend to a land of tropical isolation, Latin America's
closest approximation to Africa. Though slowly being modernized,
Paraguay is still very underdeveloped with run-down roads that are
little more than muddy paths, and splendid tree-lined avenues that
modern development has not yet erased. Asunción spreads out from
a single main street, the Calle del Paraguay Independiente, and is
dominated by the church of La Encarnación. It is hot and sultry in
the colonial city, a merciful relief from the cold thin air of the Andes.

Paraguay has avoided most of the ills plaguing Bolivia, its historic,
impoverished, similarly landlocked enemy, because the land is so
fertile and the climate so favorable. Like ancient Mesopotamia, this
tranquil, paradisiacal land lies between two rivers, the Paraguay and
Paraná. When the Spaniards arrived, the region was populated by
the Guaraní Indians, who were far friendlier than their mountain
counterparts. The Indians led a seminomadic existence, cultivating a
few fields, drinking yerba maté, smoking cigars, sleeping in ham-
mocks, moving on. As with the Bolivian Indians, the women seemed
to do most of the work. The Indians' largest problem was their
pitiable health, the result of the tropical climate and neglect. A

Rockefeller mission in the early twentieth century discovered that nearly every Paraguayan suffered from some deadly disease. After the Spanish occupation, Paraguayans were also afflicted with a succession of dictators. Paraguay was discovered by Juan de Ayolas, who sailed up the Paraná in 1535 and penetrated the Chaco to Peru. Later, the Spaniards founded Asunción, which became a rather lazy frontier town where polygamy was legal and the Indians—happily, it seemed—worked for their new masters.

A complete backwater, Paraguay attracted various groups of churchmen who hoped to use it for their social experiments. The first to arrive, in 1609, were the Jesuits, who set up thirty communities, organized along semisocialist, strictly religious lines. The Indians worked for the Jesuits, building churches and receiving classical educations. But the Jesuits somehow attracted the hostility of the government in Asunción, which tried to suppress them. They also came increasingly into conflict with the governor-general at Lima. The situation eased in 1735 when the Paraguayans under Fernando Mompóx gained independence for their sleepy paradise. When the Spanish state returned, hostility to the Jesuits grew; they were pushed out in 1768 and the communities they had created were destroyed.

Another experiment was conducted by Mennonites, a branch of the Baptists, largely of German origin, who arrived in Paraguay around 1900. One hundred and eighteen villages were set up containing some eleven thousand Mennonites and twelve thousand Indians who worked them. The Mennonites were entirely self-sufficient; they had a cooperative agricultural system, banks, hospitals and schools. They lived almost exclusively from farming, inhabiting the scrub of the middle Chaco region around Filadelfia.

The Paraguayans were so independent-minded and so neglected under Spanish rule that they resisted the attempts of Buenos Aires, which had declared its independence, to incorporate them, preferring to stage their own rebellion in 1811. By 1814, this isolated country had the first of its notorious dictators, José Gaspar Rodríguez de Francia. Possessed of a university education, an admirer of Rousseau, he was a terrifying-looking man with dark black eyes, a beak nose and a tight, purse-lipped mouth. An obsessed and lonely bachelor, he suppressed opposition brutally and closed off Paraguay from the outside world, expelling the few foreign residents. There were no schools and no newspapers. El Supremo, as this miserable madman styled himself, died at the age of seventy-four in 1840.

His successor, Carlos Antonio López, was rather different. A fat man with a limp, he reversed El Supremo's policy of isolation, sent Paraguayans abroad to universities, opened schools and started building railways and roads. But he also loved wealth: by the time of his death in 1862, he owned half of cultivated Paraguay. Francisco Solano, his son, who had been received at the court of Napoléon III, suffered from a different problem: *folie de grandeur*. He began to build pretentious houses inspired by his beautiful French mistress, Madame Elisa Lynch. In 1864 he declared war on Brazil, Argentina and Uruguay all at once in an attempt to set up a "Great Platine Republic." After thousands of his fierce, astonishingly loyal Guaraní Indian subjects had died in the war, the combined armies of his opponents moved on Paraguay, killing the megalomaniac in 1870. Miss Lynch fled abroad to squander his fortune. Of the half of Paraguay's population of five hundred thousand that survived the war, only twenty-two thousand were men.

The younger López, incredibly, became Paraguay's national hero. After the experience of the great dictators, the country's few wealthy people decided to dispense with one-man rule, and managed to elect a succession of twenty-nine presidents, until the Chaco War began in 1927. The Paraguayans proved tougher and better adapted at fighting in the lowlands than the Bolivians and, having won the war, enjoyed good government until the army, in conjunction with the Colorado Party, which represented the country's conservative elite, took over in 1940. When the civilian front man for the army appeared to falter in 1954, General Alfredo Stroessner, a tough, wily officer in his early forties, took charge.

Stroessner exiled tens of thousands, imprisoned others and killed a few of his opponents. His jails were to contain the grown children of his political opponents, born there. Absolutely intolerant of opposition, he ruled through the army and pursued modest economic development until the great leap forward of the 1970s, when the Itaipu dam, built jointly with Brazil, was completed.

The new money proceeded to create a middle class, which was soon posing problems for the dictator. Reelected seven times to office unopposed, Stroessner's regime confronted a series of violent riots that disturbed the dead calm of the republic in 1986, after my visit.

Stroessner himself showed no signs of megalomania through all this: like Franco, he ruled shrewdly and tenaciously by manipulating the power cliques around him. The most enduring modern dictator of Latin America, he was, hopefully, to be one of its last, alongside Chile's President Pinochet and Cuba's President Castro.

A light aircraft took me on a visit to Itaipu from the air. This megaproject, a huge semicircular dam, holds back more than ten miles of water. Down one side an overflow thunders, sending up huge clouds of spray, but most of the water flows through giant concrete turbines that generate Itaipu's electricity. At one time more concrete was going into a single day's construction of the dam than was used in building Rio's entire Maracaña Stadium, itself one of the biggest in the world. Itaipu seems consciously to seek to imitate, further downstream, the natural wonder of the Iguaçú Falls, with their multiple cataracts focused around a single gullet of boiling waters—hell's mouth—that sends its spray up to the highest of the clouds themselves.

This was the source of the new wealth that was challenging Stroessner's hold for the first time. The dam and the building of Puerto Stroessner nearby had generated massive corruption and mismanagement, which in turn had created economic difficulties. The government had been forced to introduce a system of multiple exchange rates to cope with its balance-of-payments problem, and the central bank manipulated the exchange rates, leading to a scandal involving at least $200 million, which the regime proved unable to suppress. Stroessner closed down newspapers and radio stations to prevent the details from leaking out. A prominent diplomat in Asunción was to tell me bluntly that "this is the most corrupt country I've ever been in, and I served in Iran under the Shah, so I know what I'm talking about."

Unable to make contact with any internal opposition, I decided to visit the Gran Chaco, one of the world's wildernesses, consisting of 100,000 people in an area of 60 million acres. The road wound through shallow puddles in a great flatland interspersed with palm forests. I found myself dropping off to sleep along that featureless drive. The only interruptions were poor mud villages and herds of wandering cattle; the Indians seemed welcoming and friendly.

My companion was a young Paraguayan driver. We were stopped

about forty kilometers out of Asunción by an army roadblock. After they had inspected the vehicle they let us through. "They are searching for contraband," my driver told me. "Actually, they want to keep the contraband trade to themselves; the military smuggles most goods through in its own vehicles. I had a friend who used to go and stay with a prominent general who has a ranch in the Gran Chaco. He used to go hunting with the general's son—you have to be careful not to get lost, because you never find your way back, it looks the same for hundreds of square miles. Anyway, the general used to get deliveries of contraband from Panama to his private airstrip and smuggle it down this road into Asunción. Most of it ends up in Brazil and Argentina, which have heavy import duties." I had noticed how well stocked the shops of Asunción were with Japanese hi-fis and American fridges. I learned that car thieves in Brazil often drive across the border to Asunción; you could pick up a car for a quarter of the price in Paraguay. About half of Paraguay's economy was a criminal one. An exiled opponent of the dictator described it as "a crook country, with a corrupt and bloody rancher in General Stroessner."

After several hours, I reached Filadelfia: it was like suddenly coming into a small German town. The wooden houses were surrounded by pretty flower gardens and orchards. The town itself was broad-avenued, but modern and comfortable, presenting a striking contrast with the desolation around. I left civilization early the following morning down the only road into the high Chaco where the desolate land for which tens of thousands had died was terrifyingly untouched. The road ran through a low thorn forest of spikes and cactuses. It was searingly hot in the car, and there were no places to stop—indeed, there were hardly any farms at all. I congratulated myself on my prescience in buying plentiful supplies of beer in Filadelfia, and told my driver to turn back.

I left Paraguay with mixed feelings: the pleasantness of the people, their very indolence, were at least partly responsible for the dreadful rulers they had endured—apart from the one gap of responsible government in the middle of the century. Yet even the toughest of these one-man governments had been shrewd enough not to resist the wind of change of the twentieth century.

It seemed a certainty that change would come when Stroessner departs. His own Colorado Party was split between its hard right and a softer group linked to the army, which felt there would have to be some accommodation with the regime's critics. The civilian opposition was surprisingly moderate; the country's most prominent exile, Domingo Laino, who was frequently turned back at the Asunción airport, appeared to be a middle-of-the-road social democrat. The country's potential armed opposition had been mercilessly extinguished by Stroessner. But Paraguay was not guerrilla country: the Chaco was too inhospitable and the fertile south too flat to provide cover, and neither Brazil nor Argentina would have helped an insurgency. All the same there was a shadowy underground communist movement that might take advantage if Stroessner clung on too long.

But in Paraguay, as in Bolivia or Peru, it seemed to me the Indians were conservative, disinclined to support extremism. The system of landholding was unequal: 20,000 families owned twenty-seven million hectares, 110,000 smaller families owned two million hectares, while the great majority had no title to their land. Yet there was no shortage of land: 95 percent of Paraguay was uncultivated. Land reform seemed less essential than an extension of the cultivated area. The new middle class seemed likely to be technocratic rather than revolutionary. The Itaipu project, costing nearly $13 billion, the largest of its kind in the world, would give Paraguay an annual income of $400 million a year in exported electricity, and seemed likely to help keep the country developing in spite of the economic difficulties that Paraguay shared with its neighbors. Whether, like Franco, Stroessner seemed unaware that development would breed a new middle class which would press for democracy, the progression seemed inevitable. Then that backwater, enjoying its idyllic lifestyle, might get the kind of government its people deserve.

I had taken the trail of the Indian across the Andes through Colombia, Ecuador, Peru, Bolivia and Paraguay, all of them poor countries, behind the general level of Latin American development. Colombia, the largest, had a per-capita income of $922 and had achieved a great deal in doubling this, in real terms, from $478 in 1960. Ecuador, endowed with oil, had more than doubled its average income, from $499 to $1,043. Peru, once much richer at $808 in 1960, had expanded much more slowly to $1,104 per head; it wasn't quite standing still, but its population growth and the economic policies of its military rulers had been ruinous for its development. Paraguay's per-capita income, in spite of the dictator, had doubled from $526 to $1,113—a success story. Poor Bolivia still struggled along with $486, compared to $382 in 1960.

Life was still nasty, brutish and short for many in these countries. Literacy in Bolivia was at 68 percent, life expectancy was 50 years, infant mortality at 151 per 1,000 live births. In Paraguay, literacy was at 85 percent, average life expectancy a respectable 66 years, and infant mortality was 63 per 1,000 live births. In Peru, literacy was 89 percent, average life expectancy 60, infant mortality a high 86 per 1,000 live births. In Ecuador, literacy was 79 percent, life expectancy 60, and infant mortality 63 per 1,000 live births. In Colombia literacy was 81 percent, average life expectancy 63, and infant mortality 46 per 1,000 live births. All told, these were the least developed countries in Latin America; but the improvements of the past twenty years had been vast, except for Bolivia and Peru.

Only Bolivia, of those five countries, has the excuse of its geography for its underdevelopment; it really is a wretched land to govern. Of the others, Peru has the legacy of its decayed colonial past to live down; and Colombia, Ecuador and Paraguay have done rather well recently. Will the troubled politics of these countries permit further development? Paraguay's future after Stroessner, it seemed to me, was unknowable, but I was guardedly optimistic. Ecuador had succeeded in moving from a technocracy under the army to a democratic technocracy. Colombia was still coming to terms with the disillusion of its masses, but its civil wars and faction fights had settled down; the chances of political stability were at least even. In Bolivia it was surprising that democrats existed at all, but exist they did, and they had put down roots against nearly impossible odds in barren soil. And Peru's boy-leader was trying to bring modern Western European–style socialism to a country of great inequality that had lost the ability to govern itself since the days it had governed Latin America on Spain's behalf. His chances are no more than fifty-fifty; but, in Peru, even that is something of an achievement.

But even democracy and attempts at social revolution have not been able to break the flat noncooperation that has existed between the white and mestizo ruling class and the Indians, who comprise nearly a third of the combined populations of five million people.

The ex-colonists who had broken their roots with their own cultures have not convinced the Indians to abandon their old tenets to work for a civilization they have considered beneath contempt. Perhaps modern technology is now creating a technocratic civilization that Spaniard, mestizo and Indian can respect, one that will allow them to develop their great natural resources and provide a proper living for their people.

PART III

THE TRAIL OF DESPAIR

Today an eagle passed
Over my head;
It carries in its wings
The storm
Nothing passes.
Death came.

RUBÉN DARÍO

ARGENTINA, CHILE AND URUGUAY, ONCE THE DEMOCRATIC AND DE-
veloped "southern cone" of South America, have now been its despair for thirty years. These countries appeared, earlier in this
century, to be following courses parallel to those of Britain and the
United States in the nineteenth century and continental Europe in
the twentieth. By this I mean the course from governments that
evolved by constitutional systems, where two or more parties competed for the votes of small aristocratic elites, to parties competing
for the mass vote. The change was to be fostered by rapid industrialization. But as happened in Europe, industrialization came too
rapidly and proved destabilizing. Before the three countries had a
chance to develop substantial middle classes, large working classes
were created, consisting of underpaid workers in new industries,
most of whom had fled destitution in the countryside and lost their
origins there.

These new working classes were politically fickle and unstable,
particularly when the Great Depression proved to be much more
long-lasting and savage in Latin America than in the United States.
And these three countries, which had seemed to be almost on a par
with Europe, fell sharply despite their advantages. They did not
suffer from difficult geographies; they had splendid natural resources; and they did not have large, suppressed Indian minorities.
Their problems were political and included appallingly misjudged
entrances onto the stage of mass politics.

In Chile the elite proved very slow and reluctant to acknowledge
the pressure building among the lower classes. As the gap between
rich and poor became wider, the left managed to capture the working-class vote and, through a series of mishaps, seized power in 1970,
plunging the country into an economic chaos. From this crisis
emerged one of the harshest tyrants in recent Latin American history.

In Argentina, the Radicals—the traditional party of the oligarchy—attempted to become a mass party with near-success under Hipólito Yrigoyen. But the Depression caused Argentina's evolution to falter. A dictator, Juan Perón, who borrowed his militarism from Spain and his fascism from Italy and Germany, came to power and dominated the country's politics for nearly thirty years, appealing both to the urban masses in his industrializing country and to the rootless immigrant masses from Europe. Under his rule, Argentina fell from its position as one of the ten best-off nations in the world, a veritable Australia of the Western Hemisphere, to a lower economic status just ahead of its unstable Latin American neighbors.

Uruguay, which had long been a small, quintessentially middle-class state, with profitable agriculture and an enlightened welfare system, succumbed to the militarization that had afflicted its neighbors in the 1960s when its society proved unable to weather a temporary economic decline.

I traveled to each of these countries expecting the worst, expecting to find evidence that even developed Latin American countries were incapable of governing themselves. In prosperous Chile I found a gifted people, among the most educated and civilized in Latin America, writhing under a tyranny that at first most had welcomed as an alternative to Allende.

During the Allende period, Chile's economy did race out of control: drastic action become necessary to avoid national collapse. But the Pinochet regime, so far beneath Chile's traditional standard in its principles and methods, constitutes an unending tragedy. And Pinochet's overriding ambition to stay in power seemed likely to so radicalize a country that has suffered deep wounds—the numbers killed in demonstrations to remove him ran into the hundreds—that blood resentment will long be felt in Chile.

In Uruguay I found a country that had just emerged from life under military rule and was determined to avoid a return to this existence, even at the risk of a lower standard of living.

In Argentina, the most difficult case of all, where people and soldiers competed for the spoils of a rich country that they had never fully bothered to develop, I found political parties that seemed to have acquired a new middle-class maturity as they stepped from under the shadow of Perón. There was an end, it seemed after all, to the Trail of Despair.

CHILE

I WAS TOO TIRED ON MY ARRIVAL TO MAKE IMMEDIATE CONTACT WITH friends in Santiago. That evening I took a stroll in the dark, past the reconstructed Moneda palace which the tyrant, General Augusto Pinochet, shared with the ghost of Salvador Allende, down to the elegant cathedral square, through the deserted modern business quarter, then back down the Alameda, in a loop. There was plenty of security on the streets, but I wasn't challenged. Back in the hotel, I took the elevator up to the restaurant on the top floor, and had dinner in the open air beside a swimming pool while an ensemble played and I gazed out over the sad city below.

Sad, but civilized. Few cities could be as social: before my visit was over I had been invited to a delightful dinner party in a prominent Chilean's house, with formal, elegantly attired guests; to the stately white elegance of the British embassy; to the pleasant suburban house of a good friend of mine, where he and his wife told me of the earthquake that had made the glass in the windows bend and ripple a couple of years before; to a delightful restaurant on a mountain overlooking Santiago; to a country estate where they made the best wine in Latin America; to a chalet in the Andes; and to the magnificent ski resort of Portillo. This blinding whirl of conviviality almost made me forget the nature of the regime outside. But the stiff, unsmiling police in the streets were always there to remind me.

On this, my fifth visit to the country, I considered the long experience of how Chile had come to its present condition.

Of Vietnam, the Middle East, southern Africa and Chile, the latter was perhaps the unlikeliest venue for one of the major cock-fights staged in the 1970s between the collectivists and the capitalists. But for three years, 1970 to 1973, the noisy supporters of each side goaded their gamecocks into battle there.

During those years, the rest of the world took a morbid interest in a country it had rarely noticed before. Statesmen gave each other lectures about the danger of meddling in Chile's internal affairs, even as their secret agents organized popular militias or plotted coups in army mess rooms. Sociologists fastidiously analyzed the country's chaotic experiments in land reform and social welfare. Editors thundered about the economic grievances of Chilean truckers.

In 1973, these tremors led to the overthrow of the Marxist government of President Salvador Allende by Chile's right-wing army in a particularly bloody coup. Latin America's anti-Marxists left the pit triumphant. They had proved themselves equal to the supposedly unstoppable revolutionary vanguard moving through the third world. Or so they thought. Today it is the Marxists who are smiling, for Chile's generals have behaved like the traditional hatchet-faced caricatures of army strongmen.

And the Battle of Chile is far from over. It is being fought in the publishing houses and newspaper offices of the world. Books bubbling with indignation (*The Murder of Allende; Chile: The Struggle for Dignity; The Last Two Years of Allende*) have poured off the presses. Fresh displays of savagery in Chile, which would hardly raise an eyebrow if committed in some other Latin American country, have gotten front-page treatment around the world. Ambassadors shuttle backward and forward to Santiago as their foreign ministers weigh the consequences of yet another outrage. American and British labor unionists earnestly debate whether to boycott goods going there.

Why all the controversy? Chile produces little the West could not do without. Chilean copper is important, but Chilean nitrates, once shipped all over the world to make fertilizers and explosives, are produced more cheaply elsewhere. There are few people in Chile, and not much of an economy, to fight over. Chile has only nine million inhabitants, producing about $11 billion worth of goods from a land slightly bigger than France. Seven other Latin American countries have larger populations and six produce more. The country has scant strategic value: no major roads or railways pass through it. Its entire three thousand miles of coastline have been ignored since the world's ships started passing through the Panama Canal seventy-four years ago.

Physically, Chile is something of a freak. Immensely long, thin as a sardine (its average width is 110 miles), it is squashed between the world's second-highest chain of mountains, the Andes, and its largest ocean, the Pacific. Chile has a geographer's cross section of climates and land, from arid desert in the north to virgin forest, volcanoes and cold, storm-swept islets and fjords in the south. Not much of the country is inhabited. Nearly half the people are crammed into the greater Santiago area, and most of the rest remain within the one hundred fertile miles on either side of the city. Chile is one of the two South American countries farthest from the United States and Europe, and is farther from Russia than any country in the world. Why did those great powers find themselves aligned on either side of the argument in that stunningly attractive, topographical oddity of a land?

The coup of 1973 was hardly unusual for Latin America. Brazil's army staged a coup in 1964, Peru's in 1968, Bolivia's in 1969, Ecuador's in 1972, Uruguay's in 1973 and Argentina's in 1976, and nobody made half such a fuss about those. Indeed, Chile was a comparatively late convert to military monasticism. Certainly Chile's coup was unusually violent: three thousand people are thought to have been killed in the fighting, or simply murdered when the army took over. More people, however, died over a longer period as Argentina's army consolidated its rule after 1976. Again, there was much less argument about that.

In the years immediately after the coup, Chile's record on human rights was one of the worst in South America. But not the worst: the rulers of Argentina, Cuba and Uruguay imprisoned proportionately more political dissidents than did the Chileans. And it was long one of the sick jokes of Latin America that the Guatemalans had no political prisoners because they were all dead. The Chilean junta tortured people. So did a dozen or more Latin American military governments. Chile's soldiers reached out to kill their political enemies living in other countries. So did Bolivia's soldiers.

Moreover, in trampling on Chilean democracy, the soldiers were acting for more understandable motives than soldiers in Peru and Bolivia, who seized power simply because they had an itch to rule. Chile's army did not move until the economy had all but collapsed. The country's democracy was being uprooted by illegal seizures of property and by the attempts of Allende's supporters to perpetuate his policies against the will of a congress dominated by the opposition; and Santiago's streets had become a murderous battleground for thugs from the political fringes.

The junta's more primeval defenders have argued that Chile has been singled out for international political opprobrium because of a worldwide Marxist conspiracy. They have pointed out that the Russians have never tired of reciting Chilean brutalities and that they have treated the exiled leader of Chile's Communist Party, Mr. Luis Corvalán (who did not play a particularly heroic role in the events of 1970–73) as Lenin's lost child. But why then did normally levelheaded governments such as those of Britain and Italy long refuse to have anything to do with Chile? Because they were Marxist dupes?

No, there were more solid, homegrown reasons why the generals became the world's pariahs. First, Chile was one of Latin America's oldest democracies, so the 1973 coup came as something of a shock. Second, the coup was directed against a Marxist president who, almost uniquely, had come to power by constitutional means. To Marxists the world over, this was final proof that democracy was a sham, which only tolerated political freedom as long as people voted for "bourgeois" parties. The Marxists conveniently ignored the fact that Allende was trying to override Congress against the Chilean constitution.

Third, the Chilean affair occurred as the spotlight was being turned on the covert activities of the Central Intelligence Agency in the United States, whose self-styled "destabilizing" operation in Chile was exposed to public view. Critics called this proof that Latin America was as sorely a nag to the United States as Eastern Europe was to Russia: any whinny of independence got a crack of the whip. It seemed to me that the anger of the Chilean middle classes against Allende had become so intense by 1973 that the coup would have occurred with or without a few words or dollars of encouragement from Dr. Kissinger, although this undoubtedly played a role. Since then the failure of American government to persuade Chile's army to be less beastly to its opponents suggests that its influence in Chilean affairs has always been exaggerated.

The fourth reason why Chile was a name to conjure with was General Augusto Pinochet Ugarte, the last of Latin America's megadictators.

To understand how Pinochet rose to power, it is first necessary to understand Chile's past: the country was so democratic, so constitutionalist, that its army lacked the tradition of ambitious men using it as a vehicle to enter politics. In Guatemala, or Argentina, or Brazil, if you lacked a power base and money, the army was a decent way into politics. In Chile the army was for those members of the upper class who lacked brains and for the lower middle classes.

General Pinochet came from the ranks of the latter, which caused him to be despised by the Chilean upper classes, who accused him of a lust for power, of a narrowness of vision, and of ruthlessness. It is unfortunate that the Chileans who cheered Pinochet's victory did not consider these qualities then. For in addition to his formidable political skills and unhesitating use of brutality, Pinochet is tenacious. At the time of my most recent visit, Chile knew no way of getting rid of him. In other countries, presidents are rotated out of office to allow other generals a spell at the top; authority is collective at the top of the armed forces. If the man in power attempts to stay on, a coup will be staged. But Chile's army was, at the time of my visit, professional and obedient to its singular leader, and loyal to the traditions of the German army, which first trained it.

On the one occasion in 1983, when I met Pinochet, I was with a small group. He had recently moved out of what was probably the best-guarded and certainly the least attractive presidential palace in South America: the Edificio Diego Portales, a towering black sky-scraper overlooking a large, almost windowless concrete bunker with giant steel girders adorning the ceiling. For years he had preferred to live there rather than rebuild the Moneda, the presidential palace where, during Pinochet's coup, Salvador Allende had either killed himself or been murdered. The elegant, two-story palace had lain wrecked in downtown Santiago, a shell-like ruin dwarfed by the giant headquarters of the American interests that had helped to ensure its fall. Here was a reproof to those who had challenged the might of the multinationals and the army.

Whether or not Pinochet had left it like that for so long as an example to his people, or because he was frightened of Allende's ghost, he had no fear of it now. Our delegation passed the green-gray jackbooted sentries, tall, close-cropped and contemptuous in their German tradition, adorned with flat caps and holster belts polished so clean you could see your reflection in them. (The march of the Chilean army was the goose step.) We were escorted through the courtyard, up a magnificent staircase and into a room adorned with chandeliers, tapestries and classical carpets. There we were greeted by the president's right-hand man, General Santiago Sinclair, reputedly his éminence grise, and his interior minister, Sergio Jarpa. The latter was Chile's last real statesman, a former prime minister summoned out of retirement, who maintained the square, loyal, yet doggedly honest appearance of an old retainer. Both men were clearly nervous as we made polite conversation. No one was offered a seat. After some ten minutes, a curtain was pulled away from one end of the room, revealing a battery of television lights; the domestic press had been kept at a respectful distance. Their cameras were trained on two elegant doors at the end of the room.

Suddenly the doors were flung back with a crash and with a heavy, measured stamp, the great dictator strode into the room wearing an immaculate white uniform, but no hat. His hooded eyes glowered at us; his lips were pursed and grim beneath his mustache. He shook the hand of each of us in turn and waved us to elegant gilt chairs. The press was shooed away. He welcomed us to his country. We asked him questions, to which he gave uninformative answers in a gravel voice. When we suggested that Chile might follow Spain's example and prepare the way for a democratic, moderate successor, he said, "We all know what happened there!" dismissing as a communist conspiracy Spain's astonishing peaceful transformation from dictatorship to democracy. It was plain that he had no thought of abdicating. At our interview, and at the subsequent lunch in the president's splendid dining room, he smiled genially on occasion and was unfailingly polite to the women around him; but he spoke rarely. Stripped of his trappings, he would have resembled an intolerant, occasionally benevolent, old-fashioned South American rancher with a mane of slicked-down white-gray hair.

But he was much, much worse than that, another incarnation of Latin American evil. He was not evil from ideological conviction, as Guatemala's Mario Sandoval was; or out of ambition, as El Salvador's Roberto D'Aubuisson was; or out of greed, as Bolivia's Colonel Arce was. He was the evil of ultimate authority, the absolute corruption of power. I had always rejected Lord Acton's pompous saying on this subject; in my experience, power often makes men more responsible, and overwhelms all too many others. But here was the real thing, a man beginning from the apparently simple motive of rescuing his country from disaster and becoming a ruler who was convinced that he alone stood between his country and communism, that all who opposed him were criminally misguided, that he was all-powerful and indispensable.

And so he was, in his own way. Everywhere he was deferred to. Even Sergio Jarpa, his chief minister, eyed him with a worried look. His chief adviser, General Sinclair, was intelligent but obsequious. "Does one have to have done military service in order to get into politics in Britain?" Sinclair questioned across the table.

Pinochet appeared to be an utterly lonely man, to whom no one spoke the truth. Yet he was sufficiently in touch with his people to have recognized that terror and fear alone would keep him in power. Many people were to die in the attempt to dislodge Pinochet, perhaps six thousand in ten years, if the deaths during the consolidation of the initial coup are counted along with the victims of torture, and of brutality at demonstrations.

As these figures testify, the Chilean regime was never as pervasive as its opponents portrayed it: a modified curfew continued a long time after the coup. Eventually whittled down to a couple of hours after 2:30 A.M., it was used by amorous boys as an excuse to stay the night in their girlfriends' houses. Moderate opponents of the regime remained in evidence and were not usually arrested. It was still possible to interview socialists and communists, who would vigorously denounce the government. In addition, magazines like *Hoy* and *Ercilla* kept up a vigorous, if occasionally censored, antigovernment tirade.

But despite these suggestions of tolerance, the regime was vicious. Demonstrations were brutally broken up, often by gunfire. Prominent opposition leaders were picked up and sometimes murdered; others were briefly detained. The sole aim was to keep Pinochet in power, despite the fact that by the mid-1980s he had lost the support of nearly every conservative and moderate group in the country. By clinging to office, he served only to radicalize the opposition. "The crisis is the president himself. He is tunnel-visioned," one of his former chief ministers told me with passion.

One moderate conservative after another failed to budge him. The president's supremacy over his fellow soldiers was firmly established in 1976 when he summarily dismissed the army commander, General Sergio Arellano, for daring to argue that the repression had gone far enough. Another potential rival, the regime's defense minister, General Oscar Bonilla, had died mysteriously in a helicopter crash in 1975. A general of the armed police who talked about reform was dismissed in 1978, supposedly for failing to protect a judge's home against one of the usually harmless "terrorist" bombs set off from time to time in Santiago. These were usually placed by the security forces themselves, to justify subsequent repression.

General Herman Brady, a top army commander who was thought to be getting too chummy with the opposition civilians, was retired. The president appointed General Carlos Forestier as his immediate understudy, in the post of army commander. His right-wing views made his boss look like a softie. No one was likely to want to push out Attila the Hun to make way for Genghis Khan.

The one man in uniform on whom the civilians had pinned their hopes certainly had his heart in the right place, but he belonged to the wrong branch of the armed forces. General Gustavo Leigh was commander of the air force when the armed forces seized power, and was one of the four original members of the junta (the others were the army, navy and police commanders). He genuinely believed in the junta's original promise to "restore the rule of institutions" interrupted by the Allende regime. In 1978, in an interview with the Italian newspaper, *Corriere della Sera*, he criticized Pinochet for failing to set Chile back on the road toward democracy.

He had made one criticism too many. The army *supremo* decided to show which service ran Chile. The following Sunday night, soldiers were stationed outside air force barracks, and air force officers were ordered not to return from weekend leave. General Leigh was informed he was out of a job when he showed up for work the next morning. The air force chief protested that there was no legal procedure for dismissing a member of the junta. Oh yes there was— the rest of the junta had issued a new law to that effect the same morning. Eight more air force generals were dismissed. Another ten resigned in sympathy with their commander. The president appointed one of the remaining two as General Leigh's successor, and replaced the rest.

With that display of tactical cunning and brute force, Pinochet dispelled any lingering doubts as to who ran Chile. He became ebulliently self-confident when three quarters of Chile's voters decided, in a question-loaded referendum in January 1978, that they preferred him to "international aggression" (by, of all bodies, the United Nations General Assembly).

Pinochet reckoned that the economy was going well, and he was buoyed up by government-sponsored polls, which purported to show that he was becoming more popular among the poorest sections of society, although less so among the middle and upper classes. This, he believed, reflected the recovery in working-class living standards after the 1974–75 depression (but what answer would you give to a government-sponsored pollster in Chile?). So, in April 1978, the president appointed several civilians to his cabinet.

The top-ranking civilian, who acted as effective prime minister, was Sergio Fernández, the minister of the interior. A tall, grave lawyer who spoke in sepulchral tones, Fernández outlined to me in 1978 his cabinet's task, which he defined as the "new institutionalization." Pinochet's government, he said, was no longer "government of transition, to restore public and economic order and then be replaced by the same old institutions." Its aim was much more ambitious. The government, he said, sought to achieve the "political, social and economic transformation" of the country through a sweeping program affecting all aspects of national life—industrial relations, agriculture, justice, public administration, health, the social services, the economy and political institutions.

The second plank of the new cabinet's policy was to improve the regime's image abroad. Here, Pinochet took a risk in appointing as foreign minister the one real civilian political heavyweight, Hernán Cubillos, a respected conservative and former newspaper proprietor. Cubillos would not have become the regime's traveling salesman unless it had improved its record on human rights.

But democratic rule in Chile was as far away as ever. The government's reforms were long-term ones. Fernández said it was trying to integrate a system of "freedom with authority." To this end a constitutional reform commission had been scratching away since 1973 with the speed of a medieval scribe. It aimed to provide the blueprint for a "protected democracy"—protected, that was, from further Marxist adventures. The draft constitution gave Pinochet a mandate until 1989; after that the junta would choose his successor, who would then be approved in a popular referendum. There were no prizes for guessing who would be running. If Pinochet can spin it out until 1994, he will have been in power for more than twenty years.

The new, moderate Pinochet proved harder to sell abroad even than Franco, though foreign minister Cubillos was the country's most welcome face abroad in recent years. A thoroughly civilized Anglophile, he was a man with a passion for pipes and the sea. His goal was to return Chile safely to democracy; in different times he might have become president of his country.

Improving Pinochet's image in the world proved impossible, however. Chile made enemies the way other countries made acquaintances. In 1979 it almost went to war with Argentina, its eastern neighbor. It exchanged angry notes with its northern neighbor, Peru, and snarls with its eastern neighbor, Bolivia. The United States briefly recalled its ambassador from Santiago, joining the club of headless delegations there, which then included Britain, Sweden, Italy, Holland and most of Eastern Europe.

The year 1979 was, admittedly, exceptional. Many of the disputes were not Chile's fault, and least of all the fault of its tireless foreign minister, Hernán Cubillos. The quarrel with Argentina was largely the latter's doing, although Britain shared some of the responsibility. The quarrels with Peru and Bolivia were, at worst, the fault of Chileans of a century before. The quarrel with America arose from some extraordinarily ham-fisted behavior by Pinochet's soldiers.

Chile's case in the Beagle Channel dispute with Argentina, which nearly put two of Latin America's most ferocious armies at each other's throats, was all but impeccable. At issue, in theory, were three microdots of land at the very tip of southern South America: the islets of Picton, Lennox and Nueva, just off the divided island of Tierra del Fuego. The argument was really about several hundred square miles of sea, which fell within the new two-hundred-mile limit on territorial waters. Both countries had found offshore oil nearby and thought the sea there was teeming with tiny, protein-rich shrimps called krill. Possession of the islands could also have had a bearing on who eventually governed how much of Antartica and its largely unexplored resources.

The treaty of 1881, which fixed the boundaries between Chile and Argentina, gave the windy grasslands of Patagonia to Argentina. In exchange, Chile got a sliver of territory right down to the toe of South America. The treaty also gave Argentina all the islands west, but not south, of Tierra del Fuego. Chile pointed out that the three islets were south of the island. Argentina said the islands were west of the Tierra del Fuego archipelago.

After years of fruitless argument, the two sides called on Britain to arbitrate. A British-appointed judicial inquiry reported back in 1977, when Britain was not so respected as it once was—indeed, it lacked ambassadors in both countries. The inquiry awarded the islands to Chile. That may have been juridically correct, but the eminent lawyers on the inquiry could have done worse than to take a course in Latin American political psychology. Deprived of even a face-saving inch, the Argentinians rejected the award. Entitled to everything, the Chileans were damned if they would give an inch—where in other circumstances they might have been prepared to give much more. Had the injured party not been Chile, the world might have sympathized with a country being pushed around by its bigger neighbor. In January 1979, battle fleets set sail, troops were rushed to the border, and air-raid practices were staged in Buenos Aires.

Only the arrival of a connoisseur of Latin political psychology, Cardinal Antonio Samore from Rome, kept the peace. Cardinal Samore persuaded the two sides to agree to talks. The papacy proposed a tie-breaking solution. Chile got the islands and Argentina was awarded a portion of the sea.

The year of 1979 also marked the centenary of Chile's war with Peru and Bolivia for possession of the nitrate-rich desert between them in the north. Chile won the war, gobbled up a slice of Peru and closed off Bolivia's access to the sea. In subsequent treaties, the Peruvians got some of their lost land back. But Bolivia remained without direct access to the sea.

In 1976 the three countries opened talks on how a Bolivian corridor to the sea might be arranged. The Chileans recognized that Bolivia had an "aspiration," though not a right, to such a corridor, which they would try to do something about. In return, the Chileans wanted Bolivian territory. The Bolivians said no. When the talks foundered a year later, Bolivia expelled Chile's ambassador.

Peru's ruling soldiers, with little enough to distract the public's attention from the unholy economic mess they had created, also found an excuse in 1979—the arrest of a Chilean spy, promptly executed—to send yet another Chilean ambassador packing his bags. An anti-Chilean campaign of surprising intensity was whipped up by the governments and the press in Bolivia and Peru. But nobody really expected either country—one almost bankrupt, the other shaken by four coups in little over a year—to launch a war to free its lost territories. Not, anyway, against a country with a war machine strengthened by Pinochet from forty-seven thousand men in 1973 to eighty-five thousand men or against a country with the highest relative military spending in Latin America—some $750 million a year, or about 7 percent of gross domestic product (compared with $180 million, or about 2½ percent of gross domestic product, when a civilian was president). Or against a country so thick-skinned that diplomatic brickbats just seemed to bounce harmlessly off.

Chile's junta, obsessed with the idea that the country's overseas detractors belonged to a gigantic communist plot, nevertheless kept supplying those detractors with armfuls of ammunition. One cause célèbre was the arrest in 1975 of a British doctor, Sheila Cassidy, for tending to a guerrilla leader on the run. Miss Cassidy, with a great deal of courage, refused to tell where she was; she was released only after being tortured for several days. Britain promptly recalled its ambassador in Santiago. Britain paid for it by losing export orders in a country where a small financial elite, sensitive to diplomatic slights, was still responsible for placing them.

The first, cynical, law in every local gestapo manual must surely be to treat citizens from other countries differently from your own. In his heyday, however, General Manuel Contreras, the head of DINA, the Chilean secret police, was a law unto himself. His operatives behaved as though the world were their hunting ground. In Buenos Aires the left-wing army commander under Allende, General Carlos Prats, was killed by a bomb in 1974. In Rome a prominent Christian Democratic left-winger, Mr. Bernardo Leighton, was badly wounded in 1975. Neither crime has yet been satisfactorily explained. The following year Allende's foreign minister, Orlando Letelier, was killed by a car bomb in Embassy Row in Washington.

At the time of the explosion, a DINA captain and an American living in Santiago were both visiting Washington, having traveled to the United States with Chilean government passports. The American was extradited to the United States, where, in exchange for a reduced sentence, he confessed to having taken part in Letelier's murder, which, he said, had been ordered by Contreras. On being indicted by an American jury, the general, his second-in-command and the DINA captain were put under house arrest in Santiago. Chile's supreme court eventually turned down the request for their extradition and freed the three men. The court said that the testimony of a plea-bargaining witness was inadmissible under Napoleonic law. The Americans recalled their ambassador for a time.

In September, in an attempt to defuse international hostility, Cubillos paid a call to some of Chile's severest critics—Spain, Switzerland, France, Germany and Britain. He was met with demonstrations in most of the countries he visited. He failed to convince Britain's Lord Carrington to send an ambassador to Chile—partly because the Chileans did not offer to investigate the Cassidy affair, and partly because it would be bad form for a British ambassador to arrive in Santiago on one airplane as the American ambassador prepared to leave on the next.

Cubillos was criticized about human rights by all he saw. France's foreign minister refused to be photographed with him. Germany's posed, looking grim. Spain's prime minister, Adolfo Suárez, who didn't seem to mind whom he met, gave Mr. Cubillos a smile as broad as the one with which he had recently greeted Fidel Castro and Yasir Arafat.

After the country's modest liberalization under Fernández, opposition began to make itself felt. The main opponents were the Christian Democrats, the largest political party, which had played a major role in the events that led to the end of democracy. Its patriarchal leader, Eduardo Frei, was accused in the late 1960s of presiding over a massive expansion in welfare spending that eventually led to the bankrupting of the country. When it came to choosing his successor in 1970, the party split, and a left-winger, Rodomiro Tomić, was chosen. A coalition of the right ran against him; under the three-way division of the votes, Salvador Allende, the Marxist candidate, won narrowly. The left never had anything approaching an overall majority in Chile. Tomić was a genial, vague, benevolent supporter of revolutionary causes whom I met in Nicaragua on a postrevolutionary visit in 1980. It was incredible that a major democratic party could have chosen a man of so little substance as its leader. Frei had been something else. I called on him in his book-lined law office in Santiago before his death in 1976.

He was one of Latin America's few grand old men. A cadaverous, yet distinguished-looking man, tall and stooped, with a genial smile and vague eyes that signaled distant charm, he spoke in elliptical, priestly tones. When I asked him for his view of the government and how it could be removed, he refused to be specific, sticking to generalities. "Authoritarian regimes," he told me, "seek to enforce order; but under the surface, ideas circulate inexorably and in no country has even the most hardened regime managed to stamp them out. The same is true of Chile. . . . Certainly democracies fall into disorder. But they recover. By contrast, look at how dictatorships are finishing up all over the world."

It was a magisterial perspective, but offered little immediate hope. He would not predict the end of the Pinochet regime, however, which implied that he felt it had considerable staying power. He was correct.

As he escorted me to the door, with the same graceful manner, pressing in my hand a copy of his treatise against Pinochet—"The Mandate of History and Criteria for the Future"—I felt that I was leaving a dying breed of wise, cultured, European politician whose optimism had perhaps been too great and had led to the emergence of that uncaged beast in the presidential palace. Frei, despairing of the pass to which the nation had come under Allende, had supported the coup but urged Pinochet to return the country to constitutional government after a short interval. The dictator had not responded— as I suspect the worldly-wise Frei knew he wouldn't. Better Pinochet than Allende, but better democracy than either. It was a view that I shared.

After Frei's death, the party divided again. The right wing, which had supported Frei, rallied behind Andrés Zaldivar, a brilliant intellectual with a great balding head and a small body; the left supported a Tomić-like fraud by the name of Ramón Valdéz. He even lacked Tomić's reputation for genuine idealism. The product of one of the best families in Chile, he was wealthy with a loud platform manner and a patronizing, genial style. Reminiscent of a slightly more benevolent version of the classic Latin American demagogue, he was a man who had reached the top by espousing all causes, who if elected would almost certainly prove incompetent and incapable of controlling the forces beneath him. Alas, he had more appeal to his party's rank and file than the intellectual Zaldivar.

Difficult as were the Christian Democratic Party's internal wrangles, the party was popular, and preferable to Pinochet. On the left, a socialist party came to be modeled on Western Europe's new moderate socialists; it was full of bright, fresh-faced lawyers wearing open-neck shirts and casual trousers, like Spain's Felipe González.

And then there were the communists. They were the underground, invisible to me except when, on the second day of my stay, I went out to visit their grass roots in Chile's dismal *callampas*, "mushroom" shanties. The place was overcrowded, like a refugee camp, but run with considerable efficiency by a section leader, a woman, and a priest. There were no drains, and the roads between the tents and shacks were dirt, but the headquarters hut was made of wood with an adequate roof and had several rooms. Compared with what I had seen in Peru and Bolivia, this was luxury. Yet it was absolutely wretched by comparison with the middle-class section of Santiago.

The tough but cheerful section leader gave me a gripping account of police harrassment in the area. "They come in and bulldoze the area where a demonstration is about to take place. Sometimes they pick up one or two people; they try to intimidate us. But we are not frightened. We go onto the streets in even greater numbers. They always come here in force; they are afraid to come in small numbers." The slums were illegal, built without permission. "Sometimes they bulldoze the area just to enforce that point. Then they move the inhabitants to another place, to break up our solidarity. We come back and rebuild."

They were the hard ones, the communists. There was always the danger in Chile that if Pinochet stayed too long, people would be radicalized in their hatred of his regime. The communists were the political arm of the poor, and there were many poor in Chile; but I could not see them ever having the support of more than a third of the population. The country was too middle-class in outlook for that.

Yet as strikes and demonstrations spread in the late 1970s, so the pressure for change grew. The man who came to embody that pressure was the interior minister of the early 1980s, Sergio Jarpa, a man of unimpeachable integrity, a conservative, who wanted to return his country to constitutional government. He tried in vain to persuade Pinochet to set up a transitional mechanism. However, Pinochet was convinced that he was the only bastion against communism and he believed that armed might would prevail against any demonstration; to a military man with the subtlety of a Sherman tank, it was a matter of the straightforward balance of force. He tossed Jarpa a few constitutional fig leaves and refused to budge. Jarpa, in disillusion, resigned. The crisis dragged on, and even increasingly overt criticism of the dictator by the American embassy came to naught.

The opposition to Pinochet grew because of the failure of his economic experiment. It had been a bold one, a kind of laboratory of pure monetarism, the fad that had swept the developed world, in a country lacking the institutional obstacles—labor unions, lobbies, political parties—that prevented pure monetarism from being applied anywhere else. It was based squarely on the ideas of the University of Chicago's Milton Friedman, and its Chilean architects were labeled the "Chicago Boys." They were mostly young, bright, yuppie-style technocrats educated on American campuses, eager to prove that economics obeyed absolute laws and that economic laws had only to be observed for all to fall in place. Lacking any grounding in politics, they failed to understand that choices are almost invariably political; that economics exist to serve, not to dictate, the priorities of man, although they can, in extremes, limit them. These young economists had free rein in a country whose politicians and unions were cowed by the guns of the army. And for a while, the experiment seemed to be working.

The main Chicago Boys included an economics professor, Jorge Cauas; a more practical type, Miguel de Castro; and a bright young foursome—Alvaro Bardon, the chain-smoking, nervous, intense governor of the central bank; Miguel Kast, the boyish, arrogant planning minister; Sergio de la Cuadra, the central bank's second-in-command; and José Pinera, the cadaverous, reserved labor minister. They were all in their thirties. Typically, the Chicago solution was stumbled on, almost by accident, by Pinochet, an economics illiterate.

Chile's longest-lasting president only narrowly avoided becoming one of its shortest. In March 1975, as Chile was supposed to be on the way to economic recovery, Pinochet was approached by the economists in ODEPLAN, the government's long-term planning department. They told him that the collapse in world copper prices would cost Chile $1 billion a year in lost export earnings; that the increase in world oil prices would cost Chile some $30 million a year in higher imports; that these increases would cut Chile's economy by 13 percent; that if he tried to spend his way out of trouble he would end up with higher inflation than Allende; that no one was going to lend Chile the money needed to stay out out of trouble (Chile's creditors, grouped together in the Paris Club, were already jibbing at being asked to reschedule the country's foreign debt); and that "shock treatment" was the only answer.

The general mulled this over for a weekend. Then he appointed a new finance minister, Cauas, to head a team of austerity-minded economists. Some of them had been to the University of Chicago, though few had actually been taught by Friedman. Never mind; to Chileans they became the Chicago Boys. They had the undimmed idealism of youth; they looked on economics as a pure science with the same fervor that a Marxist believes history obeys scientific laws. De la Cuadra said with pride, "We are so monetarist we have reached a position where the central bank is hardly in control of the money supply anymore. It controls itself."

After four years of monetarism, the government claimed that the Chilean economy was on its feet again. Inflation, the habit the Chicago Boys were trying to get their patient to kick, was down from 600 percent under Allende to some 30 percent by 1978. The gross domestic product (GDP), which shrank about 12 percent in 1974, had grown at an average rate of nearly 8 percent over the preceding three years. Annual industrial production, which slumped by more than 20 percent in 1975, had risen since then by some 30 percent. Chile's exports—particularly its nontraditional ones, wood and pulp—rose from $1.8 billion in 1975 to $2.8 billion in 1978. And at the same time, the Chicago Boys pointed out that Chile had sharply reduced its dependence on copper, which amounted to only 47 percent of Chile's exports in 1978, compared with 80 percent in 1975.

The servants of a regime that had reduced Chile's political freedom committed themselves to giving the country greater economic freedom. The first six years of Pinochet's government saw the state reversing its tradition of intervention in the economy. Price controls were abolished in 1973; under Allende the prices of many goods had been frozen; as a result, many items could only be bought on the black market. With the end of controls, prices soared, adding mightily in the short term to inflation. The government claimed that in the long run competition would regulate prices much more effectively than the government ever did.

Interest rates were deregulated in mid-1975, in order to stimulate personal savings, which had been almost nonexistent during the period of negative real interest rates under Allende. The government's monetary squeeze pushed real interest rates up to 35 percent in 1975, and nearly double that in 1976–77 (when nominal interest rates were running at a staggering annual rate of 380 percent).

Also under the new regime, Chile's clandestine capital market was allowed out in the open. Under Allende, formal credit controls were very tight so borrowers and lenders learned to bypass the banks altogether and work through middlemen called *financieras*. In 1973 these were officially recognized by the Pinochet regime. A code to regulate the new lending houses was set up in 1976 to protect the small investors after the government had come to the rescue of a *financiera* who had overlent. The government hoped that investment, which was only 10 percent of GDP under Allende, and now is 15 percent, would start to take off as the capital market grew. The banks were also freed of central bank controls. Foreign banks were allowed into the country. Minimum reserve requirements were relaxed.

Chile, long accustomed to the shelter of tariff walls and an overvalued exchange rate, was forced, by its Friedmanite managers, to look the world right in the eye. Tariff barriers were brought steadily down. In 1973, many foreign goods were in effect barred from the country by tariffs of up to 600 percent. The average tariff was 100 percent. These were the weathered buttresses of Chile's traditional policy of import substitution. Average tariffs were cut to 10 percent. Cheap foreign goods flooded the Chilean market. Bottles of gin and Scotch, for example, were cheaper than in Britain.

In the wake of the reforms, the government claimed that Chile's formerly protected, inefficient domestic producers had adapted themselves to the new competitive conditions. Bankruptcies, they noted, were lower than in the late 1960s. Companies merged to become more efficient, and changed and adapted their production lines. Many of them now bought semimanufactured goods abroad, finished them, then reexported them instead of making every bit expensively at home.

Most of the tariff cuts were made at a time (1975–76) when Chilean industry was caught in a recession. Chileans had very little spending money, so Chilean firms were forced to sell their wares abroad to survive. As the economy picked up steam again, Chileans found for the first time that they were allowed to buy the cheap things other people could produce. So reviving domestic demand was fed by imports, not by companies switching their attention back to the domestic market. Thus exports did not suffer.

There were other reasons why one of the least seaworthy industrial structures of the world stayed afloat when exposed to the gale of international competition. First, international credit began to flow into Chile, so firms found they had the money to make new, cost-effective investments. Second, many firms gave up launching new products, which often turned out to be expensive failures in Chile's tiny home market. And, third, many companies found savings could be made by buying raw materials and machines abroad to compensate for the fall in domestic prices of their own products.

But the switch toward a much freer market created more pain than the government admitted. An independent survey estimated that about seventy thousand Chileans had lost their jobs as a direct result of the liberalization of trade. Chile's sugar beet industry went bust as soon as cheaper cane sugar began flowing into the country. Chile's bevy of small, competing electronics firms had to merge into one in order to survive. Some mines closed, unable to compete with low-priced minerals from abroad. Chile's regiment of vehicle manufacturers was reduced to just four and, to keep them going, the government agreed to keep high tariffs in force for vehicles of more than 800 cubic centimeters' capacity for a further five years.

Pain or no pain, the creation of a freer economy would not have been complete (or successful) had the doors not been open to foreign investment. A foreign investment statute of quite astonishing brevity by Latin American standards was drawn up in 1977. As a result, Chile had to withdraw from the Andean Pact, a group of Latin

American countries with firm ideas about what foreigners could do with their money.

The foreign companies were allowed to step right in. From the outset, they could send all their profits back home, and after three years they could repatriate as much of their invested capital as they wanted. The Chicago Boys disapproved of any restriction on foreign investment. They said that foreign firms, like domestic firms, employed Chilean labor, paid half of their profits in taxes, and were a source of much-needed development capital. What if they did take advantage of a cheap labor force to produce goods for an outside market and skimmed off large profits which they spent back home? They brought jobs and earnings into Chile. What if they did gobble up raw materials? The country had plenty.

After a slow start, money from abroad started coming in fast. In the first six months of 1979 alone, more than $1.6 billion in proposed foreign investment was approved, compared with $1.3 billion in 1968, $900 million in 1977 and just $24 million in 1974. Of the more than $4 billion invested or proposed since the Pinochet government took over, 77 percent came from the United States and 15 percent from Canada (Britain took a surprising third place, with some $92 million invested). Significantly, of the total of 346 projects proposed since 1974, 14 mining projects tied up no less than $3.7 billion, or 90 percent, of foreign investment. As might be expected, the overseas investors were far more interested in Chile's natural resources than in its manufacturing capacity or its limited domestic market.

The gravestone on Allende's Marxist experiment was erected in 1979, when the Anaconda mining company decided to return to Chile. In 1972 its three copper mines, among them the world's largest open-cast mine at Chuquicamata in Chile's northern desert region, were nationalized. They still are. But Anaconda bought, for a modest $20 million, a copper deposit at Pelambres containing reserves reckoned at more than 400 million tons of copper ore. The company planned to spend $12 million exploring the area immediately—and said it might be prepared to invest up to $1.5 billion eventually.

Arguing that government spending was the principal cause of inflation in 1970–73 and that it starved the private sector of funds, the government indulged in an orgy of self-mutilation. The public sector's share of GDP fell from 43 percent in 1973 to some 30 percent in 1979. The public sector's deficit was brought down from 55 percent of spending in 1973 to 4 percent in 1978. The cuts were largely secured by freezing nominal public-sector wage bills, so that in real terms they fell sharply, by dismissing a tenth of workers in the public sector, and by selling off a fair (though not the most important) chunk of the government's industrial empire.

The denationalizations (the Chileans called them "reprivatizations") were carried out by the state development corporation, CORFO, under a courteous, no-nonsense, army-appointed chief, Colonel Ramos. In six years, more than four hundred companies— four fifths of the total owned by CORFO, which under Allende had acted as an industrial vacuum cleaner, were sold off to private enterprise. Fewer than fifty were left.

In the early days, said Colonel Ramos, he had to step in and rescue some of the companies that immediately went bust after being nationalized. Later he would not do so. "They must stand on their own feet," he said. CORFO would hang onto its remaining slice of GDP (amounting to some 7 percent). "Our role is not to compete with private industry but to do what private industry cannot do," said the colonel.

Chile had become a laboratory for right-wing experimentation. A social security reform was drawn up to reward the thrifty, while providing a safety net about an inch above the floor for the less virtuous. Under the government's plan, workers could set aside against retirement or unemployment a larger amount of national insurance than the minimum required by law. The government and employers had then to match it with a bigger contribution of their own. The scheme was a thinly disguised attempt to get a small savings market off the ground.

Families who saved up to $5,000 to buy their first house would get a grant for the same amount and spend the money on any house they wished. This scheme did away with the allocation of public housing by patronage; it was intended, eventually, to do away with public housing altogether. Under a health service reform, public money was diverted from expensive heart and lung machines in the big hospitals to "sanitation stations" in the poorer country areas, which would concentrate on preventive health measures—vaccinations, education, basic hygiene and so on. Many doctors, who did not like the idea of spending years in the sticks, claimed that the government was trying to boost private practice in the wealthier areas: administrators were angry that, under the new plan, their hospitals would no longer get automatic cash grants from the government. Instead, a third of the money would be paid according to the number of patients treated. The most revolutionary part of the scheme was that workers were able to buy treatment vouchers at half price from the state. They could then take these vouchers to the hospital of their choice— introducing, in the view of many doctors, an undignified degree of competition between the hospitals.

A massive reorganization also took place in education. Army generals were forced to shed the rectorial robes they donned so awkwardly after the 1973 coup to purge the universities of Marxists. The university faculties (but certainly not the students) were given greater powers to run themselves. The study of Marxism, taught in political science courses, which was taken off the curriculum after the 1973 coup, was, in the name of academic independence, again regarded as a fit subject and taught with surprising impartiality. "How is it possible to learn about political science without studying Marx?" I was asked by the education minister. The schools were given greater independence from the ministry and put under the control of regional boards. National education standards were more rigorously enforced, but the government did not seem to know what to do about growing primary school truancy and getting more children to attend secondary schools.

Bolder still, the government scrapped the agrarian reform program started under the conservative government of President Jorge Alessandri. The program had been accelerated by the Christian Democratic government of President Frei and relentlessly pushed through under President Allende. By 1973 nearly four million acres of land had been expropriated or illegally occupied, nine tenths of it under Allende. But most of the land was being squatted on "transitionally" by state-appointed bodies, and had not been handed over to individual peasant proprietors.

The minister of agriculture, Alfonso Márquez de la Plata, rejected the idea that the traditional inefficiency of Chilean agriculture had anything to do with the system of landholding. "The communists," he told me in 1980, "would point out demagogically that a single landowner possessed 500,000 acres, or a fifth of one province, but neglected to say it was barren mountainside, worth maybe $60,000."

The ministry's figures showed that in 1965, 750 landowners had some 46 percent of the land but only 10 percent of the cultivated acreage. Nine tenths of this was in the hands of smaller farmers.

Still, the government did not risk the political storm of handing the land directly back to its old owners, but divided four fifths of the expropriated territory into private holdings, giving farms to nearly forty thousand families. The rest was run by voluntary cooperatives. A lot of the new owners, however, found the plots too minuscule to support them.

Divide and rule, indeed, might have been the slogan of the reforms. The government's most ambitious plan—concerning labor relations—drew howls of indignation from the country's old union bosses. Eduardo Ríos, an eloquent Christian Democratic labor chief, told me that the new law was a blatant attempt to destroy the main strength of the labor unions—their collective solidarity. He claimed that the "atomization of collective bargaining" could have two effects: to weaken the moderate national leadership and to drive many workers, frustrated by their weakness in small units, into the hands of irresponsible far-left groups.

His anxieties were understandable. The plan was the brainchild of one of the government's most forthright intellectuals, José Piñera, and Britain's Mrs. Thatcher might have looked on some of its provisions with envy. The closed shop was outlawed; union leaders had to be elected by secret ballot; no official strike could take place without a ballot; and any group of workers could set up a union—whereas before they had to apply to the minister of labor, who was unlikely to give them permission unless the big unions approved. Political strikes were banned and the unions were not supposed to talk about politics—"even though," said Ríos, "workers are citizens. Why can't they talk politics like any other group?" As part of the same strategy of winning the hearts and minds of the ordinary worker, Piñera also introduced worker participation in industry through profit sharing rather than seats on the board.

The plan lapsed into more conventional union-bashing when it came to the regulation of collective bargaining. Workers would have the right to strike (after a ballot)—but after thirty days the management could lock them out. After sixty days the workers were assumed to have "dismissed themselves," which meant they lost social security benefits and their employers could fill their places (which

was not too difficult when unemployment was running at 14 percent). Workers in certain public and "strategic" industries—such as
the Chuquicamata copper mine—could not go on strike at all, but
had to submit their demands to arbitration.

The aim of the labor reforms was to ensure that wages went up in
line with productivity. "Collective bargaining should be a means not
of redistributing wealth but of finding the market value of labor,"
declared Mr. Piñera with missionary fervor. If pay increases ex-
ceeded productivity increases, he claimed, someone suffered—the 75
percent of nonunionized labor, the unemployed or the consumer.

The price of all this was considerable. The depression of 1975–76
hit Chile as hard as the slump in the 1930s hit Britain. At first, the
rate of unemployment just climbed and climbed. It peaked in 1975
at 16.5 percent in greater Santiago as men lost their jobs, and more
women went to look for work, particularly in domestic service, to
supplement their families' earnings. Poor families survived because,
according to one survey, nearly two thirds of them had at least one
breadwinner taking home an average of $45 a week.

As the economy picked up in 1977, unemployment dropped back
to 11 percent. But the following year it climbed again to more than
14 percent. The opposition said the new rise was the result of lower
tariffs. The government said that it was because the registered labor
force had grown by two hundred thousand during the depression
and that many of the new "unemployed" were women giving up
their jobs and returning to their families.

The unemployed workers' lot in Chile was not a happy one, even
though the government extended unemployment insurance from
white- to blue-collar workers. About sixty thousand workers drew
between half and three quarters their old yearly wage. After that
they got nothing. Anyone could earn a third of the minimum wage
by doing menial work under the government's employment program. But few Chileans were prepared to work for this pittance.
Some three hundred thousand workers got no help at all.

For those who managed to keep their jobs, real wages slumped by
about a third during the squeeze. Wages as a percentage of GDP fell
from 52 percent in 1970 to 42 percent in 1974 but recovered to some
45 percent in 1979.

After 1975, wages were indexed to the rise in the cost of living.
But the index was derived from an average of price increases, not

from faster-rising essential goods, like food, which loomed much larger in the budgets of the lower-paid. The index did not take into account the large hidden proportion of a Chilean's wage paid in fringe benefits, which had not been rising. And under the new labor law, wages would be allowed to rise in line with productivity increases.

President Pinochet claimed that during the slump he wanted to protect those "who have no one to speak for them"—the bottom fifth of Chileans. Moreover, the government argued that while social spending as a proportion of total government spending had fallen from over 40 percent in 1970 to under 30 percent under President Allende, it amounted to 54 percent under Pinochet. That ignored the fact that total government spending had been severely slashed. In the two grimmest years, 1975–77, under the army, real social spending fell by a quarter.

The fifth of Chileans who lived in third-world poverty were not spared the squeeze. They saw their share of total spending fall from 8 percent in 1969 to 5 percent in 1978. Diets became poorer: national consumption of calories fell by 12 percent between 1970 and 1978; protein consumption fell by 18 percent. This contributed to more frequent outbreaks of disease like typhoid, whose incidence per one thousand inhabitants tripled to more than one hundred cases between 1973 and 1977. Only small children benefited from the grandfather in Pinochet: infant mortality fell sharply, from sixty-five deaths to under fifty per one thousand live births. This probably reflected the efficient working of Chile's health service, which was sensibly spared government cuts. The number of children suffering from malnutrition also fell by 4 percent between 1970 and 1978.

The cuts hit hard, though, at education. The number of children completing primary education fell by about forty thousand between 1973 and 1978, as poorer families kept their children away from school so they could go to work. The government halved the number of school meals it paid for. Housing was another target: public-sector starts were cut back from an average of twenty-eight thousand a year in 1965–73 to some nine thousand a year in 1974–78. Over the same period, private housing starts fell from seventeen thousand to fourteen thousand.

Then, in the early 1980s, just as it seemed that expansion was underway and the misery had been worthwhile, it all fell to bits.

The problem—the international debt crisis, which followed in the wake of the second oil-price increase—was wholly outside the Chilean government's control. But the middle-sized Chilean economy was blown out of the water. Output fell by 14 percent in 1981; inflation went up to 58 percent; the balance of payments slumped to a $2 billion deficit. The moral was less that the economic experiment had been wrong than that a small economy, heavily dependent on the export of raw materials and, in particular, on the price of copper, had only limited room for social engineering of this kind. Some of the reforms had probably been for the good; the monetarism introduced into that political vacuum certainly went too far and caused too much suffering. But is was a strangely modern experiment to be applied by an old-fashioned hard-nosed military regime. That paradox went to the heart of the tragedy of modern Chile.

How could such a modern, developed country be ruled by so primitive a man and so crude a regime? Chile was not a Guatemala or an El Salvador or a Bolivia or even a Peru, whose political development had been stultified by racial divisions and a heavy colonial legacy. The conditions for democracy in Chile were right, and its democracy had been a model for Latin America.

I put the question to a distinguished newspaper editor, a courageous man, portly, benevolent, who had long fought the censorship under General Pinochet. "First, we are an island," he said. "Remember our geography. Behind the Andes we are cut off from Western civilization. This breeds an insular mentality, especially among our generals. Second, the army is very professional, very stupid, and has no external enemy. They are cowards, our soldiers: they shoot against unarmed people. In Chile it is the unarmed civilians who go out to face the guns who are brave. The military man has a mind all of his own: he believes political problems can be resolved by pointing a gun—bang bang. Third, we have a historic class division. In this country the ruling class, the upper class, the enlightened class was a landowning one; everyone else was poor. In the nineteenth century this class opened up a little, as the country's great wealth began to be exploited. We had a great intellectual ferment; our Catholic University and the University of Santiago were known as the best in the world. We were ruled by the most civilized autocrat in Latin America, José Manuel Balmaceda. Then came the golden age of Chilean democracy. After 1891 we had about thirty years of unbroken parliamentary democracy. But underneath it all, the great majority were impoverished and increasingly discontented. Social revolution was narrowly avoided after the first war by the great Arturo Alessandri. He was a brave man, the darling of the masses, but a conservative who broke with the ruling classes that had governed Chile. Even he became an autocrat, however, toward the end. He vied for power with a semi-Nazi, General Carlos Ibáñez, throughout the 1930s; but the army was to some extent passive. Jorge Alessandri raised the moral tone of our nation again, ruling as an orthodox conservative and presiding over Chile's greatest economic boom.

"Yet change had to come: the new middle class wanted power, and the urban classes wanted social reform. Frei, from the Christian Democrats, initiated it, with his 'revolution within history and law.' He accelerated agrarian reform and vastly expanded social spending. He went too far, and the Christian Democrats split; that gave Allende his chance, with only a third of the vote. You know the rest: it ended in Pinochet; and there seems to be no end to this particular tunnel. Our precious constitutional order was always frail, covering a terrible divide. The country of San Martín, of O'Higgins, of Diego Portales, of Alessandri, is now ruled by a political ape-man."

It was tragic, because the hauteur of Chilean life was what made it so attractive. The upper class lived on the side of the hill overlooking Santiago, away from the bustling, dingy downtown area, a long way from the shanties. They lived in ample two-story houses surrounded by gardens, served by maids and gardeners; they were laid-back and expansive. My closest Chilean friend used to drive me out in the mountains overhanging the city when I visited. We would climb up a spectacular road to the ski resort of Portillo, where he and his friends would enjoy gliding down the fastest slope in the world, an Olympic run down to a lake surrounded by dazzling white snow. The lake was supposed to be the resting place of an Inca princess, who had died of sadness at being exiled from her native Peru. (Chile's only Indians, the Araucanians, come from the fjords and islets and volcanoes of the virgin forest in the country's mountainous south.) We watched the skiers come off the slopes; they were well-built, well-heeled fellows who might have stepped straight off a prosperous farm in Europe. They were European in outlook, preferring to take their vacations there rather than in America. They loved music, and Chilean musicians were among the best in the world; they loved the arts; they loved literature and poetry.

On my last day I attended a polo match in the south of the country. It was a lovely clear day, and the match was attended by about a hundred spectators; the players galloped across the open field against a splendid backdrop of low mountains. It was a dreamy lifestyle, and I could see why they wanted to protect it. Yet I felt that unless they gave more, it might all be taken away; the thoughtful among them were aware of the possibility. But Pinochet was not a man to understand that, with his mixture of contempt for and imitation of the upper classes, with his policy of social experimentation and with his refusal to give up power, while the blood of Chileans ran in the streets. Chile, where the Beast ruled over Beauty, had gone so badly wrong, and there was little room for hope.

ARGENTINA

I took a car northward from Santiago, where the road soon branched into the Andes, to Argentina. The road wound its way through the steadily rising Andean foothills, where the white cordillera hung suspended like an ice heaven shimmering above a band of cloud. Then the road began to climb, steeply, zigzagging up a sheer rock face. The height made the climb seem interminable, and the car never seemed closer to the top. But I had a grandstand view of Aconcagua, one of the highest points in the Western Hemisphere, nearly twenty-one thousand feet up, a giant lump of whiteness. Finally I reached the border, where the Chilean soldiers were as polite and sinister as ever in their shiny jackboots and dark glasses. They let us through after a careful inspection. By comparison, the Argentine guards were lackadaisical.

From the border, the road led down from the Argentine city of Mendoza across a vast, largely uninhabited area of brown highlands. But even this seemed preferable to the emptiness of the pampas on the way to Buenos Aires where miles and miles of grassland extended in every direction, absolutely flat, and my spirits were depressed by the sadness of it all.

More lively, Buenos Aires was a splendid European city, a sharp contrast to the urban American sprawl of Santiago. It was bisected by a giant avenue, a kind of Champs-Elysées that ran to a clutch of fine French nineteenth-century buildings, which were about to be torn down. The city had a cheerful, cosmopolitan air and the pedestrians-only shopping center, filled with arcades of modern shops, made a pleasing change from the markets of northern Latin America. There was no visible poverty; smartly dressed girls window-shopped past Harrods (no relation to the London store, just a namesake) and Claridges, the town's best hotel, a monument to the *fin-de-siècle* embellished with ornamental fireplaces and staircases. Another major avenue was a mass of cinema hoardings, interspersed with *bife* restaurants.

I had visited one of these restaurants with a friend on a previous trip: the menu consisted entirely of various parts of the bullock, including giant kidneys bunched and big as a fist, and the largest steaks I have ever seen. These giant slabs, which overlapped the plates, were washed down with the rough Argentine red wine that was exported by the tankerload to Russia. I watched the Argentines eating, huge, red-faced men, devouring their *bife* with enthusiasm and loud jokes. They were a people larger than life.

Far from the diners, down another great avenue, was the congress building, built to resemble its American counterpart. But its dome appeared flat, as if squeezed by the country's succession of dictators. At the other end of the street, built to resemble Washington's Pennsylvania Avenue, was the Casa Rosada, or pink house, a pink-and-cream rococo building with extensive balconies and flourishes. It resembled the palace of a Gilbert and Sullivan colonial governor.

Yet it struck the right chord, for the country's politicians were echoes of Gilbert and Sullivan—and much worse. Behind the exterior of Latin America's most civilized society, the home of Nobel prize–winning scientists and Jorge Luis Borges, Latin America's most penetrating, puzzling writer there lurked a nation with the soul of a gangster. Or so it seemed from a glance at Argentina's recent history.

September 1973. Argentines of all classes flooded the Plaza de Mayo, in front of the Pink House, parading uproariously down the avenue, which is overlooked by the parliament house. They were celebrating the return to power of Juan Domingo Perón, eighteen years to the month after they had poured into the streets to celebrate the tyrant's overthrow. At the age of seventy-seven, after nearly two decades of comfortable exile in Madrid, Argentina's former dictator had won a staggering 62 percent of the popular vote.

The middle classes voted for him because they thought he was a bulwark against revolution. The working classes, whose view of Perón had grown rosier through glasses clouded by years of army rule, remembered him as the man who gave them some sense of dignity. The far right supported him as the world's last authentic fascist, apprenticed in the 1930s on a military mission to Mussolini's Rome. The Marxists thought of him as a gaga old man of whom they could take advantage.

Because the army had barred Perón from taking part in the elections the previous March, a left-wing stand-in, Héctor Cámpora, was elected president. Cámpora promptly freed every Argentine jailbird, political or otherwise, and invited Perón back. El Lider, as Perón was called, insisted that new elections be held and picked as his vice-presidential running mate his wife, Isabelita, a dancer with some of the looks and none of the political savvy of his second wife, the legendary Evita.

March 1976. Laconically and with a week's advance notice, Argentina's army reluctantly took power over a Hogarthian bedlam of a country. Annual inflation was 600 percent. Isabelita Perón, who had succeeded her husband to the presidency on his death in 1974, on the verge of a nervous breakdown, was being attended by Svengali-like courtiers including José López Rega, an astrologer. Politicians and union leaders had left by plane, their suitcases stuffed with looted cash. Once-tranquil Buenos Aires suburbs were reverberating to the sound of explosions and gunfire as extremist groups battled it out. The day after the army took over, many absentee civil servants reported for the first time in months to their ministries for fear of losing their jobs. Fistfights broke out between those claiming the same desks.

September 1979. General Luciano Menéndez, the commander of the Third Army stationed in Córdoba, called a press conference to demand the resignation of the army commander, General Roberto Viola. General Menéndez was angry about the government's decision to release from house arrest Jacobo Timerman, the former editor of the newspaper La Opinión. Although allegedly linked with far-left terrorists, Timerman was never formally charged with any crime after his 1977 arrest. He was tortured and, after an international outcry, placed under house arrest. In September 1978, he was put on an airplane to Israel after receiving members of the Inter-American Commission on Human Rights, who were appalled by his story. His book, *Prisoner Without a Name, Cell Without a Number*, was to bring the horror of Argentina to world notice. General Menéndez was outraged by the government's "weakness in releasing Timerman."

Menéndez was immediately relieved of his command—but not before he had set out for Jesús María, a small town in the hills, to rally his forces for a march on Córdoba. Asked by General Viola over the telephone what he was up to, General Menéndez replied, "Routine maneuvers." These maneuvers included assembling a force of 750 military engineers and antiaircraft gunners, who marched, Quixote-style, on the 15,000-strong Viola garrison in Córdoba. When his contingent was surrounded, General Menéndez was persuaded to come to his senses and surrender.

He was then forced to fly to Buenos Aires and apologize in person to General Viola in order to restore the respect due that officer. For openly attempting to overthrow the government by force, General Menéndez was sentenced (in a country where editors under suspicion were tortured) to sixty days of dignified confinement. This bizarre story of an armed rebellion, of the military feathers it ruffled, and of the magnanimity extended to the barons but not the serfs was straight out of the Middle Ages—or perhaps Bolivia.

But Argentina is neither Bolivia nor the Middle Ages. Argentina is modern and wealthy. It is the world's seventh-largest country with only twenty-six million people to share its riches. It has a mild climate and its humid pampas are considered one of the world's five richest agricultural areas. In addition, the Patagonian plateau is ideal for sheep grazing and Argentina is the world's second-largest beef exporter. The nation could be one of its largest grain producers if it cultivated its pampas, and it is its fourth-biggest wine producer. Its gross domestic product per head, some $2,000, is perhaps the highest in Latin America. Four fifths of Argentines live in cities, and nine tenths of them can read. Argentina is about to be self-sufficient in oil and has huge natural gas deposits, boundless hydroelectric potential and enormous coal reserves that it cannot be bothered to mine. The hills are rich with copper, molybdenum, gold, silver, lead, zinc, barium and uranium, very little of it mined.

The popular jibe (among Brazilians) is that God lavished natural wealth on Argentina, but other countries complained. So God gave it Argentines, to redress the balance. This is unfair to Argentines. But they did make a mess of their politics and that, more than anything else, stopped Argentina from becoming a paradise on earth.

The juntas that ran Argentina between 1976 and 1982 were unfairly criticized as the source of Argentina's ills. In face, Perón's uniquely unpleasant legacy of nationalism, populism and military might have been the source. The subsequent juntas were certainly responsible for acting with the utmost brutality, waging a savage war against the opposition that revolted the conscience of the civilized world. The report on the fate of the disappeared, *Never Again*, compiled by the democratic government of President Raúl Alfonsín, makes appalling reading. There is a nauseating voyeurism about books on torture; yet the issue cannot be avoided in any book about Latin America. This excerpt from *Never Again* will suffice:

M de M was abducted in Buenos Aires. She was taken for a long distance in a pickup truck. Judging by the sound of crickets and other details, they took her somewhere in the country. It was like a camp, a provisional setup, with canvas sheeting and tents everywhere. They left her in a sort of room where she felt terrified and started to scream. Thus alerted, her captors put her into a tank full of water. Her breasts were hurting a lot, as she was breast-feeding at the time. . . .

Then they bound her hands and feet with wires and passed electric current through them. She began to have convulsions. They said that was the breaking in she needed in order to confess. Then they stripped and raped her.

She asked to go to the toilet. They took her naked along an open gallery full of soldiers. She remembers that they all laughed. She also recalls them taking a group of people and putting them into a helicopter; they were thrown out at the end of a rope, and each time they were raised again they were questioned. . . .

Teresa Cecilia Meschiati was abducted in the town of Córdoba: "Immediately after my arrival at La Perla, I was taken to the torture room or 'intensive therapy room.' They stripped me and tied my feet and hands with ropes to the bars of a bed, so that I was hanging from them. They attached a wire to one of the toes of my right foot. Torture was applied gradually by means of electric prods of two different intensities: one of 125 volts which caused involuntary muscle movements all over my body. They applied this to my face, eyes, mouth, arms, vagina and anus; and another of 220 volts called *la margarita* (the daisy) which left deep ulcerations which I still have and which caused a violent contraction, as if all my limbs were being torn off at once, especially in the kidneys, legs, groin and sides of the body. They also put a wet rag on my chest to increase the intensity of the shock.

"I tried to kill myself by drinking the foul water in the tub which was meant for another kind of torture called *submarino*, but I did not succeed."

Nelson Dean described the effect of electric shock torture:

(a) After torture, the soles of the feet were burnt and layers of hard skin would form, which peeled off later. Obviously the skin burnt from the electric shocks.

(b) During the application of electricity, one would lose all control over one's senses, such torture provoking permanent vomiting, almost constant defecation, etc.

As for sensations, electricity begins to rise up the body. All the parts with wires attached to them feel as though they are being torn from the body. Thus, at first, it's the feet which feel as though they are being torn off, then the legs, testicles, thorax, etc. These torture sessions went on for a period of five days, increasing in intensity. During the last few days, they repeated all the above methods and, in addition, inserted wires into my anus, testicles and penis. These tortures were carried out in a diabolical setting: the torturers, some drinking, others laughing, hitting and insulting.

On three previous visits, I had met some of the people most closely involved in Argentina's evil. One was Admiral Emilio Massera, certainly the most ruthless of the nine military men who ran the country between 1974 and 1980. The admiral was introduced to me by his chief aide, a fat naval man with a mustache and belly, a man who hugged everyone to himself as though he had known them for years, even if they had only just met. The admiral appeared a little ill at ease. He was craggily good-looking—of middle height, stocky, with the square jaw of an American movie star, piercing black eyes and a direct gaze. Soft-spoken and courteous, he smiled easily. His defect was his ordinary stature. Otherwise a more different man than Bolivia's Colonel Arce could scarcely be imagined. Massera was a man's man, a matinee idol who wanted to be president of his country but couldn't be because the navy would never be allowed to run Argentina.

He tried, nonetheless. When I met him at his imposing headquarters outside the seaside resort of La Plata he was still a member of the junta, full of authority. I had expected a robust defense of the junta of which he was a member; instead he startled me with a vigorous attack upon it.

"The government should concentrate on helping the masses," he said. "We need an end to the repression, social reform, a return to democracy." For a man who was responsible for the worst outrages against human rights in Argentina's recent history, some committed on this very naval base with its air of an athletic country club, his radicalism and populism were astonishing. But the reason for his criticism was not hard to discern. The junta was coming to the end of its term of office and Massera had wanted the presidency to rotate from General Jorge Rafael Videla to himself, as navy chief. But the army would not give up the central power. So his only hope of power lay in a return to democracy, in marshaling his bombast and good looks to become another elected Perón, pushing social justice. It was too late, though; Argentina had moved beyond the stage of mass militarism, and fascism.

Videla, Massera's brother officer, represented a very different type. Shy, remote, stiff and unsmiling in public, Videla was known as El Flaco or El Hueso—"the thin one" or "the bone"—for his gaunt appearance. The first president of the military regime that followed the hapless government of Isabelita Perón, he was the very opposite of the power-hungry Pinochet. The answers he gave me in an interview were typical of his uncommunicative nature. I asked him about the restoration of democracy. "It is not our intention to restore democracy but to install it," he replied. "That is, we will not limit ourselves to returning to the situation that existed before. . . . Obviously this democracy must possess the judicial elements which will preserve it from the risks of totalitarianism, of demagoguery and other deformities. Our prime objective is nothing less than the definitive installment of pluralist democracy. There must be no doubt of any kind about this. Argentina was a country which was born in freedom when absolutism still ruled the world. This freedom is a national passion which no one can ever extinguish."

On political parties, he commented: "We cannot conceive of a democracy without the active participation of vigorous political parties. They are the natural channel for the people's expression. We had to suspend partisan activity as a purely temporary measure, in response to the gravity of the crisis our political institutions were going through in 1976. . . . But there was no limit on the free expression of personal opinions. All the channels of social communication are open for the opinions and criticism of any citizen."

About the antiterrorist campaign, he admitted: "All countries which have suffered a war—especially when the aggressor uses sordid tactics—know that, in some moments, passion can overcome reason and make mistakes possible. . . . Contemporary history is full of conflicts in which violence reached uncontrollable levels for those running operations. . . . Even if the fight against terrorism did produce some uncontrolled action, it is, and will continue to be, the duty of the armed-forces government to consolidate a legal monopoly of coercion, severely punishing those who depart from the proper norm."

On the the subject of political prisoners, he declared, "There are no political prisoners in the Argentine republic. There are only persons who performed acts of violence and terrorism. . . . The release of Jacobo Timerman is not comparable to other cases. No deduction should be made from it in relation to people arrested for common crimes."

A man who appeared to have taken on the role of president unwillingly, Videla was motivated by what he saw as his duty, which he carried out unflinchingly and sternly. Virtually everyone concluded it to be his duty, as army chief, to take over from Isabelita; he was much criticized for waiting so long while the nation's treasury was pillaged by successive finance ministers under Isabelita's necromancer, José López Rega. Yet Videla was to preside over the horror of "the disappeared."

The war against subversion in Argentina had been very different from that carried out by Pinochet in Chile. At an early stage, Argentina's officers decided that they had better, at all costs, avoid the appalling publicity that the coup in Chile had generated. So they moved cautiously in their attempt to rein in the country's wild inflation, preferring "gradualism" to Pinochet's "shock tactics," and they moved secretly in the fight against subversion. This meant that the war was undeclared. People "disappeared" when the government's notorious Ford Falcons came and whisked them off. The fight was decentralized. Each of the heads of the armed forces had his own security service, as did each provincial governor (inevitably a military man) and many intermediate officers. The war was carried out by cells of off-duty military men, imitating the cell structure of their opponents. There were some large-scale set-piece confrontations, and some massacres, notably in the Tucumán province in the north, home of the rural-based Guerrilla Army of the Poor, which at the height of its strength had about six thousand men. For the most part the war—particularly against the Marxist wing of the Perónists, the Montoneros—was carried out clandestinely.

The inquiry into the disappeared revealed the methods of the armed forces high command and Videla's role. His only defense was that, in the furious interservice rivalry at the top, he may have had no power to order any other course, he may not have been able to restrain his men. For if the Chilean armed forces suffered from an overcentralization of authority in its command, the Argentine army suffered from being a chaos of competing warlords. Even if the kindlier explanation is accepted, however, Videla was justly sentenced to eight years in prison. As a man of duty, he bore responsibility for acts that were to disgust the Argentine people when they were revealed. Videla was not hungry for power, as Massera was, but a product of his institution; he defended himself by saying that he had done his duty as a man of integrity, and that the sentence was unjust.

Was the "dirty war" against the guerrillas in any way defensible, as the military takeover in 1976 had been? Certainly Argentina at the time appeared close to social disintegration and the two rebel armies, numbering about twelve thousand men, were the biggest guerrilla challenge to a developed society. Even in Italy, Turkey and Uruguay in the 1970s, the war had been less intense. A whole generation of revolutionary soldiers, it seemed, had abandoned the route of parliamentary democracy and chosen to take on the powers who ruled Argentina through armed conflict.

In retrospect it was possible to see that angry, armed, radical surge in context, as a reaction against a political system that had undergone a form of modified fascism, successive military governments and a return to fascism that was clearly doomed. The situation seemed to invite a murderous response from the left. It had been the army's task to cope with that response until Argentina could return to something more stable. It did so with a brutality and efficiency that shattered the left, dismayed the world and gave the country a respite. Yet many innocents suffered and Argentina was too advanced a society for such barbarity to be acceptable. The parallel with Nazi Germany, drawn by Jacobo Timerman, is correct—although on a far smaller scale. Anti-Semitism was not, as Timerman claimed, the driving force of the repression; it was merely a feature of that wider evil that Nazi Germany and Argentina shared: the tyranny of a society that, for all its surface development, had failed to nurture that respect for the individual on which freedom depends. Argentina was prepared to unleash horror versus horror, because one extreme was less horrible than the other. The junta was popular, just as Nazism had been. The dirty war was popular. I remember being accosted in an elevator in Rio de Janeiro in 1980 by a well-fed young man who asked me if I was the author of a "disgraceful" *Economist* survey of Argentina. I replied that I was. He told me that terrorists had killed his father, and gave me a look I have never forgotten. To him, I was an apologist for terrorism because I had criticized the dirty war. And yet I felt that every rule of common sense as well as morality dictated that no society can turn to lawlessness to enforce the law. In so doing it undermines the law and ultimately forfeits respect.

The soldiers must have understood that. I was first introduced to the concept of the dirty war in 1979 by Brigadier General Omar Graffigna, in many ways the most attractive, thoughtful and least blustery member of Argentina's successive military juntas. I had been granted an interview in the splendid surroundings of the air force chief's military headquarters, where he was attended by his senior officers, wearing green uniforms and discreet gold braid. He responded to my questions with politeness and amiability and a glittering shrewdness in his eyes. Small, very well groomed, with an old-fashioned mustache, he explained with the patience of one speaking to a child that "few things are as dangerous as to know only part of the truth. Argentines suffered from the actions of groups of subversive delinquents of every political color and creed. They waged a dirty war against us. They cornered us into choosing life or resigning ourselves to violent death. We accepted the challenge on the ground they picked for us. We didn't choose it. . . . We have nothing to be ashamed of." At the end of the meeting he told me that he would place a plane at my disposal to go anywhere I liked in Argentina; he recommended I visit a glacier in a lake that broke off once every few years, to spectacular effect. A man with his power could afford to be courteous. But considerations of journalistic independence caused me, against my worst instincts, to decline. Even such a man did not understand the need for the state to command more respect than its enemies.

Argentina, so long abused by rulers without this understanding, suffered a tremendous stroke of luck in 1982. The generals, who, like Pinochet, had begun to enjoy power, instituted a system of successive juntas by rotation. Postponing elections—a process that was leading to polarization—they were suddenly driven ignominiously from office, giving the country's authentic democrats the chance they were looking for. The man responsible for the debacle was Leopoldo Fortunato Galtieri.

The downfall of the generals was rooted in the country's initial policy of economic gradualism, introduced in the belief that social disorder must be avoided while the campaign against terrorism was under way. The architect of the policy was José Alfredo Martínez de Hoz, who was to be excoriated by Argentina's democrats as the destroyer of the Argentine economy. That wasn't quite the case. Martínez de Hoz was a man of acute intelligence. He had unsuccessfully tried to enter democratic politics and, although a lawyer, was an advocate of gradualist economics, directly opposed to Álvaro Alsogaray, the other guru of the Argentine economy, a committed monetarist who advocated a "short, sharp shock" to cure inflation. Martínez de Hoz doubted that Argentina's sophisticated social structure would stand for such treatment; while the Perónist trade unions would accept a measure of wage restraint, they would not stand for high unemployment.

Martínez de Hoz's reply to the monetarist enthusiasts was politically pragmatic. "The form and composition of public spending are extremely rigid," he said. "It doesn't just change from one day to the next, just as the structures of central government or of state enterprise or of public investment don't change quickly. . . . You can only understand this rigidity when you're inside the public services."

And although Martínez de Hoz could not say so, the most "rigid" public spenders of all were the armed forces themselves who would have resisted even Alsogaray's best efforts to cut their budgets. Defense spending had risen sharply, partly in response to the danger of war with Chile. The armed forces had also refused to surrender to better management, let alone to private enterprise in the form of the "strategic industries" owned by their giant conglomerate, Fabricaciones Militares. This monolith jealously guarded its accounting secrets, so nobody knew just how much public money it consumed. The firm employed fifteen thousand people, invested at least $400 million a year and produced everything from steel to electric wares and cables, sulfur and electronic goods.

Good fiscal housekeeping also went by the board where national prestige was concerned. In 1978, for example, a thumping $700 million was spent sprucing up airports, hotels and stadiums for the World Cup. In a sense, that extravagance paid off—Argentina won the cup. And, for the first time, fans could watch the matches on color television, which had just been introduced at a cost of some $100 million. An investment of $20 million to build a huge underground parking lot for the Buenos Aires military academy was another example of how economy did not begin at home for Argentina's military rulers.

Martínez de Hoz was not a man who believed in sacrifice. He was not a Friedmanite, but a firm advocate of the mixed economy who believed that the modern state should "give direction and push the economy" but should "not intervene in things which private enterprise does better." True to that philosophy, he allowed state companies to embark on major investments. Indeed, under the military government, public investment ran at an all-time high. In Isabelita's freest-spending year, 1975, it had only been 9 percent of GDP; historically it averaged some 7 percent. After 1976, however, public investment was at nearly 12 percent.

Martínez de Hoz invested $20.5 billion in state projects over three years. The lion's share of the $3½ billion spent in 1979 went to the national oil company (nearly $1 billion), the state power and water company ($650 million), state telecommunications ($450 million), and the railways ($340 million). Martínez de Hoz insisted that projects already begun be finished. He said that if the state did not spend money on the major projects needed to unlock Argentina's vast potential wealth, nobody else would. Private investment was running at a dismal 8 percent of GDP.

Even the government could not hide its disappointment at failing to appreciably cut back spending in the public sector. Its share of GDP was now about 37 percent, compared to 40 percent in 1976. Some public firms were put into private hands and the state sold its 30-percent holding in 140 companies, exercised through the National Development Board and the National Savings and Investment Bank. Martínez de Hoz claimed that state enterprises had become less inefficient. The government imposed strict limits on subsidies to the nationalized industries and controlled their prices.

There were some impressive gains in productivity by state companies. Between 1975 and 1978, output per worker increased by more than half in the nationalized oil, water and electricity companies, and by more than 10 percent in state services like the railways, subways and telecommunications. An axe was taken to the (British-built) state railway network, the sixth-biggest in the world: 5,500 of Argentina's nearly 30,000 miles of track were closed down; 43,000 out of 160,000 workers were dismissed; and the $700 million annual subsidy to the corporation was cut to less than $300 million.

While public spending was proving hard to tame, the government was at least paying for much more of it. The tax authorities were collecting, in real terms, as much tax again as they were in 1975. Taxes were raised and the system of collection made more efficient. All told, by 1978 treasury revenue was covering more than two thirds of state spending—as compared with one fifth in the first quarter of 1976.

This was the carefully crafted policy of a political sophisticate, an Argentine Metternich. It fell apart in Martínez de Hoz's hands, just as Chile's had in Pinochet's, and for the same reason. The second oil-price shock of 1979 did not hurt Argentina, which was self-sufficient in oil. But the subsequent flow of international bank lending did. The money—more than $20 billion—was dumped on Argentina, for anyone who cared to ask. This tidal wave of cash sent inflation rocketing out of control, and once in Argentina, it was not put to good use. Hotels went up all over; real estate boomed. The lending that the commercial banks were splashing out was indiscriminate. It took no account of which projects were sensible, or viable, or had any prospect of a long-term return. It was guaranteed by the Argentine government, and sovereign lending was, so the banks thought, invincible. Much of the money went straight out again, in the form of quick killings by men who knew they would be burned if their borrowings stayed in Argentina. Argentina had virtually no exchange controls at the time. The carefully crafted economic plan of Martínez de Hoz was destroyed in a few months as a result of the flood of foreign money, much as Spain's economy was destroyed by Peruvian gold in the eighteenth century.

With Martínez de Hoz's policy in ruins, so was the career of the man who had masterminded the general's rule. General Roberto Viola was a tactician, the brains behind Videla. His ambition had been to take over from Videla, and push the country very slowly and cautiously toward orderly democracy, to be the architect of a new, stable Argentina; instead, he inherited economic chaos. He suffered nervous disorders within a few months. The ambitious army chief of staff, General Leopoldo Galtieri, took power in a coup so smooth it could hardly be called one.

Galtieri was a man promoted above his station. A ladies' man, fond of uniforms, parades and striking attitudes, he was in the mold of Perón and Massera, but lacked their ruthlessness. His problem was a sticky one: to resist the increasingly shrill demands for a return to democracy—in view of the army's demonstrable economic incompetence—and to restore some respect for it. He hit upon a wholly ingenious and disastrous method.

Argentina is full of Anglophiles who date back to the old British connection, when the country was one of Britain's two Latin American friends (Mexico, where the Pearson family made its fortune, was the other). To be of English descent was to be a snob. Harrods, Claridges, cricket, Scotch whiskey, golf and country clubs—all became even more exclusive when the vulgarians Perón and Evita waged war on the British connection. Argentina thus abounds in people who consider themselves experts on Britain; I had met many of this expatriate community when I visited in the past. They were well off, proud, slightly nervous, dressed in smart gray jackets and tweeds, unmistakably English. They held themselves aloof from the society to which they belonged, seeing its faults all too clearly. But they were equally critical of Britain, a country in decline that took no interest in Argentina. They were like expatriate communities everywhere, only more so.

Close to the expatriates was a community of Argentine snobs, of which Nicanor Costa Méndez, as a senior diplomat, was a prime example. Speaking impeccable English, dressed in the English style, Costa Méndez was more English than the English. And he knew how the English reacted. For that reason he was chosen as Galtieri's foreign minister, for the only way that the new president believed that the army's reputation could be saved was to pull off the foreign policy coup that had eluded Argentina for centuries: the retaking of Las Malvinas.

Whatever the historical truth, every Argentine learns as a child that the Falklands are Argentine, unjustly seized by the British through a trick. The Argentines are no more nationalistic than most people; in some respects they are less so than the underdeveloped Latin American countries, which feel that their role in the world is peripheral. Argentina is too much of a mix of immigrants, and a recent mix at that (a majority are postwar Italian immigrants) to have an exalted sense of nationalism. Traditionally its elites have looked toward Europe—France, Britain, Italy and Germany—with a nostalgia that is the very opposite of nationalism.

But nationalism, like any political passion, can be created; and as Argentina had so little sense of identity, its fervor was all the keener concerning two issues that in themselves were hardly worthy of consideration. They were, first, the argument with Chile about the tiny islets of Picton, Lennox and Nueva in the Beagle Channel, and, second, the Falklands issue. "Argentina has not even occupied most of its own territory in Patagonia. Can you imagine what it is going to do with another huge slice of wilderness?" a member of the Anglo-Argentine community scoffed in conversation with me. "What we can't understand is why the British set such store by it." He dismissed out of hand the idea that it could ever be the source of a conflict.

But General Galtieri saw it as a way out of the mess of his military predecessors' making. And Costa Méndez, who knew the British,

told him that Britain was toothless. It would protest indignantly if
Argentina occupied the islands. It would go to the United Nations.
Talks would take place; commissions would study the problem. But
nothing would happen.

The miscalculation was total, and it was not confined to a mis-
judgment about the character of Prime Minister Margaret Thatcher.
It was a miscalculation as to the mood of a nation in which nationalism seemed to be outdated and which had divested itself of an
empire without adverse domestic reaction. Try to take something—
even something worthless—by force and the British *will* react, even
if they had earlier seemed only too willing to hand the Falklands
peacefully back. They showed this by sailing into the south Atlantic
and proving themselves equal to the colossal task of taking the islands
from a poor conscript army fighting much closer to its home base.
Galtieri was exposed as a tin man. The armed forces were discred-
ited in the only asset they had left—their status as defenders of the
nation—and after a year of attempting to cling to power, they withdrew unconditionally, leaving the civilians to take charge. And to
universal astonishment, the civilians, who once elected Perón, behaved themselves this time.

To understand why this was so remarkable, it is necessary to back up
a little. What happened in Argentina was, in a sense, one version of
the earthquake that had shaken Latin America when industrialization slammed into sleepy societies long run by traditional oligar-
chies.

Argentina was an arriviste among Latin American nations: the
Spanish kings built their empire around Peru, leaving Buenos Aires
as a minor port on the edge of a vast expanse of flatland inhabited by
a few Indians. The port—the inhabitants of Buenos Aires are still
dubbed *porteños*—dominated the country. The place was an urban
slum and fairly lawless. As people moved into the interior to control
the wild herds of cattle that roamed it, a new breed of wild West
cowboys, the gauchos, evolved. They tanned leather (though their
own boots were made by putting a man's leg into a calf's hide that
was still warm from skinning), living off the meat of the cattle, even
drinking their blood.

The cussedness of these two elements—the wild men from the
countryside and the fast men from the port—caused the Argentines

to shrug off Spanish rule in 1810, at an earlier stage than other Latin Americans. When royalists from Peru tried to restore Spanish monarchy, they were soundly beaten by the Argentines as they came down from the Andes, but the Argentines lost when they chased the Peruvians back up the mountains.

The new nation disintegrated into conflict between the gauchos and the *porteños*, which was temporarily stopped by the country's first real president, Bernardino Rivadavia. The place fell apart after he departed in 1827, until a brutish gaucho, Juan Manuel de Rosas, became governor of Buenos Aires province in 1829. Having cowed the province, Rosas went back to his country farm for a while, then returned when order fell apart again. He imposed a hard, provincial conservative order upon Argentina that discouraged contact with the outside world. In 1852 he was overthrown by an equally thuggish gaucho, his lifelong sidekick, Justo José de Urquiza, who, resenting the rule of Buenos Aires, founded a new capital at Rosario. A conflict developed between Buenos Aires, whose merchant class detested the crude gaucho, and the rest of the country. After a skirmish between the two rival armies at Pavón, Urquiza backed down and the Buenos Aires leader, Bartolomé Mitre, took power.

Mitre's successor, Sarmiento, drove the gaucho influence from Buenos Aires, and the country settled down to a modest economic boom, based on industrialization using capital from the export of abundant raw materials. Immigrants flooded in, railways snaked across the empty land, and refrigerated ships created a huge market for Argentina's wealth in cattle. An oligarchic system of government was created, but below it the middle class and the working class were pressing for power. By 1916 Hipólito Yrigoyen had emerged as leader of the Radical Party, demanding universal suffrage. An able but shy man, he held the forces for a more extensive social revolution at bay during two spells as president by conceding just enough to keep the new voters happy. He was overthrown by a military man, General José Félix Uriburu, who ended the country's brief tradition of democratic politics. The army seemed ready after a time to hand power back to the Radicals, but an experiment in doing so collapsed during the middle of the Second World War, when General Arturo Rawson seized power, extinguishing the country's constitutional tradition.

The rising power in the army was Juan Domingo Perón, a good-looking extrovert who could make flowery speeches, and who sought to carve out a new and impregnable constituency for himself by dominating the army and by seeking support from the working classes. In this he consciously copied the methods of Hitler, Mussolini and Franco. Perón took formal power in 1946 and sent in the *descamisados*, the shirtless army—his brownshirts—to enforce authority, through thuggery and torture. He nationalized the railways, banks, insurance companies, the means of communication and transportation. Industrialization took place at a rapid pace, while the countryside was used to provide cheap food for the masses. Tariff barriers were imposed to allow Argentina to build up its own industries. Perón's commitment to improving the lot of the workers was, however, against the interests of the army. His economic experiment proved disastrous, and the army and his conservative opponents removed him in 1955. The army seemed motivated by high ideals, but every time it tried to hand power back to civilians, it was the followers of El Lider (he was not allowed to run himself) who were elected. When, in 1973, he was permitted to run on the grounds that he was no longer a real threat, he was too old, and his hapless wife, Isabelita, inherited the crown and presided over the shambles that brought in the army again.

With Perón gone, the mixture of right and left that was Peronism began to sort itself out. For a long time it was dominated by the "verticalists" who still looked to Isabelita—imprisoned on a lake island—to run the movement. But beneath them, the middle classes were making themselves felt. The party began to resemble the Democratic Party in the United States—a coalition of labor leaders and middle-class liberals. The Radical Party, meanwhile, unseated by the ghastly interlude of Peronism, had shed its historic leader, Ricardo Balbín. Two men fought to lead the party—Fernando de la Rúa, an ascetic intellectual from the old upper class, and Raúl Alfonsín, a bourgeois lawyer, very moderate, very independent. Alfonsín won, and went on to win the presidency.

His leadership was masterful. His first act was to put the army finally in its place. Justice against the military men was allowed to proceed, without being vengeful. The trials were slow, a demonstration of judicial fairness. The prison sentences were criticized as being too lenient, but the purpose was not to be punitive so much as to establish the supremacy of the civilian law over the military.

There were mutterings in the barracks, but as long as Alfonsín remained liked, no more than that. The sentence meted out for Galtieri's military incapacity and political misjudgments during the Falklands War was not even contested by the army, although there were later to be stirrings among middle-ranking officers.

Alfonsín moved slowly on the economic front, satisfying the growing expectations of the Peronist unions while the economy moved into deeper trouble. But once he felt secure enough he acted with decision, bringing in the shock measures of the Plan Austral, which included a freeze on wages and prices and knocking three digits off the value of the currency at a stroke. This slashed Argentina's inflation. At first no one trusted that it would work. But it proved popular in a country accustomed to an economy out of control.

Alfonsín's third move was to defuse his country's pent-up nationalism after the Falklands War. He successfully negotiated a deal with Chile, based on papal mediation, over the Beagle Channel dispute, and then submitted this to a referendum. On the Falklands issue he decided the timing was wrong, that wounds must be allowed to heal, and he declined to negotiate with Britain for as long as Mrs. Thatcher refused to discuss the issue of sovereignty.

It seemed that this bourgeois, astute leader had at last broken with the two jinxes of Argentine politics, the army and Peronism. If the two-party setup could survive, a Radical Party that resembled America's Republican Party in its conservative appeal and a Peronist Party that resembled the Democratic Party in its labor links and liberal appeal might emerge to give the country stability. The Alfonsín presidency was to be crucial to what is potentially the richest country in Latin America if only political stability could be attained.

Argentina was truly a treasure chest of natural resources. For one, Argentina had oil. In 1907, two workers near the Patagonian port of Comodoro Rivadavia, trying to dig a well, found black stuff oozing out. When the oil price jumped in 1973, Argentina was gloomily concluding that half of its reserves of 5.3 billion barrels had been used up. Five years of exploration later, Argentina found a further 2 billion barrels in the ground. The country had enough for at least another thirteen years at rising rates of production.

The largest new field was in the Gulf of San Jorge, near Comodoro Rivadavia, where reserves of some 240 million barrels were found and 530,000 barrels a year were already being produced. Most of the oil had been found offshore in the gulf or near the Magellan Straits. There were more than eighty offshore rigs operating. But oil was also being found on land. The oil was being drilled largely by private companies. Foreign oil companies reckoned that the going was good in a country that, for all its political uncertainy, had a long history of know-how and facilities for oil exploration.

Argentina already produced 93 percent of the oil it consumed. By 1985 it was self-sufficient. It aimed to increase production by 40 percent over the following five years, at a total investment cost of some $10 billion, half of which the government hoped would be put up by private companies. The state oil company, IPF, managed about two thirds of the wells. Argentina's oilmen said cautiously that the country was unlikely to export oil unless it found bigger reserves.

Argentina also had gas—some 385 million cubic meters of it, just discovered, most of it in an extensive field in the southwestern province of Neuquén. There was thought to be an equal amount still to be found. In 1979 Argentina was still importing some 6½ million cubic meters of gas from Bolivia, but was planning to build two pipelines, each one thousand miles long, to transport the gas to centers of population. By 1984 the government planned to produce 150,000 tons of natural gas a year; by 1988, 174,000 tons; and by 1997, 192,000 tons—or rather more than Argentina's industries could use, even on the most optimistic assumptions about their growth in production. Argentina wondered what to do with the surplus. Its nearest neighbors—Bolivia, Paraguay and Chile—were not likely to want it. Building a pipeline to Brazil would be expensive. So the Argentines were thinking of liquefying it and shipping it abroad—though they recognized that the cost of building plants and loading facilities would be high.

While oil and gas would run out in the end, hydroelectric power would not. And by another piece of good luck, Argentina's open-ended Andean valleys were the ideal shape for damming up rivers. Some 63 percent of Argentina's electrical consumption came from oil-burning power stations, 23 percent from gas, 6 percent from hydroelectric plants and 2 percent from nuclear power stations. By the end of the century, if the government has its way, 73 percent of electrical energy will be generated by hydroelectric power, 15 percent by nuclear power and only 12 percent by fossil fuels.

By the mid-1980s three big hydroelectric plants were almost finished: the $1¼ billion Salta Grande dam, in which Uruguay had a share, had a capacity of 1,620 megawatts; the $3 billion Yacyretá-Apipe dam, in which Paraguay shared, had a capacity of 4,500 megawatts; and the El Chocón–Cerros Colorados complex had a capacity of 1,700 megawatts. The energy minister planned to spend $22½ billion on hydroelectric power by the end of the century.

Argentina, despite its abundant natural resources, is also the only Latin American country to have produced nuclear energy. The Atucha power plant, opened in 1974, had a capacity of 600 megawatts. The director of the country's nuclear energy commission then pushed ahead with an ambitious program to give Atucha a twin and to complete three more nuclear power stations by 1997. The energy minister said that nuclear power was being developed to give Argentina self-sufficiency in energy until the year 2100. That made the government look farsighted; but how did all these proposed investments fit in with the economy minister's austerity program?

The Argentines also had eleven thousand tons of natural uranium. When the nuclear program was fully underway, the power stations would use up six hundred tons a year. The Argentines were certain that there was more uranium elsewhere. Since the power stations do not need enriched uranium, Argentina was untroubled by the anti-nuclear lobby—even though Atucha was only sixty miles upstream from Buenos Aires (and Argentina's terrorists had been able to penetrate any kind of security in the past).

Argentina had coal, too—about 540,000 tons of it at Río Turbio in the south. Of that, only a paltry 1,500 tons was mined every year. The coal was expensive to mine and to transport. "Why should we when we have so many cheaper alternative energy sources?" the energy minister asked me. "We will when we need it." I saw his point.

Argentina had a long tradition of leaving its riches in the ground. Unlike its poorer Andean neighbors, Chile, Bolivia and Peru, Argentina had left one side of the mountain cordillera virtually untouched. Total mining production reached 62 million tons—amounting to less than 1 percent of GDP. Argentina imported some $800 million worth of minerals every year. Yet surveys suggested that the mountains were well stocked with copper, molybdenum, lead, zinc and barium. Less than half of Argentina's potential mineral-bearing lands had been prospected.

The minister of mines, Fernando Puca Prota, aimed to open up the "new frontier" of Argentina's mineral wealth. Nine big mines were to be started shortly. The biggest new private mine was thirteen thousand feet up, at Pachón in the western province of San Juan, where copper reserves of some 800 million tons had been found. The mine cost nearly $1 billion to bring into production. The owners, Minera Aguilar, planned to produce 100 million tons of copper, 1,700 tons of concentrated molybdenum, 350,000 tons of sulfuric acid and a little gold and silver a year after the mine began production in 1984.

The biggest new state mine was Bajo la Alumbrera, in Catamarca province, where there were thought to be 350 million tons in copper reserves. Each year the mine was expected to produce 60,000 tons of copper, 500 tons of molybdenum, 245,000 tons of sulfuric acid, 12 tons of silver and 6 tons of gold. Needless to say, Fabricaciones Militares took a share in the mine.

Puca Prota reckoned that Argentina needed foreign money to exploit its mineral deposits fully, and his ministry tried to lure in the multinationals with tax concessions. Under a new mining law, the costs of prospecting, vehicles, equipment, buildings and technical assistance were to be tax-deductible. Value-added tax would be levied at a low rate on mineral products. For projects that got an extra seal of approval from the government, profits tax would be levied at a low rate and could be deferred. Argentine firms were offered even greater concessions than foreign companies. This meant that they needed only to pay a third of the costs of developing a mine and a fifth of the exploration costs. If nothing was found, the state would write off the debt.

Argentina thus became the test case for Latin America's new democracies. It could be a new Australia or a South Africa minus the defects. It could be restored to first place in the Latin American economy from which Perón pulled it, a society whose civic authority had caught up with its economic development. It could be a country that had recovered from populism and militarism, that had emerged from a British contest between waterfront tensions and outback cowboys' rule into a sophisticated republicanism. It is too easy to dismiss the country as a mixture of all that is worst and most flamboyant in the Spanish and Italian elements that are dominant in its makeup. The riches of the land have made it a country where the spoils are squabbled over, rather than one where people feel compelled to work hard. Yet it is finding its equilibrium.

The last call on my attempt to try to understand Argentina was down to the south, the far south where I passed up the opportunity to take the old Patagonian express. Instead I took a plane down the coast of that bleak tail of a continent. We flew past the pampas, where it merged into Patagonia, the windswept plateau covered in shallow pools of water. We saw Mar del Plata; Bahía Blanca, that seaside resort of unalloyed vulgarity; and Trelew, the Welsh port where they still speak the language of heaven. We saw Comodoro Rivadavia, and at last landed at Río Gallegos, a port with a rudimentary air terminal that resembled an air base in a Second World War film.

I took the short hop over the Magellan Straits to Tierra del Fuego on an Argentine air force plane, and felt a deep insecurity about reaching the edge of the world. Tierra del Fuego was an awesomely inhospitable clump of black mountains soaring into clouds capped by ice and glaciers slurping into the sea. Our tiny aircraft was buffeted by winds as it—narrowly, it seemed—avoided the peaks and came steeply down in a circle to put into a settlement on the sea, looking out to windswept rocks protruding into the south Atlantic.

As we came into land, I felt a sense of loneliness and desolation, which was not dispelled when I took a cab—there were only three—into town and proceeded from boardinghouse to boardinghouse to try to find a place to stay. It was cold and rainswept, and I did not fancy sleeping out. At last I found a plain hotel with cozy rooms called the Malvinas and, feeling a traitor to my country, opened its doors. As evening fell upon the corrugated iron shacks that comprised most of the town of Ushuaia, and over the gray swell of froth-ridden sea that extended round the last black rocks between South America and Antartica, I stumbled down the narrow streets where men moved quickly, huddled against the wind, to a *whiskería*, an insalubrious dive that nevertheless cheered me up and served the best sea crab I have ever eaten. I fell into conversation with the locals, who were fascinated that an Englishman should come down here and seemed to bear no resentment, although they lived as close to the Falklands as any Argentines did. I got back to the Las Malvinas hotel very merry and felt comfortable in my bed in that small warm room with the wind shrieking outside.

Next day, I took a taxi back across Tierra del Fuego. A young woman wanted to travel the same way and I offered her a lift. Pert, pretty and in her early thirties, she bore life with the provincial propriety and cheerfulness of the young officer's wife she was. (Ushuaia was mostly populated by people working at the Argentine military base.) Though stuffy at first, she soon relaxed as the journey proceeded, telling me of the loneliness of living so far south. She said the nearest community was Chilean, but because of the hostility between the two countries, very little contact took place. When she had been on a visit there, she had been surprised that the people were so like herself.

And of course they were, because they were a settler community in a cold climate, struggling to keep warm. They had more in common with the inhabitants of northern Norway than with the volatile masses of Buenos Aires. Yet she was wholly Argentine, and proud of it: she vigorously defended Argentina's cause in the Beagle Channel dispute. I kept off the subject of the Falklands. As we crossed a semitundra region toward great mountains while the interminable rain lashed a rough-water lake nearby, I reflected that national stereotypes, here as elsewhere in Latin America, were far too simple.

URUGUAY

I TOOK THE FERRY ACROSS THE RIVER PLATE, A GREAT MUDDY RED expanse sprawling across the face of Buenos Aires, and wondered how it came to be called the Silver River.

The boat plowed across that dull sea, and we landed at the port of Montevideo, which many Latin Americans consider the most civilized city on the continent. In many ways it is, being broad-avenued, leafy and prosperous, with the square apartment blocks that characterize the Spanish Riviera. Yet I found it characterless, a very middle-class city, mercifully spared the slums of its Latin American neighbors, but deprived also of their life and history and character. It was like living in an airport building—clean, efficient, practical, but nothing more.

Its politics had a similarly laundered quality. A rich country, where prosperity came from the farming hinterland in the form of wool and beef, Uruguay was frequently compared with Switzerland, but its politics had been nineteenth-century British, with that quintessential division within its middle class between liberals and conservatives. The Blancos (Whites) were the conservatives, based in the land that provided the nation's wealth; the urban sophisticates were Colorados (Reds). As the country was without an effective armed force of its own, it became the plaything of the larger powers on either side, Brazil and Argentina, which threw their support alternately to the two parties, in an attempt to turn the country into a puppet. For a century, the country was virtually divided between the two.

At the beginning of the century it was united under one ruler, President José Batlle, who instituted a kind of power sharing between the two parties and launched social reforms, including guarantees of workers' rights, a social security system, pensions and a tax system. The world depression momentarily troubled Batlle's creation, and a dictatorship took over briefly. But Uruguay returned to constitutional government under enlightened Colorados rule until the end of the 1950s, when a fall in the wool price shook the economy and returned the rule of the Blancos, who had been out of power for nearly a century. The Blancos proved utterly incompetent, and the economy crashed into debt. At this time it became apparent that the country had lived beyond its means; fully a third of the population lived off the state as employees or retirees. Strikes became endemic. Then, in the late 1960s the Tupamaros came on the scene.

In a sense, the Tupamaros (named after Tupac Amaru, the Peruvian Indian rebel, which was ironic in a country with no Indian population) were the quintessential urban terrorists. Mainly middle-class and university educated, they were frustrated by a country that had nothing to offer them beyond the faded shopfronts of a declining consumer society. They were youth revolting against a governing class grown fat, but they did not represent the small working class. They were, in fact, rebels without a cause, with romantic ideals based on Trotskyite theories of perpetual revolution. The Tupamaros set up a "parallel government" with "people's courts" and "people's prisons"—later to be copied by the Baader-Meinhof gang and the Red Brigades in Europe. They kidnapped foreign diplomats, bankers and executives. As terrorism spread and the economy bumped along the bottom, the country's democracy crumbled. Juan Maria Bordaberry, a landowner and former Blanco, became president, and used the army to crush opposition. The army used Bordaberry as a figurehead while initiating a policy of vicious repression in the fight against terrorism.

I met a prominent Uruguayan journalist at a café in Montevideo. It was nice to watch the unhurried, well-dressed people stroll past as the traffic moved at a leisurely crawl. We sat outdoors in the shade of a tree. He was a man in his late twenties, good-looking, slightly fleshy, with curly, greasy hair over the back of his collar, who looked relaxed and smoked casually. He was educated, well read, lived a comfortable existence. I asked him about torture, whether it had really been as bad as they said in Uruguay.

"Hombre," he said with macho emphasis. "*Claro que sí!*" Of course. "And the army's response was necessary. The bastards were killing people indiscriminately. They were terrorists. They had to be broken. You do not sympathize with someone who kills ordinary people for the sake of a political point. The torture was needed to find out who their collaborators were, so that fewer lives would be lost in the long run.

"Let me tell you a story. The terrorists planted a bomb. The police had a suspect who knew where that bomb was planted: they had to find out before it went off. So they tortured him. And he talked, and lives were saved. You are not telling me that was unjustified? Hurting a guilty person so that the innocent might be spared? He had the means to avoid his being tortured: simply to talk."

I replied weakly that when the state descended to the methods of its opponents, it helped to create the conditions that allowed those opponents to thrive; that it was playing into the hands of terrorism, which would exploit such examples of state viciousness to radicalize the people. *Tanto peor, tanto mejor*—that was the old anarchist dictum. It was possible, as West Germany and Italy had shown, to fight terrorism without resorting to state terrorism.

He shrugged, incredulous: "You think ordinary people oppose police brutality? They applaud it, against these monsters." He was probably right about that, and in his example, he may have been right too. Yet I shuddered to hear such a knee-jerk reaction from a well-fed scion of the middle class, and was shaken more by my inability to counter his argument convincingly.

The country's vicious response to a vicious problem—Uruguay had, by the mid-1970s, more political prisoners as a proportion of the population than any country in Latin America (altogether 50,000 people were arrested, although only 170 "disappeared")—proved effective. The Tupamaros crumbled. (Uruguay was at least to be spared the problem of the *desaparecidos;* suspects ended up in jail.) But the pressure for a return to democracy soon began to build again among the middle class, in a country that by the late 1970s was not

doing materially better under the generals than under the civilians.
The government was soundly defeated in a referendum intended to
legitimize military rule. When that pressure for change pushed the
generals out, it was the country's old democratic parties—the Colorados and the Blancos—that reemerged, for better or for worse. The
end of the military experiment left that burgher city-state chastened,
less smug, economically slightly better off, and, it seemed, more
ready to abandon its rentier existence and work for a living. In the
end it seemed, the middle classes did care about political liberty—
and also disliked police brutality as the mass campaign against the
civilian government's attempt to exonerate the soldiers responsible
for human-rights excesses was later to show; fully 550,000 people
signed a petition to overturn their pardons. This was not apparent
while the generals ruled, however.

Uruguay's importance in Latin America and the world was minuscule. But it worried many Latin American societies that even a
bourgeois society with a good standard of living and a magnificent
record of constitutional government could succumb to the ills of
economic chaos, terrorism and military rule. The concern was a little
exaggerated: Uruguay's very smallness encouraged the evils from
which it suffered: the Tupamaros were the revolt of the 1960s young
against the old, the revolt of a genuine but warped idealism against
an overmaterial existence, laced with a thoroughly Latin American
viciousness. Uruguay's overriding conservatism—the conservatism
that led even a liberal journalist to approve of torture (whatever the
rights and wrongs, how many journalists around the world would
adopt such a position?)—and its lack of frontier spirit, of any place
to go out and improve things, were breeding grounds for hard and
abstract ideologies. Chile and Argentina suffered terrorism for iden-
tifiable reasons: Argentina was emerging from an era of gangster
politics, Chile was still immersed in tyranny. But the third of the
southern cone countries, Uruguay, was too different to teach any
lessons—save perhaps that petty-mindedness can pervert ambition.
Had the country been absorbed by Brazil or Argentina in the first
place, is restless young might have found other ways of working off
their ennui than by killing people.

PART IV

THE TRAIL OF RICHES

May God not permit that I die
Without returning to São Paulo
Without seeing Street 15
And the progress of São Paulo.

GONÇALVES DIAS

THE FINAL GROUP OF COUNTRIES ON MY JOURNEY HAD PROSPEROUS futures beckoning until the debt crisis of the late 1970s strangled their promise. In the first half of this decade, Brazil, Venezuela and Mexico were vibrant with economic expansion, with citizens at work, with the exuberance of high hopes. These were countries so alive that the envy of wealth found in stagnant societies seemed nonexistent. These were countries with new frontiers, countries opening up new lands, growing at a staggering rate, engaged in a frenetic social upheaval that, while generating immense problems, was on the whole improving the lives of all residents—albeit some more gradually than others.

As in Southeast Asia, politics had in a sense become subordinate to what the Brazilians inelegantly describe as "developmentalism." Politics was the national sport in many slower-moving countries, a constant distraction from poverty for the masses, bearing the hope of better times through miraculous political upheavals that rarely came to pass. Brazil, Mexico and Venezuela, by contrast, seemed to grow richer whoever was in charge. So people got on with the business of improving their lot without taking too much notice of the political consequences. With the onset of the debt crisis, this began to change.

Brazil seemed to me a budding superpower, a United States in the making. Like America's, its economy was continental and decentralized, capable of the large-scale capital accumulation needed to create explosive industrialization. The emerging prosperity compensated for the decline of earlier periods. Unlike the United States, the great engine behind this progress was the state, not private capital; and the astonishing thing about Brazilian state capitalism was that, for all its occasionally gargantuan mistakes, it worked. When even the debt crisis of the eighties failed to end Brazil's economic expansion, it was hard to believe that this minicontinent was not on the road to becoming a country in the second league, just behind the superpowers, certainly Latin America's regional giant.

Not as large but also hopeful, Mexico and Venezuela were fueled by enormous oil revenues. Mexico's aging one-party system, based on patronage, bribery, voting fraud and, in the last resort, coercion, produced some brilliant technocrats to run the machinery of government and to channel the country's wealth. But corruption took its toll, and the inefficiencies and misdirection of a large part of the oil revenues soon piled up. Even so, Mexico might have survived the debt crisis—indeed, it might have emerged from the crisis with a more soundly based economy—but for the fall in oil prices. Venezuela's smaller population made it easier for the country to enjoy its oil boom: there were fewer people to share the wealth and more wealth to develop in a country that had been one of Latin America's most backward before the advent of oil. Venezuela, which on the whole spent its oil revenues more sensibly than Mexico, seemed likely to survive both the debt crisis and the fall in the oil price without too much trouble.

Of the three, Venezuela was probably the most remarkable because, after three centuries of rule by some of the fiercest of Latin America's military dictators, it had forged a stable two-party democracy that survived through the decades of oil prosperity. Brazil, against the expectations of two developmentalist presidents of Rooseveltian stature—Getúlio Vargas, who became a dictator, and Juscelino Kubitschek, who built Xanadu—lapsed into political silliness under a demagogue, João Goulart, who became president by accident. This provoked a coup in 1964 by Brazil's always politically ambitious army. The army embarked on its own "developmentalist" experiment, again using the formidable power of the state economy built by technocrats, who were now all the rage in Latin America. Brazil's military regime—nimbler than those of neighboring Latin American countries and much less savage—was destroyed by the debt crisis. In the ensuing years, Brazil promisingly accepted the government of a modern democrat, Tancredo Neves, and his initially lackluster successor, José Sarney.

In Mexico, the political system proved resilient in accommodating the pressure for more populist policies, while pursuing a moderately sensible economic policy; but the strains in the world's oldest one-party system were beginning to show by the mid-1980s.

Upon these three economies rested Latin America's reputation as a continent that was not only going places but overcoming the massive problems of accelerated development and the hopes of the rest of the underdeveloped world in the last quarter of the twentieth century. The trail of El Dorado might yet lead, after all the disappointments, to riches—not as great as those of the First America but perhaps not all that far off either.

BRAZIL

BRAZIL IS AT LEAST THREE COUNTRIES WITH AT LEAST THREE CAPITAL cities. But one of these cities—not the official capital—is preeminent. São Paulo, where my flight from Montevideo landed, is one of the world's great industrial complexes, a monster megalopolis, a concourse of the most hectic human activity in the world, rendering New York slow by comparison.

The city is the fastest-growing on earth and is almost undoubtedly destined to be the world's largest city by the end of the century. A small town one hundred years ago, it now has thirteen million people and its population, growing at the rate of 4.2 percent a year, is expected to reach twenty-five million people by the year 2000.

No fewer than half of São Paulo's inhabitants were born outside the city: people from all of Brazil are attracted to this magnet of wealth. Nearly 40 percent of Brazil's economic activity is concentrated in São Paulo, and a fifth of its population lives there. Wealth per capita is twice that of the rest of Brazil. Its manufacturing wealth is more than five times greater than that of the rest of the country.

To come to São Paulo as I did from small-town Montevideo is a shock. The aircraft glides over shantytowns of poor wooden huts. These endless acres lead to carpets of apartment blocks, shabby off-white concrete buildings in tidy rows with no green space between them. The aircraft glides lower and the taller skyscrapers approach, not so tall and certainly not so elegant or varied as those of New York City. Yet there are hundreds, maybe a thousand of them, a great urban cluster of featureless, gray buildings knotted together, connected by highways and overpasses and underpasses in a city that seems to function on two or three levels, with different layers of road. It reminded me of nothing so much as Fritz Lang's film *Metropolis*, this constant buzz of mechanical life, these people apparently encased in office blocks, these millions of tiny windows.

The plane landed in a gap between the skyscrapers, and I was whisked by a São Paulo taxi along the underpasses and overpasses into the city center. Here the skyscrapers are built with more imagination, shimmering black mirrors or structures of curved glass. One is heartened to see some evidence of the human spirit in this jungle of buildings that seems, from street level, to be virtually limitless. I reached the Hotel Jaragua, in the very heart of the city, and found my legs and lungs straining and my eyes smarting from the thick black grime that clogged the air and seemed to have invaded the hotel lobby.

Upstairs in my room I gazed out on the cars and scurrying figures below. Nothing of a human scale was visible, and the people for whom the city was presumably built seemed lost and utterly alone.

It was only a first impression. The next was of work, of men and women, ceaseless cigarettes and more perpetual motion. São Paulo men either wore suits or shirtsleeves; they were small, close-cropped, friendly; they were coffee drinkers, addicted to fast food, quick office snacks, getting up early and working late. The work ethic is utterly different in this country with Portuguese roots from that in Spanish-speaking Latin America, different even from the dutiful Protestant work ethic that shaped North America. A man supporting his family would think nothing of working in the same job from six in the morning to eight at night, in the effort to get ahead, to get a slightly better apartment, to keep his wife happy.

But when they play, they play hard. The shopping center—pedestrian-only—contained a throng of well-dressed women shopping for smart clothes suitable for the vibrant nightlife, evenings of theater and concerts. Some of the best rock concerts in the world take place in São Paulo; there are nightclubs of a wholly uninhibited kind, restaurants of every nationality. São Paulo is a melting pot that, in addition to Portuguese, contained Syrians, Japanese, Italians, Chinese, Germans.

Paulistas are cosmopolitan, modern; they like to grumble about their city because they have confidence in it, but they are bursting with civic pride. São Paulo's mayor, Olavo Setúbal, told me at the beginning of an interview, with a gesture toward his office window: "Don't we have a splendid city? Beautiful parks, beautiful gardens." He was pointing to a small patch of green, an insignificance in the urban sprawl; I tactfully agreed. Environment was clearly a relative matter; it seemed to me that São Paulo residents had so little breathing space that they appreciated any slight improvement in their surroundings. Yet they rarely paused for contemplation. Open-plan offices were popular in the city because they allowed direct communication with other offices. This saved time, even though most people would have preferred personal offices. This was not a city built for human pleasure, but for work.

In the city center there is little time to think of the plight of the lower classes. There are, in fact, two separate urban centers , the city of the workers and the city of those who want to work—the "marginals." The workers are an upper class, and tend to be accommodated in apartments provided for them by their companies. The marginals, a large pool of labor, occasionally employed, partly employed or unemployed, live at the low end of the social system of a country that has vast planning problems, because of its uncontrolled growth. There are 4.5 square meters of green acre per inhabitant, compared to an international minimum of 8. Only two fifths of the roads have been paved, and twenty-six thousand roads have been built by private developers without government permission. Half a million inhabitants live in houses without electricity, while only half have piped water and a third have drains. Three quarters of the houses on the "periphery," as the shantytown around São Paulo is called, throw their sewage into open holes, or just on the ground.

Transportation is chaotic because, as the housing and the factories have been built far apart, roads have been constructed across the city and the workers have to fight their way through the traffic in the daily rush for work. The buses carry 6.8 million passengers per day, at a rate of 130 per bus, double the official maximum. The newest slums are as desperately poor as anything to be found in Santiago or Bogotá.

But the workers in São Paulo's booming industries live better. The

ABC complex is the city's biggest, and includes the suburbs of Santo André, São Bernardo and São Caetano, huge industrial suburbs where the city's factories grind on, day and night. In 1980 I had visited São Paulo in the middle of a series of strikes staged by Luís Inácio da Silva—"Lula"—which did for Brazil's workers what Solidarity's protests did for Poland's. The scene had all the dignity and pathos of those first strikers for workers' rights. Inside a grim stadium, hundreds of thousands of workers had gathered, clutching statues of the Virgin Mary and other religious objects. They were quiet, well disciplined, in open-necked shirts but otherwise well dressed, with all the dignity of respectable working men.

They stood and listened as their leaders harangued them: Lula was a giant beer-bellied man with a bushy black beard, a loud laugh and abundant curly hair plastered to the top of his sweating forehead. He looked like Captain Bluebeard with his T-shirt riding high up his black hairy stomach; he was loud-voiced as a speaker, born to the part; and yet his words were actually conciliatory, despite his tone. He urged the workers to remain calm, not to take things into their own hands, not to fight for their rights.

As he stepped down from the podium in that quiet stadium filled with people, a helicopter gunship suddenly swung low, clattering loudly over the strikers' heads. "Your friends have come to pick you up," exclaimed Lula in sour humor to me, as the only "gringo" present beside him on the podium. In fact the helicopter was probably on a routine photography trip to intimidate the strikers. No one moved; there was no panic. It disappeared like an angry wasp in the hot blue sky.

Afterward at the strikers' headquarters, the camaraderie was something to be witnessed. Great crowds of beer-swilling, good-hearted union members kept their vigil with nothing to do, holding song-and-dance sessions to while away the time. As I watched the cheering, clapping revelers in that bright room in the industrial heart of the world's fastest-growing country, I could see through the large plate windows a great red glow illuminating the sky from the steel furnaces that ran through the night using nonunion labor. These were dark Satanic mills where great new wealth was being created; out of it a working class was growing, struggling for its rights.

And struggle it was. São Paulo's strikers were bedeviled by the fact that, with the city's vast pool of unemployed, it was possible to find substitutes without difficulty. The employers even sometimes gave in to strikers' demands, then fired the workers and reemployed them at a lower wage to maximize their profits. To maintain an effective strike, São Paulo's unions had to create a vast sense of solidarity among the work force and keep the unemployed from taking the jobs. Inevitably, strong-arm methods were used, but they were no worse than the tactics used against the strikers.

The strike leader, Lula, himself was too important, and too moderate, to be murdered; he was arrested and later released. The strike, the largest in Brazil's history, was finally broken through the use of nonunion labor. It was a primal struggle to establish the rights of the working man in a capitalist system based on pure profit accumulation and an inexhaustible supply of labor. Unlike Poland, Brazil did not need the power of martial law to suppress the strike; it was a freer society than Poland, and what was born in São Paulo that year was later to express itself in a major political party, Lula's Workers' Party, which established itself as a major force of the left when democracy came in 1985.

The next day I took a trip down to Rodovia dos Imigrantes, the highway built to link São Paulo with the port of Santos on the coast. It was a remarkable construction sweeping through mountains and dense swampy land below, to relieve the hard-pressed two-lane road where traffic barely moved. One of the construction managers told me with pride: "Only eighty people were killed building this road. That is a record."

From nearby I took one of the shuttle aircraft that linked São Paulo with Rio de Janeiro, only a twenty-minute flight. The plane was full. São Paulo's business class took the plane to Rio as a London city gent might catch the commuter line to Surrey. Soon we were engulfed by a tropical thunderstorm, with lightning flashing all around; Rio's main airport was too badly flooded for us to land. We circled for an hour and a half in the heavens run amok, and then landed at an airport close to central Rio. Air travel in a country as large as Brazil is all-important, yet surprisingly disorganized; it took more than an hour to get a taxi from that ill-frequented airport.

To travel from São Paulo to Rio is comparable to traveling from Milan to Rome, or from Chicago to Miami. The climate is not all that much hotter, but it seems so, as the steamy tropical heat of the coast massages the tension of the hypercity out of the system. Going straight into Rio from the inner airport, I missed the usual madcap rush from the international airport, which lies on an island in the estuary of the Janeiro River. On previous visits the ride from that airport always took me through a cross section of the city—through a large stilt slum built over germ-ridden water through the working-class apartment blocks near the Maracaña Stadium, then, as the road narrows in an agonizing crawl, past the *favelas*, past the slums that cling like limpets to the sides of the mountains, which the authorities are clearing into soulless apartment blocks, and finally into the tunnel that leads to the heart of the city.

I missed that experience and drove ahead under the recurring thunder, under clouds that rolled and billowed as a muddied light illuminated Rio's scenic mountain, the Corcovado. Rio is one of the most modern cities in the world, yet it is built between the fingers of a great mountain dominating the sea, so that, unlike São Paulo, the natural environment is very evident. The mountain has a diminutive statue of Christ at the top, gazing out over the immense expanse of city, the bay into which the estuary disgorges, the mountains on the other side of the city, and the islands in the bay.

The taxi coasted easily along the front of dangerous Copacabana, once the smartest beach in town, now a haven for muggers; and down to Ipanema, a white expanse of sand in front of a row of skyscraper hotels. My hotel was well furnished, with comfortable rooms instead of boxes. There were only a few colonial houses, daubs of charm, in a seafront of towering buildings, reduced by the size of the mountain.

Life in Ipanema was relaxed. That night I was picked up by a friend in shirtsleeves who took me to a fashionable party high on the hill where the women were dressed with a breathtaking mixture of elegance and exposure. The people of Rio were quite simply the best-looking I had seen on earth. The men all appeared to be young, athletic, well built, vital; the women had voluptuous figures, and their looks were a combination of everything that was best in the looks of white and black. They were also frank, articulate and uninhibited in a way that came as a surprise to a European. Conversation was often a perfunctory preliminary to sex.

The following morning, caressed by sleep and the sea air, I went out onto the beach; it was clean, with Cariocas of both sexes playing ball. I swam, then lay down on the sand. A few yards away an American businessman and his wife were doing the same. Kids started kicking a ball to waken them. He took it good-humoredly, until they started making a ring around him and his wife. He got angry. There were thirty or so of them, closing in, laughing, taunting. He became flustered. I thought he should make tracks; unforgivably, that is exactly what I did. He saw sense at last and left the beach, before it got too rough, under the jeers of the mob. On the way back to my hotel, two boys, no more than fifteen years old, accosted me: "Shoeshine?" Unsettled by the previous scene, I hurried past. "Look," said one—my shoe was covered in shit that his companion had dropped. "Shoeshine?" I brushed angrily past. The scene disturbed me more than it should have—because I was in no danger. Yet there was always an undercurrent of street-level violence in Rio, as recession drove the unemployed to rob. The police were helplessly inadequate, so revenge killings, lynch mobs and death squads became common.

After breakfast, I went to see one of the men on whom the future of Brazil depended: the governor of Rio de Janeiro, Leonel Brizola. He was a man with a strong handshake, a wide smile and eyes that watched and did not smile. His cool, colonial governor's palace with its potted plants was one of the few relatively attractive buildings in the city. He managed, throughout our conversation, to say absolutely nothing; he agreed with me that foreign debt was Brazil's most terrible problem and insisted that all of Brazil's difficulties could be laid at the door of the debt. Yet he declined to say what he would do about it. The smile resembled that of a shark, it was so insincere. I left, appalled that such a man might be Brazil's future.

In 1980, the last time I had been to Rio, I came face to face with Brazil's past, the man most identified with the transformation that was then turning Brazil into a world power. Antônio Delfim Netto was the busiest person I have ever observed. When I had met him in London at one of his innumerable conferences of central bankers, he was relaxed, witty, chatty. But in Brazil, it took hours to arrange a meeting; on a single day he might be in São Paulo, Rio and the capital, Brasília; I eventually caught up with him on a brief stopover in Rio. When "O Ministro" arrived, all the officials present stood up, and he walked through the room at unbelievable speed.

He was comically small and well fed. Apart from a quick handshake, there was no ceremony about him: the eyes behind the thick spectacles flickered quickly, as though working out the question I was about to ask; he never talked without purpose, as so many politicians do. It was a fast, quiet voice. I asked him about the soaring foreign debt. "Of course we will pay. It is not a problem." He showed me graphs to demonstrate that Brazil's debt would taper off and go away. I was unconvinced. I asked him what he thought about the possibility of a Falklands war. He beamed: "There will be no war. Can you imagine Britain and Argentina fighting for such a place? It is science fiction. The Americans will knock their heads together."

O Ministro was then the most powerful man in a country of more than 100 million people where all power came from the top. He had prepared a detailed paper setting out his views on the debt and he said he would arrange for me to receive a copy of it in Brasília. It didn't come; but when I got a plane out of the capital, there was an unaccountable delay. Then an announcer asked me to go to the front of the aircraft. Nervously—Brazil was still a military dictatorship— I did so; they had held up the plane so that Delfim's paper could be rushed to me. There was enormous power in the hands of that short man with his stubby fingers fidgeting on the table in front of me.

O Ministro, the busiest man in the world, the man of action, the supreme technocrat, the man who could hold up planes and lightly dismiss a debt of (then) $70 billion, had been responsible for the greatest successes and the greatest mistakes in Brazil's recent history. In that respect he had been the reverse of the other creator of modern Brazil, Roberto Campos.

Campos was as unlike Delfim as it was possible to be: informal, worldly-wise and amusing, with the girth of a prosperous cattle rancher, he was a lover of the good things in life. Campos was nevertheless an honest man brought in by the generals in 1964, after the military coup, to clear up the economic mess left behind by the populist government of João Goulart. This he did, within two years, with exemplary speed and efficiency, and without inflicting too much hardship. He introduced the concept of indexation into modern economics; his theory was that, in a developing country, inflation was an endemic result of the need to create more capital. Indexation of most prices, salaries and pensions would insulate Brazilians from the social consequences of inflation. Campos was a "developmentalist" who was committed to keeping Brazil growing, but in a limited and controlled way.

His archenemy, Delfim, denounced him as a cautious conservative and took power, with the backing of ambitious military men who wanted the country to grow fast. He pushed Brazil hell-for-leather toward economic growth, and the devil take the consequences. Campos was undoubtedly right in his caution, and Brazil's economic growth would have been a less chaotic affair if his advice had been heeded. Delfim's recklessness was, however, quintessentially Brazilian, and, as seemed always to be the case in modern Brazil, he pulled off the impossible.

Delfim loved to insist that he was not a politician. Yet his personality harked back to an eminently political figure, Juscelino Kubitschek, the first developmentalist, the man who had founded a new capital and bankrupted the economy in doing so. His transfer of the seat of government from Rio to Brasília had been desperately unpopular: Rio was the pleasure capital of Brazil, Brasília a hideous, artificial creation in the windblown interior, from which civil servants fled every weekend as soon as their generous office hours would allow. Yet Delfim's aim was inspired: his goal was not just to open up the huge undeveloped heartland of Brazil, the three quarters of a country whose only significant population clusters were on the coast, but to wrest power away from the rival power centers of São Paulo and Rio to the heartland of the country. Since Brasília was new, no one could be jealous of its predominance. Because it was removed from the rest of the country, it remained uninfluenced by the fevered demonstrations that affected the two big cities. The seat of government was thus removed from the masses. It was an elitist decision, and it worked well: it was hard to riot and shake up a government seven hundred miles away.

It was with reluctance that I took the plane to Brasília. Brasília, Kubitschek's creation, "a pharaonic waste" as one angry Brazilian friend of mine described it, is one of the ghastliest cities in the world, in a wholly different way from São Paulo. Brasília is a horrible testimonial to the avant-garde that had become jaded and out of date almost as soon as it was created. The city is literally, in the middle of nowhere, in the Brazilian *mato grosso*, a land of red earth stretching thousands of miles in every direction whose main crop is cactus or occasional grass, inhabited by a few herds of wandering cattle.

The city itself is designed in the shape of an aircraft, which may be an encouragement to those whose first thought on arrival is to arrange their departure. It is divided by function into a diplomatic sector, a civil-service sector, a shopping sector, a red-light sector and so on. The east of the city—its fuselage—is the area where the ministries were built. It consists of two rows of buildings, blue concrete structures opposite each other, a giants' causeway. At one end there is a cathedral, which looks like a glass tepee with girdered fins sticking out of the top. It seemed small until I entered and realized that most of it was underground and the glass was only the top of the roof.

Further along is the foreign ministry, the Itamaraty. The most elegant construction in the city, it rises behind a moat of stagnant water adorned with statues and houses offices in which no one ever seems to do a stroke of work. The building contains a central hallway and staircase on which it was judged unaesthetic to build a balustrade, so that tipsy visiting politicians have to be kept away from the edges by the ushers.

Not far from the ministry is the presidential palace, a one-story building with the look of a giant bungalow replete with concrete walkways and guarded by a ludicrously plumed presidential guard, who seem sharply at odds with their surroundings. They reminded me of the futuristic emperors so beloved by science fiction writers.

The *pièce de résistance* of this strange tableau is the congress building, a juxtaposition of two skyscrapers dominating a flat surface on which sit two enormous saucers, one upside down. These structures were meant to symbolize the relationship between the two houses of congress. The building is a remarkable place. Until the return of democracy, the powerless representatives and senators boasted large suites of offices that they rarely occupied, and congressional proceedings were broadcast on loudspeakers to all ends of the building, a perfect nightmare of rhetoric. Beyond the congress building was an artificial lake on the shores of which the senior generals and politicians of the new Brazil constructed comfortable houses and went riding.

In 1979, I had been here to visit another of Delfim's rivals, the man who, for a long time effectively ran Brazil from the presidential palace—General Artur Golbery do Couto e Silva. Golbery was the architect of the generals' coup in 1964, and subsequently became head of the civilian household to a succession of presidents whom he effectively controlled. Acutely at odds with his grandiose surroundings, he was a wizened man with spectacles, wearing an old-style suit. He had the charming manner of a seasoned diplomat. He was unpretentious, unassuming.

He spoke with great vision about the need to take Brazil "safely to democracy, which had been the intention of the generals when they had first taken power." The plan had been postponed. He spoke of the country's need to improve its social services, to share the wealth more equally. He was as civilized and well respected as the best of contemporary European politicians and completely antique in manner, utterly at odds with the strident newness of Brasília.

I walked back from the meeting to my hotel. It proved to be a mistake. Because there are only large buildings in Brasília, they give the illusion of being smaller and the distances shorter than they actually are; and there are no walkways for pedestrians under the four-lane highways. It took me an hour, instead of fifteen minutes, to reach my hotel, at the end of the avenue of the ministries.

Brasília had been built by Kubitschek at a cost of at least $10 billion with an army of workers who squatted in a slum outside. A gaucho politician from the state of Minas Gerais, Brazil's long-civilized outback, Kubitschek was smooth and skillful. He helped create Brazil's inflation with his massive spending but those who found employment under him were grateful. He was the prophet of growth; Brazil's annual GDP was accelerated from 3 percent when he first took office in 1956 to 8 percent in 1957 and 10 percent in 1960: the Brazilian miracle of economic expansion was underway. Surviving two attempted coups, Kubitschek bowed out in a blaze of popularity by breaking off relations with the International Monetary Fund, which was trying to bend Brazil to more orthodox economic policies. The man who had squandered billions building a new capital in a country of extreme social division, he was beloved by the people. It was left to his successors to pick up the tab.

Kubitschek's successor as presidential candidate, Marshal Henrique Teixeira Lott, was an earnest soldier who was easily defeated in

1960 by the more charismatic right-wing candidate, Jânio Quadros—
one of the most interesting political figures of recent times. Quadros
was a tall, gangling, highly intelligent man with a bristling mustache
who won the election by defying the conventional political machines
and preaching honesty, efficient administration and progress. His
symbol was the broom, with which he would sweep corruption from
office. His main backer was Carlos Lacerda, Brazil's most prominent
right-wing activist and newspaper publisher. When he won the
presidency, Quadros emerged as a conservative who proposed to
control the inflation caused by Kubitschek through strict controls on
government spending and on wages. Quadros also rather cynically
tried to appeal to the left by forging relations with the Soviet Union
and by awarding Che Guevara Brazil's highest honor, in a display of
independence from the United States.

He soon found himself in conflict with congress, which was made
up of the party politicians he despised. Quadros hit on the idea of
resignation, in the hope that the army would step in to back him
against congress and give him a free hand to run the country. The
decision was wholly absurd, and Quadros found himself precipitat-
ing the military coup that was to deaden Brazilian politics for two
decades.

When he resigned, his intellectual pygmy of a vice-president, a
free-spending populist with ideas rooted in the thirties, took control.
This was João Goulart, the scion of a landowning family. Goulart's
plans were hopeless: he tried to prompt growth by printing money
and through intensive government spending; the unions meanwhile
embarked on a wage explosion to keep ahead of inflation; and peasants demanding land in the northwest went on the rampage. The
middle classes recoiled from the spectacle of demonstrations. The
uprising was sparked in Minas Gerais, where a column of troops set
off toward the capital, Rio de Janeiro, in March 1964. Forces that
Goulart sent to stop them deserted. The president flew to Brasília
and then to exile in Pôrto Alegre.

The new president was the army commander, the shadowy general Humberto Castelo Branco. He was backed by a skillful tactician, General Artur Golbery do Couto e Silva, who was in many
ways the architect of the coup and the man who had taught many
senior officers at that finishing school for army plotters, the Escola
Superior da Guerra in Rio.

Golbery and Castelo Branco installed Brazil's most brilliant economist, Roberto Campos, to rescue the country from the long-term consequences of Kubitschek's extravagance and Goulart's folly. Campos proved highly effective. Within two years the economy was back under control. Inflation, which had been about 400 percent, fell to 50 percent, and Campos initiated the policy of indexation that allowed him, through fiddling, to reduce the wage pressures on inflation. But politics is an ungrateful profession: as Golbery and Castelo tried to pave the way for a return to democracy, elections they held resulted in a victory for the opposition.

A hard-line faction in the army believed that Castelo was too soft on communism, and anyway wanted to run Brazil, claiming legitimization from the success of the economic policy. This group forced Castelo out of office, and General Artur da Costa e Silva, a blunt old conservative, took power. By 1969, Costa e Silva had fallen ill, ceding power to the leader of the hard-liners, General Emílio Médici, who installed Delfim Netto as finance minister. The hyperactive Delfim built on Campos's achievement, allowing the Brazilian economy to grow quickly, also enriching the ruling clique of generals.

These were the years of the Brazilian miracle. From 1968, growth ran at 10 percent a year, inflation was down to 20 percent, while the balance of payments was running a surplus of $2.3 billion. The new regime also resorted to thoroughly un-Brazilian repression: a series of guerrilla attacks led to strong retaliation by Médici, including the use of torture, which had been more unusual in Brazil than in Spanish-speaking Latin America. The "dragon" chair, in which electric shocks were applied to the victim, the "operating table," a type of modern rack used to stretch people, and the "parrot's perch," which forced the victim to sit astride were Brazilian tortures; the death squads, set up under the monstrous Sergio Paranhos Fleury, murdered guerrilla suspects and could be hired to kill private enemies. Not until 1974 did a more moderate group, under General Ernesto Geisel, take control and slightly rein in the repression, now that the guerrillas were defeated. Geisel also fired Delfim, just as the economy began to overheat, and as Brazil reeled under the impact of the oil-price shocks.

Geisel, a plodder, missed the opportunity to set Brazil on course to democracy and, instead of opening up Brazil's large potential oil reserves, committed the huge blunder of embarking on an expensive oil substitution program. This was denounced in a book by one of Brazil's best journalists, Alberto Tamer, *Oil: The Price of Dependence*.

In the later years of Geisel, the court vizier, Golbery, who was the president's chief adviser, began to steer the country toward democracy once more. Congressional elections were held between the only two parties permitted by the government, the governing party, ARENA, and the opposition Brazilian Democratic Movement (MDB). The MDB scored spectacular victories. The army narrowly deferred the pressure for direct elections, installing as president General João Figueiredo, a jolly cavalry officer who expressed the view that he preferred the smell of horses to that of people. Figueiredo presided over the collapse of the economic miracle under the pressure not just of the oil crisis but of the debt crisis.

Figueiredo tried to hand-pick a successor, but even the proarmy party in congress would not support him. Instead, in 1984 it split and one half joined with the opposition in voting into power a wily man from Minas Gerais, the state that produces most of Brazil's leaders. He was Tancredo Neves, benign and conservative but a social democrat, who told me in 1980 that Brazil "would always honor its debts." He, however, fell ill before taking office and died, being succeeded by a conservative machine politician, Jośe Sarney, in the task of building Brazil's fragile democracy and overcoming the effects of the debt crisis. To many it seemed that Brazil was about to go through another cycle that would leave Latin America's one budding superpower busted again.

Cycles seemed to dog Brazil's history. Brazil had been the most fortunate country of all in the method of its independence; her institutions stayed intact, and no war was required against the colonial power. The Brazilian independence movement began when the Portuguese royal family fled to Brazil after Napoléon's invasion in 1807. The Portuguese court settled in Brazil under Prince João, who opened up the New World to the culture of the old. When Portugal was freed, the king decided to return, leaving his son Prince Pedro in Brazil. When Portugal turned republican, Pedro found himself at the head of the Brazilian independence movement, finally becoming emperor of Brazil in 1822. At first highly popular, Pedro was too distant to retain the affections of his people, and he abdicated in 1831, leaving his five-year-old son, who was to become Pedro II, as regent. Astonishingly, Pedro proved to be earnest, sincere and widely respected as a benevolent autocrat: he presided over the first industrial revolution to affect this undeveloped land of four million people.

But the cause of republicanism, in a continent of republics, proved too strong even for this man. On the night of November 16, 1889, he was taken prisoner in his palace and then bundled unceremoniously aboard a ship, to die soon afterward. There was no one left to support the monarchy, it simply collapsed. The early years of the republic were much more peaceful than those of Spanish America; the army stayed in the background, propping up a succession of aristocratic and well-educated republicans in presiding over the nation's efforts. But slowly the army came to assert itself, rigging the election of 1910.

This political degeneration was mirrored by economic trouble. Brazil's economy was dependent on the export of coffee and rubber. As coffee production expanded in Central America, Colombia and Argentina, the price collapsed. The rubber boom provided a new prosperity to the impoverished northeast. The cities of Bahia and Manaus became flourishing, beautiful tropical cities; Manaus, a thousand miles up the Amazon, boasted its own opera house. But a trader had smuggled Brazilian rubber plants to Kew Gardens in London, and they made their way to Malaya, where they were cheaper to grow than in Brazil; the boom collapsed. The economy enjoyed a brief respite during the First World War, then slumped during the postwar period. The army moved in again, staging a series of military coups between 1922 and 1926. As communism spread in Europe, Luís Carlos Prestes, an army captain, led a band of two thousand men to raise the impoverished rural areas in revolt. His long march lasted two years and covered eighteen thousand miles— long before Mao's long march in China—but got nowhere. In the late 1920s, Brazil's economy started to move again, but the world slump soon intervened.

In 1930, as Brazil faced financial collapse, the defeated presidential candidate, Getúlio Vargas, claimed that the election had been rigged. Vargas was a pint-sized man who claimed to be of gaucho stock but looked like a country doctor with a cheerful, amiable bedside manner. Vargas became minister of finance and governor of Minas Gerais, the breeding ground of Brazilian politics. He proclaimed a revolution and marched on Rio—although he himself took the train. A military group seized control in Rio on his behalf, and he marched in to a hero's welcome.

He became a Brazilian Roosevelt. Public works projects, minimum wages, a forty-eight-hour week and a massive program of economic diversification were instituted. Vargas also sought to raise coffee prices by burning three years' crop. He faced a challenge from São Paulo, whose leaders felt that Brazil's premier city should run the country. An army of fifty thousand men was assembled, and Vargas marched on São Paulo. After a standoff the Paulistas surrendered with only desultory fighting.

In 1933 Vargas was democratically elected, and he became Brazil's most popular president to date. Although constitutionally barred from running again in 1937, he produced evidence of an alleged communist plot and called off the elections. He set up a new constitution, called the Estado Nôvo, which contained many features of Italian and German corporativism; a secret police was set up and political prisoners were taken. But Vargas's authoritarianism was nowhere as severe as that of his European models, or indeed as that of Perón in Argentina. The next stage of his government was to industrialize the country, setting up textile companies, newspapers, household appliance firms, chemical factories and so on. As industrialization moved on apace, Vargas, believing himself still popular, opened the system slightly toward democracy. An election was scheduled for 1945. As the election approached it seemed probable that he would annul it and stay in power. The army marched in and put Vargas on a plane back to his Rio Grande do Sul ranch.

General Eurico Dutra presided over an economic boom based on huge electric power projects like the São Francisco Valley project. In 1950, Vargas ran again as the candidate of the left; to everyone's surprise, o pai do povo—the father of the people—swept sixteen of the nineteen states. Yet the economy was fast getting out of control. The main cities were swamped with millions of immigrants from the poor northeast; steel, car and truck plants were built at breakneck pace. Rio and São Paulo bristled with skyscrapers. Vargas, once the great modernizer, began to seem dated. When an air force officer close to Vargas was killed in an attempt to assassinate a prominent conservative opposition journalist, the army decided to force the old man out of office. The generals decreed that he must take a permanent

leave of absence. At eight o'clock in the evening in the presidential
palace in Rio, Vargas went to his room and shot himself, leaving
behind a burning indictment of those who "did not want the world
to be free. They do not want the people to be independent."

Vargas was a great man who had outlived his usefulness, the
instigator of change who had himself been bypassed and could no
longer control events. The process of growth that started in the
1930s continued at a fast and furious pace through to the 1970s,
interrupted only by the crisis of the mid-1960s. Brazil was on its way
to becoming a superpower, one of the largest, strongest economies in
the West. The opera house in Manaus and the decaying cities of
Belém and Recife had been the symbols of promise gone to seed; but
even they were rediscovering a new, more solid prosperity founded
on competitiveness and industrial development.

And then the debt crisis threatened to overwhelm it all. The origins
of the crisis are not mysterious. External public debt first piled up in
Latin America in order to cope with the yawning balance-of-payment
surpluses caused by the first oil-price shock. Brazil's debt rose from
$10 billion in 1973 to $47 billion by 1979; Argentina's from $3.5
billion to $11 billion; Colombia's from $2.7 billion to $5.5 billion;
Peru's from $2.4 billion to $8 billion; Chile's, more modestly, from
$3.4 billion to $5.5 billion. Even petro-plutocratic Mexico and Venezuela fed at the same trough. Mexico's external public debt rose
from $7.2 billion to $37 billion; Venezuela's from $2 billion to $10
billion. The debt increases, said the planners, were comfortably in
line with world inflation and nothing to worry about.

They probably were—until the second oil-price shock of 1979–80,
which did three things to Latin America. It punctured the self-con-
fidence of the non-oil-producing Latin American economies by imposing an almost intolerable strain on their balance of payments.
Simultaneously, because the immediate response of the developed
world to the second oil shock was medium-to-sharp deflation, world
money markets were saturated with petrodollars in search of a home.
Latin America's third problem was that, owing to depressed demand
in the developed countries, the bottom fell out of the market for the
commodities the continent produced.

The response of the non-oil-producing Latin American countries
was to borrow to cover their growing trade deficits. The response of

the oil-producing countries was to borrow because the money was there for the asking and they had oil, the best of securities, to borrow against. By the end of 1982, the Latin American debt stood at around $300 billion, with Brazil owing some $90 billion, Mexico $80 billion, Argentina $38 billion, Venezuela $32 billion and Peru $10 billion.

The response of the international banks and, behind them, the central banks of the developed world was to send for the sheriff, the International Monetary Fund, to tell that saloonful of free-spending Latinos to sober up. The trouble was that at least five countries—Brazil, Mexico, Venezuela, Chile and Peru—found it extremely hard to service their debts and afford the imports they needed for economic growth. Economic recovery in America and some parts of Europe was a help, but recovery alone was not sufficient to deal with the scale of Latin America's debts.

Enforcing laws against borrowers is difficult. Any bank offering a loan usually wants to be sure that the debtor (a) will put the money where it will yield a return that will pay off the interest and eventually the debt, and (b) has security that the bank can grab in case something goes wrong. In lending to sovereign countries there was no such security, except a country's concern to preserve its creditworthiness (bankers could lay their hands on a country's financial assets only when most of these were held abroad, as was the case with Iran in 1979).

Creditworthiness was a limited asset: there could come a moment when the cost of borrowing could outweigh a country's wish to be able to go on borrowing more. So a lot depended on the bankers' sense in lending money where there was some prospect of real return. That meant that borrowed money needed to be invested to boost exports or to save on imports. In the world of 1980–81, where sober-suited bankers were chasing scapegrace adventurers in Latin America, there was never any prospect of a return on much of the debt.

Much of the money went to new government spending. Brazil's hard-pressed government, wincing from the grumbles provoked by the country's 1979–80 recession, sighed with relief when it gained access to new foreign money just in time for a preelection year. Not only could the minimum wages of those the Brazilian government had most to fear from, the employed urban working class, be promptly underwritten; the financing was there to polish off a host of projects, from the São Paulo subway to the Itaipu hydroelectric scheme.

The Mexicans, themselves in an election year, poured money into construction (up 12 percent in 1980–81) and electricity generation (up 10 percent). Even Mexican manufacturing registered a 6 percent growth. In Chile Pinochet eased his spartan economic disciplines to give workers real wage increases of 14 percent, and splashed out $700 million on improving the Santiago subway.

Much of the money went to pure speculation. The worst examples were in Argentina and Chile, where a plethora of *financieras*–barely regulated financial holding companies–were set up to channel money largely into booming property markets. It was possible at one time for a more or less penniless *financiera* to borrow $1 million to buy a property in downtown Santiago and sell it for $2 million after a few months. That was all right for some, but when the boom came to a stop a lot of people found themselves stuck with properties bought on borrowed money.

Quarter-occupied luxury hotels and office blocks were the lingering monuments to the loan boom. Most Latin American countries enjoyed a short-lived construction boom: total value added by construction in Latin America jumped by some $8 billion between 1978 and 1981. In Argentina and Chile, many of the *financieras* and property companies went down with a resounding crash in 1981–82.

A lot of the lending went straight out again. Many Latin American countries had no exchange controls; where they existed, they could be evaded fairly easily. Western bankers estimated that as much as $100 billion was recycled back from Latin America to the United States and Western Europe in 1981–82. Mexicans were believed to hold some $30 billion in assets abroad, Venezuelans some $18 billion. At least $12 billion left Brazil in a single year. Even in an economy as small as Chile's, the capital flight in 1981 was about $1 billion.

The worst thing was that after four years of squeezing, the Latin American economies were no better off than before. The squeeze had eliminated much of the advance of those economies over the previous years, yet they were more indebted than ever.

And then in Brazil the miracle happened. The ruling class flinched before the financial prescriptions of the IMF, fudged the figures to keep it happy, and embarked on a policy of economic experiment that allowed a resumption of development. By 1985, Brazil was growing at 8 percent a year. The IMF could do no more than look skeptically at the figures and continue to provide the credits that allowed it to pretend that Brazil was not defaulting but fulfilling its international financial obligations. The financial strictures of the IMF had been shown by the Brazilians to be paper tigers—because if the IMF exposed the sham, the world financial system would be undermined. Few outsiders understood that if it came to a showdown the Brazilian economy was unlikely to suffer more than it had had to suffer in repaying the debt. Economic sanctions were unlikely, although Brazil would certainly have to pay a percentage point or two more for suppliers' credits. And the banks' threat to deny Brazil credits would not work, because Brazil was being denied credits anyway.

The pessimistic view of the debt was relayed to me by everyone I saw on my current trip, from foreign diplomats to local officials. A priest who is now a member of the Workers' Party told me, "We're suffering. It can't go on." Brizola told me, "We need to audit the debts and pay only those which have been legitimately incurred. Many of Delfim's debts were used for purposes other than the ones they were borrowed for." A lively congressman, Senator Severo Gomes, insisted that "if we declare a moratorium, the Americans aren't going to seize our assets abroad; if they do, we'll help ourselves to a multinational."

Despite its economic problems, I found Brazil more confident on my latest trip than ever before, maybe a consequence of the new democracy, of the new freedom of expression and above all of the government's freezing of prices under the Cruzado Plan. In my experience, such a plan would not last long, but it had dented the psychology under which Brazilians had grown accustomed to an inflation rate of upward of 50 percent a year, and had bought the government breathing space to introduce more lasting policies. The trouble was that a democratic government was under even more pressure to spend and to increase incomes than Brazil's expansionist authoritarian one. If both of these were not brought under control, the country's price freeze would be temporary. It was hard not to get caught up, though, in the mood of euphoria that accompanied the creation of Brazil's "new republic," harder still not to be skeptical about its prospects of lasting. If the economy does crash, the obvious way out, with unknown consequences, seems to be a repudiation of the debt—and I, for one, would not condemn the Brazilians for resorting to it.

From Manaus I flew to Caracas, the capital of Latin America's very first El Dorado, and my next-to-last stop.

VENEZUELA

YOU HAVE TO LOOK VERY HARD TO FIND ANY EVIDENCE THAT CARACAS has a history at all. Large modern tunnels carved through the mountains that slip down to the Caribbean on Venezuela's northern coast set the scene: a three-lane highway coasts into the city entirely without pause, slicing through the middle; the city itself is set in a long, narrow valley with high mountains on both sides; and on both sides of the motorway stand skyscrapers, sentries of the new age, an avenue of buildings that somehow form a stately accompaniment to the road. The Caracas skyscrapers are—unlike those in Bogotá—aesthetically impressive and complement the green majesty of the mountain range behind them; they do not look intrusive and silly. The reflecting glass of the two tallest skyscrapers gives the city's downtown a flashy streak. Caracas is elegant and new and like the Venezuelans themselves, one might suspect, lacking in much respect for the past. The great procession of skyscrapers makes the valley in which the city is situated all the more distinguished.

It is a well organized city, too: in place of the lines of slow-moving traffic that plague other cities, the main highway and the roads that spin off it are fast-moving and well planned. The shopping district and parking lots are accessible. Well-heeled Caracas seems a justification for modern living. There is a downside, of course. The hills on the approach roads to the city are packed with the inevitable shanties, tumbled down one on top of the other like mushroom outgrowths even more precariously so than in Brazil. But here, the slums merely seem in less glaring contrast with the city's progress, and wealth.

Venezuela was not always so fortunate. When Columbus discovered the "Spanish main" on his third voyage, he believed he had found a perfect colony, and the discovery of villages built on stilts near the Orinoco River caused the colony to be called "little Venice"—Venezuela. But further inspection revealed that the region consisted of a tropical jungle that cloaked the declining eastern spur of the Andes, and then plunged into an extensive swampland around the Orinoco, merging with the Andean rain forest in the south. So unexplored were parts of the Venezuelan jungle that mountain outcrops with rock- and bush-covered plateaus were later discovered to contain species that had survived from primeval times in "lost worlds." Successive attempts by the Spaniards to subdue the Indians of the area came to naught. The country was populated along the coast by blacks and Creole slave owners who moved inland as far as Caracas.

Venezuela experienced a slight economic boom in the late eighteenth century, when hard-working Basque immigrants arrived from Spain. Indeed, the country was linked to the mainstream of European thought by its geographical proximity to Spain and its trade with the mainland, and it was always a seedbed for new ideas. But by 1810, the local aristocracy had had enough of Spanish misgovernment and ousted its governor-general, although formally continuing to swear allegiance to the Spanish king, Fernando VII; a royalist reaction left the rebels in control only of the heartland.

But two educated, well-connected Latin Americans had sailed from Europe to take charge of the revolution. The first was the sixty-year-old Francisco de Miranda, El Precursor, who had long fought for Latin American independence and been exiled to London; the second was Simón Bolívar, El Libertador, a handsome, aristocratic youth, who had imbibed the ideals of revolutionary France. The two gradually assumed control of the Venezuelan rump republic, and, on July 5, 1811, declared its formal independence, the first in Latin America—a lasting source of Venezuelan national pride.

The republic soon fell apart as Spanish forces closed in. Miranda tried to sail away, and Bolívar turned on his friend, handing him over to the Spaniards, who imprisoned him until his death.

Then, Bolívar himself marched with a column out to the highlands of New Granada (Colombia), which by now was also in revolt. There he assembled an army, ostensibly to protect Colombia from invasion by the solidly royalist country of Venezuela; unexpectedly, he led a band of six hundred men back across into it, seizing Caracas by 1814, and imposing a dictatorship.

The royalists rallied, however, with the help of the rough cattlemen of the llanos, the Venezuelan outback, the land between the mountains and the jungle. The cattlemen's leader, José Tomás Boves, set up a "legion of hell," which dashed about the country, committing a hurricane of atrocities. By 1814, Bolívar abandoned Caracas again, and fled to Bogotá. By 1816 the Spanish forces had re-entered Bogotá itself after a long march, and Bolívar fled to Jamaica.

In 1816 he set sail again for Venezuela with two hundred men; but no one on the mainland joined him, and he abandoned his plans. He then hit on the idea of trying to win over the *llaneros*, the thugs who had ousted him years before; these people had come to resent the central government and the royalists who controlled it with as much intensity as they had once detested him. He landed at the mouth of the Orinoco, took over the town of Angostura, and set about convincing the brigands to support him. Over the next few years, Bolívar built up a force of four thousand with this unpromising material; he set out in 1819 for the uplands of Colombia, where he surprised the royalist forces, inflicting a major defeat and taking the capital. At about the same time the Spanish monarchy fell, and General Pablo Morillo, who had beaten Bolívar once in Caracas, made his peace and sailed for home. After a campaign against the remaining royalist forces, Bolívar returned in triumph to Caracas in 1826. He then set off for the rugged uplands of Peru, delegating a smaller force under General Antonio José de Sucre to liberate Ecuador. In Guayaquil he met the liberator of the southern part of the continent, José de San Martín, who acknowledged his subordination in front of Bolívar. It fell to Venezuela's Bolívar to wage the final battle in attempting to free Peru, the seat of the Spanish viceroyalty.

Venezuela was left under the control of the leading llano bandit,

José Antonio Páez, who turned out to be not a bad ruler. After setting up a tolerable dictatorship over the torrid, impoverished coastal state, he withdrew from power in 1835; the country was promptly taken over by brigands, and Páez returned in 1839; after he again withdrew in 1843 in favor of an ally, another dictator, José Tadco Monagas, eventually took power, quarreled with Paez, and plunged the country into civil war. The main division was between the Blues, loyal to Caracas, and the Yellows, who consisted largely of *llaneros* and favored a more federal system.

It took another dictator, Antonio Guzmán Blanco, to restore order and a degree of economic development. He decided to retire to Paris, however, and left the country in the hands of puppets for two years. He was finally overthrown in 1889, and the country lurched back into civil war. One of his henchmen won power for a time, but was pushed out by a vicious Blue leader, Cipriano Castro, who looted the country, sending most of his money abroad while posing as a Venezuelan patriot. He persecuted foreigners, and when the Germans, British and Italians set up a blockade against the country to defend their interests, he defied them. The United States, alarmed by the European intervention, put its fleet out, the Europeans withdrew, and Castro became a national hero.

He was overthrown—incredibly—by an intemperate subordinate, Juan Vicente Gómez, who took advantage of the dictator's absence abroad for medical treatment. Gómez was less falsely moralistic, but was otherwise a friend: he was said to have magical powers, and his men indulged in appalling tortures and invented innovative punishments for those who wronged him. He once closed the University of Caracas after a demonstration and sent the students to pound rocks on the roads as forced labor. In this fashion, the monster presided over one of the poorest countries in Latin America, funnelling some $30 million into his personal bank accounts.

Then the discovery of oil at the hottest spot in Latin America, Lake Maracaibo, suddenly propelled the country into undreamed-of wealth. The exploration and exploitation of the oil was left to foreign companies, which paid the government handsomely; Gómez lavished the money on the eighty children he had fathered, or on lavish projects in the countryside. The poverty of most people remained absolute; Gómez made no pretense of helping the poor. When he died in 1935, the country went wild with spontaneous joy.

At that point, the defense chief, General Eleazar López Contreras, assumed the presidency and appealed for calm. López was a run-of-the-mill military ruler who handed power over to an even more moderate successor, Isaías Medina. The new president allowed political parties to establish themselves and a left-wing group called Acción Democrática, under Rómulo Betancourt, a long-standing opponent of Gómez, was formed. Betancourt was a shrewd, down-to-earth man with high ideals. He managed to seize power in 1945, as the popularity of Medina's benevolent autocracy waned, and installed a government dedicated to spending the oil wealth on improving the lot of the masses. Betancourt was a true democrat, and robustly anticommunist, but his first attempt to govern was hopelessly idealistic; in 1948, after he had decided to embark on a radical land reform program and to disband the army, setting up a peasants' and workers' militia in its place, the army seized power, installing a figurehead president.

Soon the real strongman took over: the bespectacled defense minister, Marcos Pérez Jiménez. Unprepossessing in the extreme, he was only thirty-six and spoke with a stammer. Believing he was liked, the general held an election in 1952, which he lost dramatically. But he rigged the ballots to claim a large victory and installed all the traditional machinery of a Latin American dictatorship, with the army as a privileged caste. He gave the air force an airfield in the middle of Caracas (it is still disconcerting to see light aircraft flying down the avenue of mountains, past the skyscrapers, to land in the middle of the city) and an extensive security apparatus. Pérez Jiménez spent much of the country's growing oil wealth on public works, creating the basis of the city that is Caracas—in particular of the highway network that runs through the city. But by 1958 his repressive policies had made him so unpopular that his own army supporters decided to overthrow him, in a bloodless coup.

Despite that relatively tranquil transfer of power, the Venezuelans seemed to be in a dangerous frame of mind. Richard Nixon, the visiting American vice-president, was nearly dismembered in a riot on the main street during that same year. An election at the end of the year resulted in victory for Betancourt again. He walked a tightrope between the right and left, which was in a militant mood after Castro's accession to power in Cuba in 1959; but he succeeded in creating a moderate opposition party, COPEI (the Christian Democrats), and in protecting civil liberties.

Betancourt was succeeded by a member of his own party, Raúl Leoni, who had a tempestuous presidency, but survived. The opposition won the next election, a sign that Venezuela was, truly, a two-party democracy. Acción Democrática won the presidency in 1973, under a flashy youngster, Carlos Andrés Pérez, who administered the increase in prosperity brought about by the 1974–75 oil price increase. Pérez decided to raise Venezuela's profile abroad, using his country's wealth to buy influence in major organizations, including OPEC, to which Venezuela belonged. His administration was severely criticized for corruption, and was succeeded by the COPEI government of Luis Herrera, which benefited from the fresh windfall of the 1970–80 oil price increase.

The country was on a high: its GDP was $46 billion, which made it one of the richest countries of the region, alongside Brazil, Argentina and Mexico. Its GDP per capita, $3,000, put it right at the top of the league. The country's social welfare system was one of the most advanced in the Americas, although slums still rubbed shoulders with skyscraper affluence. Venezuela had also embarked on an intelligent policy of trying to diversify its economy, pouring money into developing iron ore, aluminum, steel, cement and the motor industry. One weakness was its dependence on imported food.

Venezuela was so rich it could afford to live well and prudently at the same time. And yet none of this would have been possible without its remarkable political recovery. Venezuela is a country absolutely devoid of a democratic tradition—indeed, possibly, the scene of the worst misrule in South America until around the middle of the century. Absolutist tyranny by the most vicious and capricious of men was almost all it had ever known. Within a generation, a democratic political leadership had sprung up that was democratic and noncommunist (Latin America's successive military leaders usually claimed that universal suffrage would bring in the communists) and that had managed to preserve its democracy and freedoms in the face of threats from the army.

It was the reverse of the Argentine experience, which suggested—frighteningly—that the wealthier the country, the more crooks it was likely to breed. Corruption certainly existed in Venezuela, but its political class was as moderate and thoughtful as that of any

Western democracy, and the army and the left abided by the system. Once Latin American countries attained a certain level of prosperity, the Venezuelan experience seemed to suggest, guerrillas and despots were things of the past.

The country's luck, and soaring prosperity, temporarily receded at the beginning of the 1980s. Despite its riches, Venezuela proved unable to resist the offers of money from overliquid Western banks: borrowed money poured in, and the country ended up $29 billion in debt. When oil prices dropped, Venezuelans suddenly realized the size of the debt they had amassed. The irresponsible Herrera administration was driven from office and Acción Democrática, under the most sober leader it had ever had, Jaime Lusinchi, took office. He promised to honor the debt, in Venezuela's own good time. The country was further buffeted by a crash in oil prices in 1985. Still, the oil wealth was enough to guarantee a continuing income of $7½ billion a year, and Venezuela's exports of nontraditional goods had marginally increased. On almost every count, Venezuela had performed admirably; what remained was to create an industrial base before the oil ran out some twenty years hence.

I asked a Venezuelan political scientist the key question, as we sat in the flashy luxury—so typical of Caracas today—of the Hotel Tamanaco, with its luxurious pool overlooking the highway that curves through the city, beneath green slopes. How had Venezuela achieved the impossible? How had it survived as a democracy through two of the most tyranny-strewn decades of Latin America's history, when its own history had been one of tyranny?

Venezuelans are a relaxed people. He smiled and sipped his piña colada, and the cries of children in the pool mingled with the unceasing boom of traffic along the highway below. "Obviously, the money played a big part. But there is another factor: our army has a slender tradition of coups. The dictators, Pérez Jiménez apart, were not military dictators. They used the army, but they were not created by the army. The army respected their rule, just as it respects the rule of democracy now. Perhaps we owe something to the dictators, who kept the army in its place.

"Another thing: we are a more regionally divided society than you would guess. The handful apart, we were all equally poor in the days before oil, and since then we have all been equally rich. There is no exploiting or exploited class.

"We are an independent people. There was the tradition of Bolívar, there was the tradition of our coastal region, there was the tradition of the *llaneros*. We put up with dictators when we were poor. We could dispense with them when we were rich. And we could never accept totalitarian rule. We are too independent," he repeated. Perhaps.

I put a similar question to a young university student in a noisy restaurant one night. The band was loud, playing Venezuelan country music—a mixture of West Indian calypso and traditional South American music. A crazy, skeletal Creole jumped around the room like a man possessed. Why hadn't the student been seduced by the attractions of the far left? Why, in fact, had the left not pursued a campaign against the old dictators, and now the corrupt democrats?

He was one of those intellectuals with thick glasses who don't look you in the eye but speak to someone behind you, someone who isn't really there. He had a curious, apologetic way of talking, slightly simpering, as though one should excuse him for his views, even though they turned out to be moderate.

"Communism is not for Latin America. We Venezuelans understand that. We are socialist, we want a better redistribution of wealth; we want to punish the corrupt. But we believe in democracy. Only a small minority on the campus have ever been Marxist; the rest want to achieve change by peaceful means. As for armed struggle, it causes much suffering, and it never succeeds. Never in all the places where it has occurred. In Argentina, Uruguay, Chile, Brazil, Bolivia—"

"How about Cuba and Nicaragua?"

"They were both countries with dictators. Venezuela is a country with democracy. Venezuelans are a hotheaded people." He gestured expressively around the room, where people were jiving in a frenzy to the band. Even a colonel type, with white mustaches and sombrero, was jumping up and down with a jolly, plump, middle-aged woman. "But we are not very political. We put up with the dictators for so long for that reason. We have no reason to let the communists ruin our democracy."

"Some people tell me Venezuelans are independent; others, that they are subservient."

"Hombre, they are both. In the city they were long subservient. For too long. But poor people—and we were really poor—are subservient. In the llanos they are independent, but the *llaneros* do not take much interest in politics, except when some centralist wants to impress his rule upon us. Go into the interior. See how different they are. If you do not like the life of the city, there is a good life to be made there. The future wealth of this country is in the interior."

So I decided to take a trip into the interior, to sample the spirit of independence, which my friend had suggested made Venezuela so different.

First, though, I went to Mass in one of the smartest residential quarters of town, a place with comfortable two-storied houses, where armed guards patrolled the streets against crime. The church was engagingly antique against the backdrop of the city, a puny assertion of the spiritual against the material. It was filled with the pious newly wealthy—well-dressed, pubescent girls accompanying their grandmothers to church, serious-minded fathers at their devotions, wearing slacks and open-necked shirts. They were casual, familial. I wondered whether this country would avoid the Uruguayan problem: that of a society where so many are wealthy that the young react violently against their elders from sheer boredom. The youth of Venezuela were an unknown, and when the attractions of wealth had passed for a future generation, they might become frustrated.

Then I thought of the underdeveloped interior, and how much more there was to achieve, beyond enjoying the proceeds of the natural wealth gushing from the ground.

I left early the following morning, by car, along the splendid tarmac road that wound its way in a great ascent into the overhead greenery of the Venezuelan mountains. One had grown so used to the bump and rattle of dirt tracks that to be riding along a road that would have done justice to West Germany or Italy was a marvelous experience. The road went past towns with dirty shopfronts doing a roaring trade, past the petrol stations where gas could be bought at ten cents a gallon (cigarettes cost only twenty cents a pack), past the grubby picnic areas where Venezuelans liked to come and court or, if married, offer their children rides on the shaggy-haired ponies that stood in groups by the side of the road. Still we climbed, and Caracas itself was reduced to a shimmering mass of white skyscrapers far below the imposing greenery, while the jungle-clad mountains—there were occasional clusters of palm trees—rose all about us.

After an hour or so, we reached Colonia Tovar, a German town built in quaint Black Forest style, constructed around a square with a black and white church. German settlers had founded the colony as long ago as 1843; the name derived from the landowner who had given them the land to settle on. The shops sold European ceramics—beer mugs, the usual crafts. The food shops sold wurstel and sauerkraut. I felt disoriented in this German town perched on a Venezuelan jungle hillside.

I went into a restaurant, and searched about in vain for any sign of the blond, blue-eyed German settlers I had been told to look for. A couple of small girls with golden locks came out of one shop, but I could not make out whether they were visitors or locals. On a side of the road a youth with passably fair hair and blue eyes was selling bags of apricots and onions. In the middle of towns, gangs of youths on motorbikes and in American pickups acted cocky and aggressive, as though they had been transplanted from an American town. Two boys rode past on oversize horses, with three or four Alsatians trotting at their heels. The mixture of German quaintness, latent violence and mountain jungle was very Latin American, a reminder that the region is as much a melting pot as the United States.

We drove on, through the greenery, across the highlands. After hours, the road wound down into a town, San Juan de los Morros, where I was told the local sport was cockfighting. After spending the night there, we traveled across rather bare, dry mountains into the llanos, the outback of Venezuela, where the men who have such contempt for the city come from. It was a bare land although there were clusters of trees, usually alongside rivers, and occasional table-lands that the road never seemed to get close to. It ought to have been a tiresome territory, but its openness, save for wandering herds of cattle, gave it grandeur.

I learned later, when I stopped in the town of El Tigre, that the llanos contained some five million cattle, regularly driven by the herdsmen away from the floods that affected the area—about three hundred thousand square kilometers—into the mountains, and then moved away from drought into the basin of the Orinoco. In El Tigre, I saw up close some of the riders on horseback I spotted from the car: long-haired, with keen eyes, chiseled features, slow gestures, and for the most part taciturn. They were a kind of savage cowboy;

more urbane John Wayne types seemed in short supply. They were hard to draw into conversation.

Across the llanos, I got my first view of the Orinoco. It was a disappointing, sluggish, curving river with deep jungle on either side; it was much less wide than the Amazon, and lacked the native settlements that made that river interesting. There were squalid wooden shacks along the banks. The water was a muddy brown.

Ciudad Bolívar, further along the Orinoco, did not disappoint. It is situated on a low hill on the edge of the river, with a plain cathedral surrounded by some colonial buildings; most of it was new and extended along the riverbank. It was busy, a town built on the river, for the river. Boats did brisk trade there. The town had recently become the nub of a minor gold and diamond boom, and had a brawling reputation. Bolívar had come here to recruit the *llaneros* and through sheer force of personality acquired a following among these roughnecks. It used to be called Angostura, because the river was so narrow at that point; a doctor invented the bitters here. Much of the world has forgotten Bolívar, but it has not forgotten Angostura bitters.

From the city it was a short drive down another good highway—a constant surprise in such arid landscapes—to Puerto Ordaz. We passed a seemingly endless artificial lake that slipped in and out of the meandering valleys through low hills like a designer Jacuzzi. This was the Guri Dam, where a thundering cataract of water passing through a complex of hydroelectric plants and pumps was to generate some six million kilowatts of electricity a year. This inland sea was attractive in contrast with the green, yellow and brown lowland beside it, and was more, rather than less, impressive for being a man-made creation. Venezuela appeared to be investing in its nonoil future rather well.

Puerto Ordaz was a new town on a red-earth site with an opencut iron ore mine. The Orinoco, in its continuing sluggishness, now more than ever resembled the river in V.S. Naipaul's *A Bend in the River;* so did much of its waterfront. Yet the difference was development. The cities just behind it, earth movers and industrial estates and multistory housing in the middle of nowhere—all these formed major contrasts to the vacuous countryside. Soon the tropical setting of the Orinoco would be home not just to gold and diamonds but to power generation and manufacturing.

From Puerto Ordaz I took a plane to my last destination in Venezuela, the outback country that made up a third of the nation: the Guyana highlands, which were actually not particularly high. They were an area of semidesert scrub, interrupted by forest and jungle down the middle of which ran the *mesetas*, the table mountains that comprised one of the wildest parts of the Amazon-Orinoco basin.

The plane landed at a postage-stamp airstrip, Canaima; the airport terminal consisted of wooden props holding up a canvas covering. I was taken in an open-topped jeep that bumped up and down a dirt road to an off-white house, with straw thatched roof, standing in a cluster with others. I appreciated the spaciousness of the rudimentary rooms. I checked the windows to make sure the mosquito netting was pinned down.

The food in the local restaurant was filthy, so I resorted to the plain-looking bar, where they advertised a Canaima cocktail. I asked what was in it; the barman, a short man, gave me the easy, innocent smile of the lowland Indian (in contrast to the sullen, suspicious mountain Indian). He said, "It's gin, rum, brandy, grenadine, vermouth and bitters." He added, "A man's drink." I didn't doubt it, and settled for a watery Polar beer.

Gazing out from the bar one could see the cataracts of Canaima lagoon, a roly-poly waterfall, quite low, maybe fifty or sixty feet high, but bearing such a volume of water, sending up clouds of white spray, that the torrent seemed overwhelming in its force. That afternoon, I climbed up beside the surging water and glanced across the large, mirror surface of the river above, which gave no warning of the crash to come. After walking through great heat, I came to the site of three other cataracts, higher still, one a slightly muddish brown color, the others straight falls that showered me with their spittle and soothed my brow. At a waterfall, all the hidden strength that could only be guessed at beneath the surface of a big river (and this was only a minor tributary of the Orinoco) revealed itself, in cross section, its guts exposed, so to speak. Later I paddled upstream with an Indian guide to a shallow where I searched, in vain, for alligators. The water, he claimed, was drinkable. I didn't make the test. Instead I paddled, and got bitten by ticks which left marks that didn't fade. Later I watched the gentle surface sweep past and peered at the table mountains that dominated the horizon.

That evening, after dinner, I fell into conversation with a local businessman who supplied Canaima with fuel. He was in his late thirties, a straightforward, blunt-spoken man. He asked me how I liked the place. "Very much," I told him, "but I wouldn't want to live here."

"It's the best land on earth."

"It's too wild for me."

"That's what I like about it."

"It still seems to me the Venezuelans are too Caracas-oriented. They haven't made enough effort to open up the interior. I was told by a friend in Caracas that the interior was the great challenge facing the country. It hasn't been resolved."

He turned serious. "That'll come. All the opportunity is here. It's hardly been scratched. The potential wealth is enormous. That's why I came. I used to run a garage business in Caracas. I couldn't see opportunities there; the government has all the wealth from the oil and gives it to its friends. Here one day the agricultural and mineral wealth will be exploited. There may even be oil. Canaima is just a beginning. Anyone who was out here from the beginning will be in a good position."

I liked his drive, the pioneering, enterprising spirit of the man. But I was unconvinced. "There isn't anyone out here. There are the cowboys further back; and there's this little camp; and there's the dam and the steel mill, which a lot of people say is just a waste of government money. That isn't the right kind of enterprising spirit."

"Those projects have shown Venezuelans that there is an interior, on the other side of the mountains; they hadn't grasped that. These are early days. But I predict the interior will one day be more important than Caracas."

My Indian guide, whom I encountered on my way back to the cabin in the cool, humid evening, said, "This is unspoiled, unlike Caracas. It will always be that way, because Caracans like the good life too much; they do not enjoy the wilderness. Most of the people who come here, like you, are foreigners."

Next day I took a light Cessna plane out to the Angel Falls, the world's highest. The pilot was a man with a mustache, a swashbuckling expression and a receding weak chin of the kind that one associates with the cad or villain in a Rider Haggard book or a Tarzan film; he wore a safari hat, shirt and shorts that might have come straight off a film set. He sat silent and shifty as he maneuvered the flimsy thing into the air.

We left the ground with none of the effort and groaning that accompanies a commercial airliner: the Cessna's nose simply sniffed the air and was off the ground, ascending fast over the waterfalls, then following the river upstream through the dense jungle that sat at the base of the tablelands. As these came toward us, mists clung to their flanks like children to a mother's skirt. We buzzed the crags and shoulders of dark rock that crashed thousands of feet down a sheer face to the jungle below. In that tiny plane, one felt some of the freedom of a bird: we dived in around those huge, angry rocks thousands of feet above the valley floor, contemptuous of the height or of the forbidding crags before us. Then we reached a cut in the cliff, and the Angel Falls lay before us.

They could not have been more different from the squat, powerful cataracts we had just seen, or the mighty waterfalls of Iguaçú. From what seemed to be a puny source—just a trickling stream at the top—the water curved in and down in a single stream, fanning gracefully out, then closing in again, ending in a spectacular splash of spray to the bottom, where it trickled, exhausted, onto a lower shelf. The beauty was the thinness of the torrent, its height, its curvature, the grace of the plunge; the fall of that dazzling white stream against the brooding black precipice was one of the most attractive sights I had ever seen: the highest free-fall in the world, nearly three thousand feet of uninterrupted drop. We flew over the scarred mossy rock top from which the water came out over the very lip cascading, and my heart seemed to plunge as we peered straight down the cliff, with the eyes of an eagle going over the edge, down absolutely sheer rock into the green forest far, far below. Then the plane, so light against the enormity of nature yet able to defy it, turned for home and flew cheekily, lightly away.

Four hundred miles further on, on just such a tableland—with a peculiar, coarse vegetation layering a surface of pitted rock—was Roraima, whose flora and fauna had been found to be significantly different from those of the neighboring region, retarded by thousands of years of loss of contact between the plateau above and the forest below. It was said to have given Conan Doyle the idea for *The Lost World*. Robin Parish reported in *The South American Handbook* that it was about a two-day walk to the jungle at the foot of Roraima and there it is possible to climb to the plateau along the "easy" gully which is the only route to the top. The gully is the more central of the two which run diagonally up the cliff face. The ascent takes 3–5 hours, and it is possible to camp on the eerie plateau, but beware of lightning from the frequent electrical storms which the mountains attract. There is plenty of water en route, but no accommodation. Full camping equipment is essential and we took thick socks and boots to protect our legs from snakes. The whole trip can take anywhere between one and two weeks.

That night the rains came and they pounded on the roof of the cabin where I slept, overpowering the noise from the cicadas and birds and the distant roar of the cataracts. I felt a very long way from anywhere, in this deserted outback where nature was at its most formidable. Yet with so much frontier to cross and exploit (apart from the region's hydroelectric resources, the area was extremely rich with untapped reserves of iron ore, manganese and bauxite), it seemed to me that Venezuelans would never want for a purpose. The oil had merely been a key with which to unlock the country's riches, providing the capital whose absence was the single biggest obstacle to Latin America's development.

Silly old men and Indians believe in the legend of El Dorado, that there is a city of fabulous wealth waiting to be discovered, somewhere on the continent. Venezuela was El Dorado, a true source of natural wealth beneath its inhospitable territory. (Bolivia is another, unexplored.) The torrid, dirty oil derricks around Lake Maracaibo, where the first wealth was found, wasn't everyone's idea of El Dorado. But the money was beyond the dreams of any mere gold digger. In 1973, Venezuela had been earning a handsome $4½ billion from oil exports; by 1981 this had risen to $19 billion for a much lower volume of exports. Most of the money had been channeled to opening up the country and improving its standard of living without sending inflation through the roof. Venezuela was an example to Latin America, the country with the highest and probably best-distributed per-capita GDP (around $2,500), and 80 percent urban population, a literacy rate of 88 percent. The country had been given an opportunity, and its fifteen million people were making the most of it.

MEXICO

I DECIDED TO RETURN TO MY STARTING POINT, MEXICO, TO SEE whether I could draw the threads together, whether I had the answers to the questions I had posed in Tijuana.

Mexico City. The aircraft came in past the soaring, perfectly majestic cone of Popocatépetl—white-capped except where the volcano's smoldering heat had melted the snow. From the gaping hole at its summit, smoke drifted languidly over the city, a reminder that this was truly a monster in repose.

It seemed to me that there could have been nothing more spectacular than the first Spanish sighting of Emperor Moctezuma's city, built on a lake, the city from which Hernán Cortés and a tiny band of Spaniards ambushed by the Aztecs had to fight their way down the causeway to escape, the scene of one of the most terrible chapters in human history: an advanced though ruthless civilization in mortal combat with another more advanced in warfare, just as savage, yet backed by a humanist religion.

These are but a few chapters in the history of Mexico City, where the Pyramids of the Sun and the Moon, surrounded by carvings of snarling lions, sit in primitive splendor just beyond the confines of the city. Here is real history of a kind not felt in upstart Buenos Aires or flashy Caracas, a history rich with events dating back long before Columbus and encompassing events, from the Battle of the Alamo to the strange emperorship of Maximilian to the revolution of 1917.

A taxi took me along a jammed four lane highway from the airport. It was bumper-to-bumper all the way: where was the lake? "Oh, there are a few marshes, no more," the driver told me. "It is all built over. Actually the city is sinking, because we are drinking the old lake dry. One day we will have a terrible earthquake when the ground cracks. Who knows? You know, the city is built on the San Andreas Fault. I will show you." A little later he pointed out a building that exhibited a larger crack than most of the others. "That is the San Andreas Fault." I had no way of knowing whether he was telling the truth.

The taxi moved slowly along an urban highway that ran between lines of utilitarian skyscrapers, unsculpted concrete blocks, unlike those in Caracas. My hotel was spacious, built in the shape of a latter-day pyramid; I felt isolated from the city outside. But there was no other trace of Mexico in its style: it was up-to-date, anonymous. I went out that evening, and my eyes struggled with the film of thick pollution all around, a pollution spawned by the exhaust of millions of cars that gushed down the clogged highways, and by the industries that spewed out their filth in this hollow mountain bowl were the air barely moved. To get anywhere, I needed a car.

I went to the Pink Zone, the Zona Rosa, the red-light district, which is said to harbor Mexico City's soul. It consisted of a few blocks of low-level buildings just off the highway. Removed from the fumes and pollution, you can watch jovial fat men in ten-gallon hats and braided suits, wearing Zapatalike mustaches, strumming merrily away to café audiences. It was at least a bow to the old Mexico.

Mexico City had become a nightmare, densely populated, congested, a mess on a high plateau. It lacked the vibrancy even of São Paulo, the business city that never pretended to be anything else. Mexico City was the capital, and it had gone hopelessly wrong: it was a mixture of industrial zone and political capital, and a magnet for all who lived anywhere near. I wandered through the Pink Zone to the city's splendid presidential square, with the colonial cathedral along one side and the presidential palace at a right angle, and I realized what it must have been.

Next day I called on a middle-class banker and his wife with two small children and a nanny, whom I had known in London. The house was fair-sized, a haven from the noise, although not from the pollution. We were served hot Mexican foods by maids, and I enjoyed a long afternoon in the garden. I asked about the lake. My friend's wife said she would take me there; Mexicans liked to go boating on the lake in the afternoons. I was surprised that the lake existed, after all. We drove down to a church, and parked the car, and then went to a jetty that joined onto a canal system, with deeply vegetated green banks. We hired a boat painted in as many hues as one of Guatemala's buses, and the punter pushed us through hordes of other boats. On another boat, a floating band steamed toward us. This canal was all that was left of Mexico's lake. That evening I went to the disco at the top of my hotel. It was okay, but it wasn't the Mexico City of Moctezuma and Cortés I had hoped for. It was what Mexico City had become.

Next day, I drove out past the workers' quarters, with their lines of unemployed youths standing around the bars or playing pool; idleness was the order of the day. They were lucky: they lived in decent houses; that is, they didn't have running water or lavatories, but they had properly built roofs and walls. Backed up against the hills were shanties, rickety contraptions just like the ones in Bogotá or Rio, except there were many, many more of them, repetitive acres of them. And all of these people were becoming worse off because of the debt crisis.

Mexico had become the most politically stable of Latin American nations. That was remarkable when considered against the terrible history of violence in the years after independence from Spain lasting until the middle of the century. The country's size, its poverty, its racial mixture, the United States—all had been responsible for the carnage. The initial period of independence was played out under a reckless, good-looking, womanizing layabout, Antonio López de Santa Anna, who lasted until 1855. His main feat was the loss of Texas, which need never have happened. After his forces had taken the Alamo, massacring all inside, his army was surrounded on a riverbank during their siesta while he was making love to an Indian girl, and he only just escaped with his life. War with the United States was to follow.

The fecklessness of Santa Anna enraged idealists in the generation that succeeded him. They were liberals, the most prominent a full-blooded Zapotec Indian, Benito Juárez. They drew up a constitution and a program for reform, which included a moderate measure of land redistribution to reduce the power of the church, the most conservative force in Mexican society. The reform proved far too dramatic: by 1858, the country was in the throes of a full-scale civil war of the utmost savagery. It lasted three years. Churches were pillaged, nuns and friars butchered; the conservative forces proved as savage to the heretic liberals.

Juárez won, only to inherit a bankrupt country. When he defaulted on Mexico's debts, which were mainly owed to France, the angry, autocratic Napoléon III decided not just to teach the country a lesson, but to make Mexico a French colony. A puppet of Napoléon, Maximilian, the Hapsburg emperor, was sent to rule. The United States fretted about the European intervention near its territory, and as soon as the end of the American Civil War allowed, supplied arms to Juárez. Abandoned even by the French, against whom he was trying to make a stand, Maximilian was taken prisoner and shot in 1867. Juárez died in 1872. After a brief interval, he was succeeded by Porfirio Díaz, a cruel despot, who nevertheless ushered in peace and economic development. The country made foreign investment welcome, and three thousand silver, zinc and copper mines were opened. And then, in 1900, oil was discovered, and prosperity began in earnest.

The conservative and repressive Díaz overstayed his welcome: the pressure from the new classes began to mount for change. By 1911 he had been forced out by a constitutionalist, Francisco Madero, just as bandits began to rampage across tracts of the country. The two leaders of the insurgency were Pancho Villa, no more than a brigand, and Emiliano Zapata, a land-reforming peasant whose ideals found support among many other peasants. Madero was betrayed and shot by a drunken general, Victoriano Huerta, who looted the city's treasury and debauched himself. The insurrections grew stronger, and at last a constitutionalist, Venustiano Carranza, pushed out Huerta and engaged in a long and bloody civil war against the peasant chiefs. The 1917 constitution, which the Mexicans call their revolution, was drawn up.

It was, the Mexicans never tire of pointing out, a revolution that

anticipated the conflicts of the Russian revolution. In fact, the imposing of constitutional order upon a lawless, desperado society was
very different from the sweeping away of an old order by proletar-
ian-based intellectuals that took place in Russia. The constitution
did, however, specify that the state, not the individual, was the
source of authority—thus harking back to Aztec days. It gave many
formal rights to the peasants and workers. In order to guard against
tyranny, presidential terms were fixed for four years and presidents
were ineligible for reelection. To preserve continuity they would
appoint their successors; and in that country ravaged by private
armies, power would emanate from the center, from Mexico City.

The objectives of the Mexican revolution were never fully put into
practice; reform proceeded slowly and most peasants lived exactly as
before. Workers were strong-armed into joining the official unions.
The government made scant use of its powers of collectivization,
except in nationalizing the country's enormous oil reserves. Mexico's
social fabric remained in a precarious state. A vicious president,
Plutarco Elías Calles, tried to defuse some of the tensions that persisted in Mexican society by a relentless campaign against the church,
while protecting the power of the landowners. But only with Lázaro
Cárdenas, who set about a major land reform program and increased
real wages to the workers, did a genuinely populist presidency get
underway. But the presidency was soon returned to a conservative.

And so, after 1917, Mexico's system was established: one-party rule
by the Institutional Revolutionary Party. To some it was a model of
third-world government—benevolently autocratic, allowing for
some change but not too much, at least partly representative. The
ruling party's labor-union wing was powerful, and a system of
bosses, inherited from Díaz's day, saw to it that the views of grass-
roots voters in the cities and the countryside were passed up the
pyramid of power in Mexico City. At the same time, opposition was
ruthlessly suppressed by these bosses; election results were fiddled
with, so that the legally permitted opposition won only a pittance of
the vote. The largest legal opposition was a middle-class conservative
party, the National Action Party (PAN); the Communists had poor
support. The government controlled the press, and its extensive
patronage ensured loyalty among its supporters. When opposition
manifested itself directly, as it did in the riots during the Mexican

Olympics in 1968, the army moved in. Casualties were much higher than the three hundred supposedly left dead, and the massacre was emotionally to scar the minister of the interior who ordered the troops to go in, Luis Echeverría, for the rest of his life. He became Mexico's most left-wing recent president in order partly to compensate.

The real genius of the system was, however, the way it straddled conservatism and socialism. The ruling party was institutional in that it controlled power and wanted at all costs to protect the power system (its leadership was stuffed with Latin American technocrats, able men who ran the economy and administration), and revolutionary in that if there was any swelling of popular disaffection, it would dance to the tune and up its revolutionary rhetoric, particularly in the field of foreign policy and sometimes in that of land reform. The system was a synthesis of right and left, a bureaucracy that was much more pervasive than those in most one-party states. And in spite of the fraud and corruption on which it was based it had lasted, because its political antennae were sophisticated.

The system lasted, too, because Mexico was developing, the Mexican economy was growing, and Mexico was proud of itself, in spite of the fact that its growth was unequal and unplanned. From being the tacky third-rate country beneath America's border with only sixteen million people in 1934, Mexico had thirty-five million in 1955; by 1970 there were forty-eight million Mexicans, and the growth rate of 3 percent a year would double that number at the end of the century. That made Mexico, in its own eyes, the largest Spanish-speaking nation on earth and the focus of the Hispanic world, more so than Spain or Argentina.

In a sense the claim was bogus; Mexico sought, as in most things, to have it both ways: it valued its Spanish heritage as well as its Indian and Mexican heritage. It claimed that its Americanism, rooted in its Indian culture, was much more authentic than gringo Americanism or the proto-European cultures of South America. The semiprimitivist murals of Diego Rivera and José Clemente Orozco restated this Mexican culture in the 1920s, as did the poetry of Octavio Paz and the nationalist puffing with which Mexico showed off its pre-Colombian heritage in its great ethnological museum. Yet it also claimed to be the center of Hispanic tradition. It was revolutionary, yet it was conservative. It was hostile to the United States's domination of the continent, yet it pointed out that it was a North American country, enjoying a special relationship with the United States. The Mexican system took pride in facing both ways at once.

Mexico's greatest prosperity came as the consequence of the oil boom in the 1960s. Its wealth exploded, as a consequence of the price hikes made by OPEC, a cartel of which Mexico, in deference to its great neighbor, was not a member. Between 1960 and 1970, Mexico's GDP doubled, from $40 billion to $80 billion. The GDP nearly doubled again by 1980, to $153 billion. Population growth made the achievement somewhat less remarkable; yet per-capita GDP grew by nearly half, from $1,103 in 1960 to $1,580 in 1970, and up to $2,228 by 1980. Mexico had become, by 1980, the second-largest economy of Latin America, after Brazil, more than twice as big as Argentina. Its per-capita GDP had gone ahead of Argentina's by 1980, was well ahead of Brazil's, and was behind only those of Uruguay and Venezuela. Yet, fatally, its prosperity was founded on oil, and then on borrowing. Oil contributed only $186 million to Mexico's trade account in 1975; by 1982 the figure was $15.8 billion.

The government of Luis Echeverría was lucky enough to inherit the first oil bonanza. Echeverría was a sallow, muddled man, given occasionally to violent rhetoric and fickle idealism. He engaged in an energetic attempt to give Mexico leadership of the third world, an ambition frustrated when he failed to become U.N. secretary-general. A series of irresponsible financial measures and a last-minute land reform were introduced before his successor, José López Portillo, elbowed aside his mentor.

López Portillo started out as the most reasonable of Mexico's recent presidents, and ended up the most spendthrift. This was partly an accident of fortune. After nearly putting right the Echeverría mess, he found himself the beneficiary of the 1979–80 oil price increase and the huge lending spree that followed, as petrodollars showered Latin America. Because Mexico was a petrocurrency, its credit was fairly good, and López Portillo saw no reason to miss out on the bonanza being enjoyed by the rest of Latin America. Brazil's debt, the largest, had gone up quite slowly, and much of it consisted of sensible borrowing. In Mexico, the state went out of control, increasing its borrowing from nearly $14 billion in 1975 to $55.5 billion in 1982, when the bubble burst. A large proportion of the money went overseas, while much was spent on expensive petrochemical industries that were later to lose much of their markets. López Portillo's sideboards grew longer and his smile larger as his country stumbled further into debt. He left office before the reckoning.

His successor was a managerial type. Miguel de la Madrid was more sober and less political than either of his predecessors: he inherited an economy that had a 17.6 percent deficit in government spending, an inflation rate of nearly 60 percent, and a current account deficit—for an oil-exporting country—of nearly $5 billion. This he turned around, with backing from the International Monetary Fund, with a vengeance. Wages were slashed by a third, unemployment went up by half, the government simply stopped buying abroad. In one year, imports were reduced by half, to produce a balance-of-payments surplus of $5 billion. Government spending on housing and health was squeezed to a deficit of just 7 percent. Inflation fell to 100 percent in 1982 and to 65 percent the following year. And the foreign debt continued to mount. There was no way Mexico could begin to pay it back, because however hard the nation squeezed, it could barely afford the interest—that is, it could barely prevent the debt from continuing to mount. Since much of the original money had gone on speculation, or had left the country altogether, it was the poor of Mexico who had to shoulder the burden. Yet they did not take to the streets and riot; the political system was still stable. But it was being stretched, and unless some hope was offered, it would be remarkable if there were not a blowup.

In my contacts with ordinary Mexicans, they insisted they were different from other Latin Americans. They were North Americans, but of course not gringos. Their Indian culture made them special, the most enduring civilization on the continent.

"You must go and see the ethnological museum," a friend told me. "It is revealing. You can only understand us if you appreciate our former civilization. There is our political order. It is like a pyramid in structure, it is almost Asian in concept. We do not really sympathize with the idea of competition; it seems wasteful and envious to us, in politics as well. And of course we reject the crudeness of the military regimes further south. We live in a unity, a whole, in which people work together to produce a consensus. This is the only country in the Americas where the system that existed before Columbus is, in modified form, still in place, and has prevailed over the newcomers."

I was not so sure that the idea of political pluralism was so unappealing to ordinary Mexicans.

"Of course that is nonsense," claimed a peppery, middle-aged leader of the National Action Party, the small middle-class group tolerated by the ruling party because it was never likely to appeal to the masses and win elections. He was very European in outlook, middle-aged, well dressed, with a cultivated, yet impatient, manner. "We are a very diverse society, and we need political parties, just like anywhere else, to express those divisions—of class, of racial background even, of politics. You cannot generalize about us. The reason why the Institutional Revolutionary Party stays in power is through voting frauds, through controlling the press with subsidies, through massive patronage and corruption and ultimately, when necessary, through violence. Of course Mexico has a strong national identity that is neither North American nor South American. But it is not a national identity that favors one-party rule."

I said, "When the rest of Latin America is democratic—as it nearly is already—Mexico will look behind the times, as a one-party state dating from the year of the Russian Revolution."

"That's right. Then Mexico will in one respect be behind its fellow Latin Americans."

That evening, when it was cooler, I climbed the huge Pyramids of the Sun and the Moon outside the city, and I felt, in the still of that ancient site, that after all the pyramid structure—a wide-based society narrowing in power and wealth to the absolute rule of the emperor-president at the top—perhaps did partly explain the ancient obeisance that had kept the structure of Mexican society in place so long.

I went back to a hotel in the Zona Rosa, and had a tequila on the patio, in that slight respite from the pollution and noise and squalor and bustle of Mexico City, and I thought I understood the answer to the question I had asked at the beginning of my long odyssey. The depression of travel-weariness and homesickness had cleared my mind.

Why was Latin America so far behind North America? Because it had had so much more to contend with. First, it had an impossible racial mix, a subdued forty-million-strong indigenous population, unjustly suppressed through centuries of bloodshed.

Second, Latin America had its awesome geography. The United States was a heartland of fertility, with a partially hospitable western desert and mountain chain. Latin America was a long desert strip in the west, a mountain chain, the largest swamp in the world and a rugged plateau in the middle. Only in southern Brazil, Uruguay and Argentina did the land become gentle.

Third, Latin America had the weight of its own colonial inheritance to shed. Founded as an empire, it had evolved from a top-heavy bureaucracy and a landholding system based on an idle upper class and chattel labor; the independent, work-ethic tradition of America's colonists was alien to the older colonization. The Spaniards had been driven out by warlords, and then these newly independent countries had been ripped apart by their rivalries, only gradually emerging into an eighteenth-century European-style clash between conservatives and liberals a century later. When industrialization and the mass society caught up with Latin America, the oligarchy was elbowed aside and chaos followed for a time—chaos that could only be ordered by despots. As a large middle class emerged and the economies took off, it seemed that the age of the despot was passing; Latin America was becoming developed enough for democracy.

In particular, Brazil was blazing a trail across the skies of economic development. The southern cone countries are at last behaving more sensibly and becoming potentially one of the most prosperous regions of the world. Even the Andean republics are allowing progress to submerge their centers of decay and racial grievance. And Central America is emerging from its bloodshed as a developing and democratic isthmus.

Yet one terrible obstacle remains, an obstacle not of Latin America's history, but a freak, an accident. Three hundred billion dollars had been taken out of the pockets of the non–oil producers of Latin America by an oil-price increase. Most of the money had gone to fabulous follies; I remember the anger I felt when I once visited Saudi Arabia and saw palaces being built in the sand and cows shipped in by air and the exotic lifestyles of a people who preferred to live away from their homeland, and thought of how hard the Latin Americans were working to pay their oil bills.

With far too much to spend, the oil producers had put the money on deposit and the Western banks had sought people to lend it to; they found outstretched hands from those countries still seeking to better themselves. Of course the Latin American countries were at fault for not borrowing more sensibly; but the lenders bore the responsibility for turning a blind eye to the scale of the borrowing, and for making the cash so readily available. If the money had not been there, or had been more carefully handled by the lenders, issued only for safe projects, instead of for any projects whatsoever in a desperate attempt to maximize monthly profits by lending the maximum, there would have been no debt crisis.

In the order of blame, the banks shared equal responsibility with the borrowers. But there was a third responsibility. Most of the charges that Latin American countries made against the United States rang hollow, and were an excuse for their own underdevelopment. The charges of raw material depletion, of multinational exploitation, of support for troglodytic military regimes—this was just the rhetoric of the Latin American left. The export of commodities had given Latin Americans the capital base with which to foster industrial development. The multinationals left jobs and skills in their wake. The military regimes were homegrown Latin American affairs, which would have seized power with or without America's help. Indeed, the Americans labored with difficulty to control native excesses.

One charge against the United States did stick: that of neglect. The appalling wars that ravaged Central America from 1979 onward would not have happened if the Americans had earlier played a more active role in urging primitive regimes toward democracy and in toppling dictators. Through six years of debt crises, the United States government persisted in its neglect: its case-by-case approach, using the IMF and the banks to do the formal negotiating, was a classic failure of responsibility. The government of the United States had a duty to weigh the long-term effects of a continuing debt crisis upon the world's financial system, and upon the politics of Latin America. This it failed to do.

The consequence has been a reining in of Latin America's late-twentieth-century leap forward, and the transfer of $100 billion from the developing to the developed world. Other consequences have been to endanger the region's new, hopeful, progressive democracies, encouraging populist demagogues and then, perhaps, military coups. The consequence, here in Mexico at least, was an economic crisis of unparalleled proportions that was driving Mexicans across the Rio Grande to the prosperity up north. The United States's only hope of sealing off the border is to encourage economic development in Mexico to a point where the poor no longer need to go north to survive. Until the debt crisis, that was beginning to happen.

And so the consequence of not writing off those debts and settling the world financial crisis once and for all at a cost of possibly adding a percentage point or two to world inflation was to reencourage despotism or revolution in South America. The First America bears a heavy burden of guilt for postponing the flowering of Latin America. But it has merely been postponed, because the recent surges of the region suggest that Latin America can achieve a prosperity that will not equal that of the First, but not fall far short, either. When Latin America achieves its prosperity, it will be able to look the First America in the eye, as a partner and a friend.

I finished my tequila, enjoying its strength and taste through the bitter salt on the rim of the glass. The four paths still pointed toward prosperity. Part of the third world was not far off joining the first. I had enjoyed the trip. I flew back to London, direct from Mexico City, the following morning, and there was little turbulence on the journey home.

INDEX